Peter Hamilton

Rambles in historic lands

Travels in Belgium, Germany, Switzerland, Italy, France and England

Peter Hamilton

Rambles in historic lands

Travels in Belgium, Germany, Switzerland, Italy, France and England

ISBN/EAN: 9783337210229

Printed in Europe, USA, Canada, Australia, Japan

Cover: Foto ©Andreas Hilbeck / pixelio.de

More available books at **www.hansebooks.com**

CASTLE OF CHILLON FROM LAKE GENEVA.

RAMBLES
IN HISTORIC LANDS

TRAVELS IN BELGIUM, GERMANY, SWITZERLAND
ITALY, FRANCE AND ENGLAND

BY

PETER J. HAMILTON, A.M.
LATE FELLOW OF PRINCETON COLLEGE

ILLUSTRATED

G. P. PUTNAM'S SONS
NEW YORK   LONDON
27 WEST TWENTY-THIRD STREET   24 BEDFORD STREET, STRAND
The Knickerbocker Press
1893

COPYRIGHT, 1893
BY PETER J. HAMILTON
Entered at Stationers' Hall, London
BY PETER J. HAMILTON

Electrotyped, Printed and Bound by
The Knickerbocker Press, New York
G. P. PUTNAM'S SONS

AFFECTIONATELY DEDICATED
TO
RACHEL BURGETT HAMILTON
MY WIFE
THE SHARER OF THESE RAMBLES
MY INCENTIVE TO AUTHORSHIP
AND MY FRIENDLY CRITIC

PREFACE.

WHEN a new book of European travel is announced the three questions naturally arise, Who is the author? What is his point of view? What new has he to tell?

In reply it must be confessed that he is no distinguished man. He is a resident of Mobile, and a graduate of Princeton College in 1879, where he took the Mental Science fellowship and went to Leipzig University for courses in philosophy and law. In the vacations he travelled a good deal, ranging from Stirling to Pompeii, from Berlin to Paris. Not yet recovered from the systematic training of his *alma mater*, he observed carefully while abroad and kept full journals, being interested more especially in everything connected with history. On this occasion he lived abroad over a year.

In 1891 came the pleasure trip of four months recorded in this volume, in which the route was somewhat varied but the historical point of view maintained. This book follows the footprints of the second visit but includes much of importance gleaned on the first. It has been almost two years on the anvil.

What new has he to tell? Well, it will not do to pretend in these Columbian times that an American discovered Europe. But there are several things which if not absolutely new can be told in a new manner.

For instance, German University life is told as experienced by one studying in the largest German University, just as it appeared to him fresh from one of the greatest of American colleges. He loves art and describes galleries as they struck an amateur. He gives a careful if short sketch of the art development of Europe, derived from various sources, because others may like himself have been unable to find any that is at once measurably accurate, brief and interesting. Something like a philosophic study of the Roman Empire, ancient and modern, is made in connection with visits to historic centres, because many yet think of the Empire as ceasing A.D. 476 and have not mastered Bryce's views of the middle ages. Historic sites are described from sheer love of archæology and desire to realize the surroundings of epoch-making races and individuals. He relates what was seen of nature in Switzerland when he walked its passes, before railroads came to whirl one along too fast for good views and deaden enjoyment by making it too easy. Venice, Paris and London have certainly been much written about, but they appear different to different temperaments, and, possibly, still admit of systematic, if brief, treatment. Somewhat so, too, of great men. The greatest men of modern times are Luther, Shakspere, Goethe, and Napoleon, and everything of interest found relating to them has been described, because in one way or another they have made modern history.

Americans are getting to be as great travellers as their English cousins, and it may be that to some people of each nationality this volume, without belonging to the useful but prosaic class of guide books, may relate experiences by land and sea of some interest and value and be a useful complement to guide books. It at least embodies general views and descriptions which the detailed guide book does not give and which the author has realized himself only from the air, surroundings and life of the places themselves.

It has not been thought necessary to cite authorities, for while the authors to whom the book is indebted are many they are mainly such as are familiar to most people of general information.

The illustrations, it may be added, are from photographs secured on the spot and are meant to reproduce places of interest not commonly pictured.

Such are some of the aims of this book of travel. How far it has succeeded its author cannot judge, for this he must leave to the candid critic and to the reading public.

There are of course several kinds of moneys mentioned, and it may not be amiss to remind the reader that the German mark and English shilling are each worth about twenty-five cents, and the franc, used in France, Belgium, Switzerland and Italy, about twenty cents. These are all silver. The mark is divided into a hundred pfennigs, the franc into a hundred centimes. The copper five centime piece is commonly called a sou. In Italy the franc is called a lira, but the currency is largely paper and somewhat depreciated.

MOBILE, ALA., August 20, 1893.

CONTENTS.

CHAPTER I.

ON THE OCEAN 1

Cousin Dan's proposition—Itinerary—Off on the trip—S. S. Rotterdam—Meals—Amusements at sea—Fire—Storm—Bow, stern and hold—Arrival at Boulogne.

CHAPTER II.

AIX, COLOGNE AND THE RHINE 13

Brussels—Waterloo—Aix-la-Chapelle (Aachen)—Town hall and cathedral—Charlemagne's empire—" Reclamation "—Cologne—Cook's Tours—Characteristics of Gothic architecture—Cologne cathedral and churches—Queen Louise—The Rhine trip to Mainz—Castles and Legends—Lorelei—National Monument—Sunday at Wiesbaden.

CHAPTER III.

HEIDELBERG TO WEIMAR; THE LUTHER AND GOETHE COUNTRY 29

Mainz (Mayence) and Worms—Heidelberg castle—The Palatinate—Frankfort—The Electors—The Ariadne—Railroad travelling—Luther's country—Wartburg—Erfurt—Wittenberg—Weimar—Goethe and Schiller.

CHAPTER IV.

LEIPZIG : ITS UNIVERSITY AND ITS BATTLE FIELDS . 42

Museum—Old Leipzig—New quarters—German Supreme Court—Visit to Frau Paetzel—The University—Student life —Lectures—Wundt—Windscheid—Other celebrities—Battle field of Breitenfeld—Battle field of Lützen—Battle of Leipzig—Napoleonstein—Celebration of Sedan Day.

CHAPTER V.

DRESDEN : ITS COLLECTIONS AND HISTORY . 58

Museum—Sistine Madonna—Other great pictures—King Albert and Queen Carola at church—The Green Vault— Historical relics—Porcelain collection—Brühl Terrace— Rietschel—Sketch of Saxon history.

CHAPTER VI.

CARLSBAD, NUREMBERG AND MUNICH . . 70

Saxon Switzerland — Carlsbad — Bohemia — Nuremberg— Torture as a fine art—The Iron Virgin—Munich—Handsome streets—Picture galleries—Rubens and Murillo—Sculpture gallery—Hall of Fame—Sketch of Bavarian history.

CHAPTER VII.

CONSTANCE AND NORTH SWITZERLAND . . 83

Outline of Swiss topography—Constance and its lake—Huss —Upper Rhine—Schaffhausen—Falls of the Rhine—Zurich —Zwingli—Lake dwellings—Lucerne—Thorwaldsen's Lion —Glacier Garden—Rütli—Tell—The Eidgenossen—The Rigi—Pilatus—Brünnig Pass—Interlaken and Grindelwald.

CONTENTS.

CHAPTER VIII.

BERNE AND FRENCH SWITZERLAND . . . 99

Berne—Swiss railroad cars—Sunset on Lake Geneva—Lausanne—Geneva—Famous citizens—Calvin's sway—Genevan history—Voltaire at Ferney—Lake Geneva—Chillon—Chamouny—Zermatt and the Matterhorn—German again.

CHAPTER IX.

THE SIMPLON PASS AND ITALIAN LAKES . . . 111

Brieg—Diligences—Simplon road—Hospice—Italian custom-house—Grand Hotel at Pallanza—Lake Maggiore—Borromean Islands—Lake Lugano—St. Gotthard railway—Lake Como—Villa Carlotta—Monza.

CHAPTER X.

MILAN AND ITALIAN HISTORY 121

The Last Supper—Cathedral—Roman history : 1. The Republic of Rome, Development of the City ; 2. The Empire of Rome, Cæsars ; 3. The Roman Empire, Its division ; 4. Holy Roman Empire, Pope and Emperor—Milan's history.

CHAPTER XI.

VENICE 133

Grand Canal—Gondolas—Pension Anglaise—Square of St. Mark's—Streets, canals and bridges—Sketch of Venetian history—St. Mark's—Campanile and its views—Frari Church—Titian and Canova—Venetian architecture—Shylock at home.

CHAPTER XII.

FLORENCE AND ART 148

Our financial troubles—Description of Florence—Its history—Italian Gothic—Cathedral—Campanile—Baptistery—Historical sketch of modern painting—Uffizi gallery—Venus de' Medici—Niobe—Pitti gallery—Madonna of the Chair—Salvator Rosa's landscapes—Michael Angelo's sculptures—The New Sacristy—Loggia dei Lanzi—Church of Santa Croce.

CHAPTER XIII.

ROME AND ITS RUINS 166

Marble and dirt—Via Nazionale and the Corso—Topography of ancient Rome—Columns of Trajan and Aurelius—The Forum—Via Sacra—Mamertine Prison—Trajan's cut—Palatine Hill—Capitoline Hill—Colosseum—Baths of Caracalla—Pantheon—Lateran church and palace—The Sacred Stairs.

CHAPTER XIV.

ST. PETER'S AND THE VATICAN 182

Pasquin—The Borgo—St. Peter's—Its interior—Statues and paintings—Graves—Tasso—The Vatican—Sistine Chapel—Raphael's Stanze—Transfiguration—Sculpture galleries—Apollo—Laocoön—Tapestries.

CHAPTER XV.

ENVIRONS OF ROME 195

Graves of Keats and Shelley—Appian Way—Catacombs—Grotto of Egeria—Circus of Maxentius—Tomb of Cæcilia Metella—St. Paul's—The Alban country—The Alban Lake—Tusculanum—Lost in classic woods—A night at a peasant's—Lake Nemi—The Alban Mount—Passionist monastery—Pompey's tomb—Emissarius—Terni—Falls of the Velino.

CHAPTER XVI.

THE RIVIERA ROUTE TO PARIS 209

The Campagna—The Maremme—Pisa—Cathedral—Swinging lamp—Baptistery—Campo Santo—Leaning Tower—Mediterranean coast—Genoa—Columbus—Hotel Smith—Riviera views—Monaco—Nice—Marseilles—Avignon and the Popes—The Provençal cities—Lyons—Railroad express—Disagreeable neighbor—Fontainebleau—Arrival in Paris.

CHAPTER XVII.

PARIS: ITS HISTORIC MONUMENTS AND ENVIRONS . 222

History of the city—How Paris made France—Place de la Concorde—Champs Elysées—Hôtel des Invalides—Napoleon and Josephine—Eiffel Tower—Column Vendôme—Tuileries—Louvre—Hôtel de Ville—Bastille—Palais de Justice—Sainte Chapelle—Notre Dame—The Morgue—Pantheon—Cemetery of Père la Chaise—St. Denis—Visit to Versailles—St. Cloud.

CHAPTER XVIII.

PARIS: THE LOUVRE AND THE STREETS . . . 239

Hotel meals—Our landlady—Magasins—Omnibus travel—Boulevards—Opera—Lohengrin and the Boulangists—Louvre collections—Recent Persian discoveries—Greek sculptures—Venus of Milo—Diana—Louvre picture gallery—Sketch of French painting—Crossing the Channel.

CHAPTER XIX.

LONDON 253

Outline sketch of London—West End—Westminster Abbey—Its chapels—English Gothic—Parliament House—Westminster Hall—The palaces—"To the Bank" on a 'bus—Trafalgar Square—National Gallery—Turner and English painting—Law Inns and Courts—St. Paul's—Tombs of

Nelson and Wellington—Famous sites—London Bridge—
The Tower—Regalia and armor—State prisoners—Bank of
England—Route back to West End—South Kensington
Museum—British Museum—Elgin marbles—Underground
railway—Tussaud's Wax Works.

CHAPTER XX.

HOMEWARD BOUND 279

Windsor — Oxford — The colleges — Stratford-on-Avon—
Shakspere's birthplace—His home—His grave—Chester—
Liverpool—On the City of Paris—Jaunting car at Queens-
town—Description of the ship—History of ocean travel—
Journal of our voyage—The storm—The engine stopped—
Custom-house inspection—Arrival at New York.

INDEX 295

ILLUSTRATIONS.

	PAGE
CASTLE OF CHILLON, FROM LAKE GENEVA	*Frontispiece*
CORONATION HALL AT AIX-LA-CHAPELLE	13
RHEINFELS CASTLE, ON THE RHINE	26
THE COURT OF HEIDELBERG CASTLE	31
WHERE NAPOLEON STOOD ON THE FIELD OF LEIPZIG	56
WHERE HUSS AND JEROME WERE BURNED	86
CALVIN'S CHURCH AT GENEVA	103
THE ARSENAL AT VENICE	133
THE ROMAN FORUM, FROM THE CAPITOLINE HILL	166

    (Arch of Septimius Severus, Temple of Saturn and Basilica Julia in the foreground; Comitium, Colosseum, Arch of Titus and Temple of Castor and Pollux in the background.)

THE PALACE OF THE POPES AT AVIGNON	218
NOTRE DAME, FROM THE SEINE	233
INTERIOR OF WESTMINSTER HALL	261

RAMBLES IN HISTORIC LANDS

CHAPTER I.

ON THE OCEAN.

"WHERE do you intend to go on your wedding trip?" asked cousin Dan at the dinner table one day, when that not distant event was under discussion.

"To Niagara, I suppose," I replied laughing, "but I would like to go to Europe."

"How much would it cost for two," he said.

I had spent thirteen months abroad eleven years before, mainly studying at Leipzig University. All told it had cost $800.00, but I had lived economically. I rashly thought that on even a more liberal basis a trip of four to five months could hardly exceed $300.00 apiece.

So I answered, "About six hundred dollars."

He slapped his hand on the table and said, "I will make you a present of the trip!"

I had not expected that, even from him, but recovered my breath enough to thank him, and then rushed down town to tell *her* about it.

The next few months passed on, and while she was busy about dresses I was fixing up our itinerary. I had when abroad priced at Cologne some of the tours offered by Thos. Cook & Son, the tourist agents, but found that I could travel cheaper third class on my own account and so never bought their tickets. This time I thought I had better try them again so as to save the trouble of buying tickets at every stop.

I got into correspondence with them and soon arranged for second-class tickets for two on a long tour selected by ourselves. I felt a little hesitancy as to how to speak about Rachel in these letters, as I did not care to talk of the trip as an intended bridal tour, and yet could not say that I was married. But I did resolutely mention "my wife" nevertheless. I suppose Cook knew no better, although he may have noticed that I especially declined to go with any party, personally conducted or otherwise. I never told Rachel about it until we were married and on the ocean, when she was much amused. It was finally all arranged, $484.00 remitted, and I was to obtain the tickets when we arrived in New York. They were first class on steamers and second class on railroads.

The itinerary as finally corrected gave days and places and was as methodical as Haydn's Dictionary of Dates. Here it is:

ITINERARY.

July	8	—Leave N. Y. (S.S. "Rotterdam.")
	17	—Arrive Boulogne.
	18	—Brussels.
	19	—Aix-la-Chapelle. (Sunday.)
	20	—Cologne.
	21	—Rhine Steamer to Mainz.
	22	—Heidelberg *via* Worms.

23-24—To Leipzig *via* quickest route, &c.
25-26—Dresden. (26, Sunday.)
27   —To Munich *via* Carlsbad.
28-29—Munich.
30   —Lindau and Lake Constance.
31   —Constance and to Zurich *via* Schaffhausen.
Aug. 1 —Zurich.
2   —Lucerne. (Sunday.)
3   —Steamer, Rigi and return to Fluelen.
4   —Railway to Goeschenen, Diligence to Rhone Glacier.
5   —Meiringen and Giessbach.
6   —Brienz, Interlaken.
7   —Faulhorn and Grindelwald.
8   —Thun, Berne and Lausanne.
9   —Lausanne and Geneva. (Sunday.)
10   —Steamer to Chillon, Railway to Brieg.
11   —Simplon Pass to Arona.
12   —Steamer by Borromean Islands to Luino, Lugano.
13-14—Menaggio and Lake excursions, to Bellagio.
15-16—Como and Milan. (16 Sunday.)
17   —Milan to Venice.
18-19—Venice.
20-22—Florence and to Rome 22d.
23-30—Rome.
31   —Pisa and to Genoa.
Sept. 1 —Nice to Avignon.
2   —Avignon and to Lyons.
3   —Lyons.
4   —Fontainebleau.
5-12—Paris. (to Rouen 12th.)
13   —Rouen. (Sunday.)
14   —Dieppe—Newhaven to London.
15-22—London.
23   —To Melrose *via* Peaks of Derbyshire, &c.
24   —Melrose Abbey, Abbotsford, Dryburgh.
25-27—Edinburgh. (27 Sunday.)
28   —Trossachs.
29   —To Liverpool.
30   —To New York by Steamer " City of Paris."

I showed it to my mother. Her comment was that it was good, but that I had named no days for headaches.

. . . .

The important event finally came off and we left for our trip. We spent a few days, of course, at Niagara and New York, and then prepared to take the steamer. We called at Cook's office and obtained our ocean tickets and an order on the Netherlands line office at Boulogne for others.

We had chosen the "Rotterdam" of the Netherlands line in order to go direct to the continent and avoid crossing the channel on a small steamer. While this is one of the smaller lines and not ranking first in speed, we were assured that it was safe and comfortable.

Our first sight of the steamship was on the night of the seventh of July, 1891, when we took a cab from the New York Hotel across the ferry to Jersey City in a driving rain and were let out at a pier covered with a spacious frame warehouse. We climbed up the staging to the big black steamer, looming up indistinctly before us, and were shown down two stairways to our little state-room on the right or starboard side. An incandescent lamp was burning, but there was also a port hole not far above water line, which lighted and ventilated the room in the daytime. Below the port hole was a seat or berth and opposite were the upper and lower berths for ourselves. Opposite the door was the ingenious washstand arrangement that was pulled down for use and at pleasure shut up to empty the water. Everywhere was the green Dutch flag and "N. A. S. M.," the initials of the Company.

Then we explored the dining saloon above our state-room and found two long tables on each side, with stationary seats upholstered in red velvet, and at the forward end discovered a good piano and music. While there an agent gave us the gratifying information that Messrs. Cook & Son had let us pay too much for our ocean tickets. We had paid at summer rates, which are higher, when in some way July should according to Dutch calculation be in the winter schedule. As the result was $26.00 in our favor we agreed to reform the calendar. Evidently the topsy-turviness of an ocean trip had affected the Zodiac too. As the price was only $80.00 for the two at first, this made the cost about equal to the expense of boarding for the same length of time at a fair hotel on land.

After this pleasant episode we went out again on the covered pier and promenaded, watching with interest the preparations for leaving. We saw our lone trunk and big satchel, with labels attached, go aboard, and tried to guess who of the arriving people would be our particular associates on the voyage. A pleasant surprise was meeting in the surgeon of the ship a Mobilian and friend, of whom we had lost trace for some years and whom we now hardly recognized in his jaunty blue uniform.

We went to bed after a while in our narrow berths. The novelty of the position, the noise of the steam winch and the shouting of orders by apparently every one on deck banished sleep for a long time. When we awoke there was no noise, and daylight streamed in the port hole. We looked out and found that we were moving. We were off Sandy Hook and our trip to Europe had begun.

The official introduction to sea life was at breakfast. Our friend the surgeon was at the head of one table and put us on his left and carefully attended to Rachel. Almost every one was out to breakfast and we found that we helped make up a passenger list of forty or fifty. The food was excellent and when our appetites had recovered from the uneasiness of the first two or three days the principal pleasure of the day was the gong to meals. The dishes were French (*à la* Dutch) and after we had become used to the singular appearance of some of them we liked the cooking very much. The favorite dishes were currie and similar combinations, and gravies and good pastry were part of every meal. At 7:30 A.M. was a cold breakfast with coffee, at noon a hot lunch, at 5 P.M. a formal dinner of many courses, and at 9 a cold supper. The service was excellent. At our table were two handsome Dutch boys who were very attentive waiters.

For the first few days sea-sickness was prevalent and as the patients gradually came on deck their pale faces and weak condition marked them out. They were not all ladies. I recall one young man who did not come out on deck for a week. During an excitement which I will describe he was told that the ship was on fire and he must save himself. He languidly replied, "Let her sink," and turned over in his berth. Gradually, however, the breezes and salt air brought all the invalids around, and the services of the chambermaid in bringing up meals were less and less demanded. She, by the way, was quite pretty and a great favorite. All called her Jungfrau for short.

In our usually placid life on shipboard the first thing in the morning was getting steamer extension chairs located in a shady place and lashed to some fixed part of the vessel. The next important matter would be vigorous promenades after breakfast, and indeed after each meal. Up and down one side, or up one side and down the other, they went in couples until onlookers, like themselves, were tired. Walking was often no easy work. We gradually, however, got our sea legs and learned to navigate the uncertain deck, balancing to accommodate ourselves to the roll of the ship, and after a while we could promenade at all angles, in humble imitation of the sailors and of Captain Van der Zee, the commander, whom no lurch surprised. We became so accustomed to the motion of the ship that on reaching land we walked for days with feet some distance apart to guard against possible disturbance of the *terra firma*. At noon we learned the vessel's progress from a little chart daily posted up near the dining room door, and the unquenchable betting propensity of some of the passengers would be gratified by pools and wagers on the speed. We generally made in the neighborhood of 200 miles a day, but often somewhat less.

In the course of a few days the passengers gradually became acquainted and divided off into congenial groups. We took as naturally here by ourselves in mid-ocean to sets and criticism as on land, and in fact as we had more leisure we noticed things that on shore we would not. We were taking up prejudices and having them removed all during the trip. The ship was a little world and as we could not escape each other we got closer together in those twelve days than we would in years of casual intercourse on land.

We were sitting out on deck by the ladies' cabin one evening at twilight, the chairs lashed to the house, holding on as the ship rolled. It was not far in front of the forward smoke stack and its smoke sometimes blew down on us. We then noticed more of it than usual and suddenly found ourselves enveloped in a choking cloud. We instinctively rose to our feet. There was a great commotion below the gratings about the smoke stack and we were able to make out that the smoke was pouring up from them. We hurriedly grouped towards the ladies' cabin, losing each other on the way. The electric lamps were burning and there we saw an assemblage of blanched and silent people gazing with wide open eyes at the black volumes rolling past the cabin door. I went out to discover what I could and found the captain by the gratings shouting orders,—in Dutch. The officers had neither time nor inclination to talk, and as they hurried about on their several duties we looked at them and tried in vain to make out the probable result from their manner. I went down on the main deck and found the crew passing buckets of water from the side down into the boiler room, but they were all Dutch and I could get nothing out of them that I could understand. It looked very serious. I gazed out on the angry ocean and felt that if the fire got beyond control and we took to the boats, they could not live in so high a sea.

The suspense lasted at least an hour and then the captain came to the ladies' cabin and in his usual bland manner announced that everything was all right again. Some tar barrels which had been carried to the boiler spaces to be heated for use had been upset by the motion of the vessel and caught fire, but only burned themselves out. He said he was proud of the behavior of his passengers. None of the ladies had exhibited any undue emotion. He then considerately ordered up some champagne from the ship's stores and a glass around did much to restore equanimity. Not a few, however, had a suspicion that the fire was only half smothered and slept lightly for some nights. These regaled us with stories of how fire had been found in vessels' holds and raged for days unrevealed to hapless passengers.

We had hardly become re-assured and cheerful again when a night or so later the steamer broke her shaft near the stern at a point hard to reach. We lay to all of that night mending it and the splice made in mid-ocean under these circumstances was said to be remarkable. The accident was not made known generally, but the daily record of only half as many knots as previously told the tale, and we finished the voyage at half speed.

The chapter was not even yet complete. We had to endure also a severe storm, and during it the passengers were locked below in the cabin while the ship toiled on under bare poles against high wind and wave. The Rotterdam's promenade deck does not run the length of the ship, and standing at the forward port holes of the dining saloon we could gaze out across the open main deck at the mountainous green sea through which our ship was painfully working her way. Every now and then a wave would sweep over the deck immediately before our eyes and the scuppers could hardly carry off the water before another deluge came, or the sea would strike the ship a blow sounding like thunder and under it she would quiver from stem to stern. The view of the mad waves fighting each other as well as pounding the ship, rising high to dash into spray, and then falling away again, was grand. The ship would careen so far to one side that we had to hold on to keep our feet, and it was with recurring relief that we felt the roll cease and the vessel gradually recover. There were many passengers sick and frightened that day and night, and meals were eaten under difficulties. Even the racks for dishes and plates were insufficient, and soups and liquids were liberally distributed over the passengers, while solids slid across the tables like avalanches. At some of the rolls all of us would instinctively stop eating to wait and be certain that the ship was going to regain the perpendicular. Sleep at night was out of the question. The sideboards to the berths were up, but to stay in the box thus made one had to remain awake and hold to its sides. Fortunately the spliced shaft worked all through this pounding and no actual injury to the good ship occurred.

The storm gradually subsided, however, and in a few days it was but a disagreeable memory. One bright morning a party of ladies and gentlemen went forward and sat in the bow. We watched the beautiful lacework of the spray as the ship cut through the green water and for hours gazed lazily out at the dancing waves around us. In fine weather this is the most enjoyable place on the vessel. Behind us the masts and ship rocked steadily from side to side almost as if a different thing from the part where we sat. We saw no sail, and in fact seldom did on the voyage, for it is rather an event to sight one or even detect the smoke trail of a distant steamer. Outward bound ships pursue a different track from inward in order to avoid collisions, and so they are not often in sight except near shore. We went also one day to the extreme stern and stood in the railed place where they throw the log. This is now not of wood or even the triangular piece of canvas which they used on the Erin when I went over some years ago, but a little brass screw attached to a line. The line registers on deck the revolutions of the screw, and, as each revolution means a certain distance forward, this tells the speed. At both bow and stern one is so far from the life of the vessel that he feels strangely lonesome.

But the most interesting part of the ship I thought was the boiler room, away down on the floor of the hold. The surgeon took me there one day and I had to hold on to such steep ladders in the descent that I forgot to count the landings. Finally we were on the bottom before the hot furnaces, into which blackened, half naked stokers were continually throwing coal. There was much less rocking perceptible there than on deck, but the heat was intense despite the ventilators. As this is below water level, ashes and the like have to be put in buckets, hauled up to the main deck and thrown overboard. We crept through between the boilers and found some more furnaces, for they are placed end to end and fired from opposite extremities. Above us we saw iron stairways and gratings in several floors, and it was on one of these landings that the tar had burned and so alarmed us. I was glad to go up on deck at last and escape from the heat.

Finally the voyage neared its end. From day to day we had been platting our progress on the little charts and were told to expect land about noon of July 19th. True enough, about that time the officers on the bridge saw it a little off the port bow, and excitement ran through the whole ship. Glasses were in demand. There indeed we saw sticking up out of the sea at the horizon a pencil, which we were told was the lighthouse on Bishop's Rock. All faces were wreathed with smiles, and Columbus hardly saw America with more joy than we did this outpost of the Scilly Islands. Gradually we came nearer and could see the rocks and breakers and then the main land behind, and all that day and the next we were in sight of the south coast of England. Cliffs, parks, towns and green fields again became familiar to the grateful eye. France was invisible off to the south, but we were told that we would arrive at Boulogne late that night, and we prepared again for land. We passed many vessels, and at last sent up rockets off Boulogne, answered in turn by a green, then a white, and then a green rocket from the Netherlands people ashore.

Then came farewells, the inevitable donations to waiters, packing of satchels, and at 3 A.M. July 21st we changed to a Netherlands line tender amid kind words and the singing of "Good night, ladies." The long black ship was stationary, while our little side wheel boat steamed off with a dozen of us who did not care to go on to Amsterdam. We looked back with regret as the Rotterdam faded into darkness, but were soon absorbed in the French jargon of the crew and in the lights gleaming from the shore.

We entered Boulogne between two long piers, disembarked on one of them, and passed a perfunctory customs search for whiskey and tobacco. Then we were led in a solemn procession to the railroad depot, where our trunks also were delivered, and last of all we were conducted by an alleged interpreter to the little Hotel du Luxembourg, where they were evidently not expecting us. Mr. Luxembourg seemed to be sleeping very soundly, as it took a long time to ring any one up. At length, however, we succeeded and were shown up a winding stairway, to enjoy our first sleep in Europe.

CORONATION HALL AT AIX-LA-CHAPELLE.

CHAPTER II.

AIX, COLOGNE AND THE RHINE.

THE morning of our arrival at Boulogne we had a pleasant breakfast to ourselves in the neat dining room and the amusement of practising on the waitress the French which we had been studying and rehearsing aboard the steamer. We then changed a pretty gold Napoleon, paid the bill and started off down the quaint, narrow street. Tiled brick houses, old women with huge baskets of vegetables, hard working men with blue blouses hanging outside their pantaloons, sidewalks so narrow that almost every one takes to the stone roadway,—these were the first impressions we had of Boulogne. It is remarkable too how the same characteristics cropped up in every city of continental Europe that we visited. The old towns were all alike, regardless of country.

Our first care was to find the office of the Netherlands Company, whence we sent a cable, mailed letters, and we also arranged to forward our big trunk to await us at Paris. We obtained the tourist tickets to Cologne, where we were to get the remaining books for the summer trip. As the first train left at 11 A.M. we had no time to lose. At the quiet station we got from the trunk such clothes as we thought would be needed for two months and put them in our two satchels, of course in such a hurry as to give me for outer clothing only the gray suit I had on, destined to rival in color before we came to Paris the black one in the trunk. The polite porter examined our tickets and from admiring and asking about my engraved watch let us miss the through train to Brussels, and then passed us through the locked doors separating the stuffy waiting rooms from the car shed just in time for us to get into cars that stopped at Lille, and we were off on our travels. We had to wait at Lille for another train, which finally landed us in Brussels in the afternoon.

On arriving at Brussels we took a cab and were driven to what Baedeker said was the "unpretending" Hotel Vienne, but the description was true only in the sense that the hotel was in a back street and had no elevator. It was comfortable, however, if rather expensive, and our day of rambles in Brussels was very pleasant. The 21st of July, the date of our arrival, is the anniversary of the separation of Belgium from Holland in 1830, and was celebrated by illuminations. The designs in colored lights on the high fence of the park opposite the royal palace were particularly fine. The vast and enthusiastic crowds showed that Belgium is a patriotic country. Indeed this densely populated little state, organized as a buffer on the north-east against French ambition, and whose very existence has to be guaranteed by international treaties, was regarded, up to the recent agitation for universal suffrage, as rather a model for the rest of Europe. The form of government is constitutional. King Leopold I., uncle of Queen Victoria and long her guardian, was its first ruler.

In our strolls we had some amusing struggles with our French, and the shopkeepers and street car people enjoyed it as much as we did. St. Gudule there was our first experience of cathedrals and the beautiful effect of its stained glass windows and lofty arches has never been forgotten. The old high roofed city hall, the Exchange and the fine art gallery were like others we were to see, but the imposing Palais de Justice, by Polaert, situated on a commanding hill, is a modern architectural wonder.

We left for Aachen (or Aix-la-Chapelle) the next day and had a pleasant but uneventful ride. On the road the lion monument crowning the huge mound in the valley at Waterloo may be seen, miles away to the right. There June 18, 1815, the allied army and the French were separated by this depression, across which a highway ran towards Brussels. In the hollow, some distance apart, were the famous Hougoumont and La Haye Sainte, so desperately charged and fought over by the two armies until the arrival of fresh Prussians on Wellington's left resulted in the total defeat of Napoleon. The huge mound covers the allied dead and was erected as their monument.

On passing out of Belgium into Germany, as on coming into it from France, we went through a lax customs examination. Everything now became military. Police, postmen, guards, all wore uniforms and had an erect carriage. Indeed the difference between soldiers and all other men in Germany seemed but a difference of degree. All were soldierly.

Our stop for the night was at Aachen, the native name for Aix-la-Chapelle, the seat of Charlemagne's government and last resting place of his body. Our hotel was near the station and sleep was taken on the instalment plan. It was grateful to my ear to hear German again, but we do not recollect the hotel pleasantly, because, strange to say, they had wine and no bier, and, worst of all, for an omelette gave us a mountain of white of eggs which crumbled at the touch. This was our introduction to Germany.

The two places of chief interest at Aachen are the Cathedral and Rathhaus or Town Hall built on the site of Charlemagne's palace. The cathedral is made up of massive octagonal tower and dome 104 feet high, erected by Charlemagne as a chapel to his palace, and a later Gothic nave or choir back of it, with beautiful stained glass windows. Otho III. ventured in A.D. 1000 to open Charlemagne's tomb in his chapel, and found him seated on a marble chair. Frederick Barbarossa opened it a second time, transferred the remains to an ancient sarcophagus and dedicated the chair to the coronation of future emperors. Fortunate Charlemagne was canonized, but his unfortunate remains were yet a third time disturbed, on this occasion to be removed by the grandson of Barbarossa to a golden reliquary, their final resting place. This is still in the treasury and is shown by a priest with caskets containing the robe of the virgin, the swaddling clothes of the infant Jesus and other trustworthy relics.

Charlemagne is claimed by both French and Germans, but with more justice possibly by the latter, as the Roman Empire which his coronation in Rome A.D. 800 re-instituted survived in the East Frank division of his German kingdom until our own century, although it is true that it was little more than nominal from the death in 1250 of Frederick II., the Wonder of the World. Under Frederick's grandfather Barbarossa, who prefixed the word "Holy" to the "Roman Empire," and bade Saladin retire from *his* Asiatic Roman provinces, it was anything but nominal, and in fact it was not until the seventeenth century that the emperors conceded the title "Your Majesty" to the kings of France and England. Here at this cathedral, in the presence of its dead founder, in the magnificent Imperial Chamber of the adjacent Rathhaus, ornamented with frescoes of the early emperors and itself the place of their coronation, the old empire seems indeed real again. The Saxon Othos, the Franconian Henries battling with such popes as Hildebrand, the Suabian Fredericks trying to make their sovereignty over Italy a practical domination, whether in our opinion wise or not, were great men according to their mediæval ideals, and did their best in the impossible task of building up a new universal Roman Empire. The German King, when crowned at Milan with the Lombard iron crown and by the Pope at Rome with the golden imperial crown, became the Roman Emperor, supreme in temporal affairs as the Pope was in spiritual. Pope and Emperor were to be the two swords of God's rule on earth. Modern history begins, however, with the growth of the distinct German nationality from the time of the interregnum and quarter century of anarchy which succeeded the death of Frederick II. From the time that the election of Rudolf in 1273 ended the interregnum until 1806 the old empire was vested in the house of Hapsburg and of Austria; but it was merely a titular precedence of a so-called kaiser over all but independent dukes, electors and margraves, an appanage of the one family which had sufficient hereditary possessions to support the title. As Voltaire said, the Holy Roman Empire finally became anything but Holy, Roman or Imperial. German development is independent if not hostile to this phantom empire, for the historical chapters of modern German history are the growth of Austria, the Reformation, the Thirty Years' War, the growth of Prussia, the era of Napoleon, and the later supremacy of Prussia.

While on the train to Cologne our historical musings were disturbed by the guard's discovering that I had not had our tickets stamped at Boulogne, a fact which the railroad people in France and Belgium had not noticed. I could not for a long time make out what he meant by "stempel" and "reclamation," but finally understood that I had to buy tickets over again from the German frontier to Cologne and trust to Cook's refunding the price of our dishonored book. Rachel thought at first that we were arrested for something, but I bought new tickets at one halt, and we then had no more trouble. The Cook agency at Cologne promptly refunded the money on our arrival, although it was all my own fault in not studying the directions.

At Cologne we spent several delightful days, housed at five marks (or $1.25) each per day in the pleasant little Hotel Paris across from the church of the Minorites. This church contains the tomb of Duns Scotus, the eminent Scotch theologian, who flourished at Paris in the thirteenth century, and from whose name is inappropriately derived our word *dunce*.

Cologne, Koeln in German, is a city of 260,000 people, with a history dating back to the time of the Romans, from whose *colonia* of veterans, placed here by the mother of Nero, it derives its name. Like most of the old Rhenish towns it is on the west bank of the river, the side whence came Roman civilization. Aachen, the seat of the Carolingian Empire, was near, and Cologne in that period became an important place, subject to its own archbishop, who was an elector of the German emperors from about the twelfth century. Mediæval Cologne was rent by contests between archbishops and citizens, its nobles and guilds, but the archbishop was finally driven out and Cologne was for centuries a leading member first of the Rhenish and then of the Hanseatic League. The first meeting of the Hanseatic League is said to have taken place 1367 in the Hansa Saal, still shown in the imposing Cologne Rathhaus, which we visited.

The most interesting study in Cologne, however, is its churches, Romanesque and Gothic. Greek architecture in its origin reproduces in stone or marble the artificial wooden house, with posts and beams. The Roman added the arch and dome. It was left for the races of the north, after imitating through Christian influence the classic work in its general tendency, but not in detail, to strike out a new and not less beautiful style, the Gothic, which seems to copy trees in its spires and the meeting of the forest boughs in its arches and interiors. Christian churches were originally the flat roofed basilicas, with side aisles and at the rear a raised circular apse, adapted from the use of the Roman judges to that of the bishop and his assistants. Sometimes in the Romanesque period transepts gave the building the shape of a cross, and occasionally, as at Ravenna and Aachen, the church was round or polygonal and domed, rather in the style that architecture had taken in the east. The western Romanesque architects added a tower for bells (which were unknown to the ancients), generally a separate structure near the church, called a campanile. People could not read, and therefore the church was filled with paintings or mosaics of sacred subjects, just as later the

Gothic stained glass windows continued to make the church the people's Bible.

In the Gothic style the ground-plan is normally a Latin cross, the nave and aisles constituting the long arm, the choir the short arm, the transepts the cross-piece. As the nave is higher than the aisles, a walk or triforium went around it at the height of their arches, and there were windows in the higher clerestory elevation of the nave. Sometimes the choir, too, as in Westminster Abbey, has around it a series of lower chapels, and the transepts are generally of the same height as the nave, but often without side aisles. Without between the windows the piers, whence spring its pointed arches, are fortified by buttresses, which rise above the roof. Against these rest the round arches flying across over the aisle roof to support the clerestory at the place where the pointed arch of the nave roof begins. The tower or lantern over the intersection of nave and transept, and the double bell towers, which were part of the front, facing west, complete the principal constituents of the Gothic church. The ribs, groins, tracery, statues and other ornamentation are different in each case, while the acuteness or flatness of the arch, and particularly of the great outside windows, is the main test of the early or late age of the structure, and marks the periods of the Gothic. Gothic architecture, originating in the twelfth century in the north of France, soon spread over the world, leaving some of the noblest examples in Germany, indeed possibly its grandest result in the cathedral here at Cologne.

A description of any church, and most of all of this, the noblest of all Gothic cathedrals, is difficult if not impossible. To say that we found it of brown stone in the form of a Latin cross, about 450 feet long, the towers

512 feet high, the roof of the nave 201 feet from the ground, the stained glass magnificent,—conveys an indefinite idea of vastness, perhaps too of color, but in this dissection the harmony and life of the building escape. Any Gothic building must be seen to be appreciated, and of this church even pictures are inadequate. Its large court is insufficient to show it properly in front, and the most satisfactory view is from the open places to the south, and from the spacious bridge over the yellow Rhine in its rear, whence the flying buttresses and lofty choir loom up above everything else in Cologne. The towers are as usual in the front façade facing west, each divided into four stories, crowned by high open spires. The main portal, 93 feet high, is between the towers and above it is a noble stained glass window. Inside one sees but to admire the lofty nave and the choir with double side aisles, and transepts north and south terminating in external portals. Much of the stained glass is modern, presented by Ludwig I. from the Bavarian or by Wilhelm I. from the Berlin factories, and is nobly drawn and executed. A peculiarity which we noticed everywhere in colors on glass is that figures in red and yellow seem to stand out, and those in blue retreat, particularly when seen through the opera glass, so useful in travelling. When the Virgin's dress is red and her mantle blue, the lower part of the figure seems to be walking away from the rest, as Rachel said.

The cathedral was begun in 1248 by Meister Gerard, but has been centuries in building. By the fifteenth century the choir and nave were partly finished, but little more was done until the nineteenth. In all old pictures of Cologne a huge crane is seen on the south tower, a landmark of the city for four hundred years.

The gradual absorption of the north German states by Prussia has its questionable features morally, but at least the government is always better, and old public works are carried out. During the French occupation the cathedral was a hay magazine. As soon as Prussia seized it her kings made plans to finish the edifice, and the actual work has gone on from 1823, the government paying most of the expense, but much coming also from donations and some even from a lottery. In August, 1880, I saw the spires enveloped in platforms and scaffolding, and the completion of the structure was celebrated by appropriate ceremonies October 15th of the same year in the presence of the kaiser.

There are not quite so many relics as usual in this cathedral, probably because it is largely modern. The bones of the three wise men from the east, discovered with so many other things by Helena, Constantine's mother, and brought first to Milan, rest in a reliquary in the treasury, and of course many local worthies are buried in the church. The heart of intriguing Marie, the exiled widow of Henry IV. of France, also reposes there under a slab.

At Cologne are, however, other relics. In St. Gereon's church the bones of the Theban Legion of 318 Christians are in boxes around the walls. They were massacred here under Diocletian. In St. Ursula are the bones of that English princess and of her 11,000 virgin attendants, murdered at Cologne on their return from a pilgrimage to Rome. They are arranged in glass cases and make the church resemble an apothecary shop. However, I never question legends and relics. True or not they have edified and instructed many generations, and at least they show us what our ancestors believed and like other poetry can if read aright touch our hearts too and make our own lives sweeter and better.

Of greater interest, though, we found the excellent museum, built with money given by the merchant Richartz. Its collections originated with the bequest of the artist Wallraf to his native city. Roman pavements, sculpture and architectural remains found at Cologne are here exhibited, and the stiff but famous mediæval Cologne schools of painting are well represented. But the gem of all is Gustav Richter's beautiful picture of unfortunate Queen Louise of Prussia as she gracefully descends some steps, a star on her forehead, her white drapery sweeping behind her. The queen insulted by the first Napoleon was mother of the Wilhelm whose victories drove the third Napoleon from his throne and recovered German provinces which France had held for almost a century before Louise became queen. Camphausen's Wilhelm and his generals at Sedan and other good paintings and frescoes are in this museum, but the lovely face of Louise impressed us most and lives in our memories as among the most beautiful things of Europe.

At Cologne, when we made our " reclamation " for dishonored tickets, we obtained also the rest of our continental tickets, a series of thin slips clamped together, those of each country making up one little book. Cook's Tourist Agency, despite the retirement and lately the death of its founder, has in the hands of his descendants grown into a great and well managed system, with prominent, if small, offices in all large places. The Cooks are also bankers and we used their facilities with much satisfaction. With Cook's tickets and Baedeker's guide books we were well equipped.

Early in the morning of July 24th we went aboard the long, narrow steamer for a trip up the Rhine, and found there several friends from the Rotterdam, just arrived from Holland. The satchels were piled up around the smoke stack and we went forward to seats on the open upper deck to eat cherries and enjoy the views. When the swift steamer got under way we had to wrap up and indeed in the afternoon retired behind the funnels to avoid the sharp wind. It was colder than on the ocean.

The Rhine generally runs between high banks terraced into vineyards, and on the heights are picturesque castles, mostly in ruins but some in use, and all with legends. The part of the river most travelled is the 119 miles from Cologne to Mainz, above which are few attractions, and even between Cologne and Bonn is not much of interest. I visited a friend once at the university of Bonn and could well understand his love for the long buildings, shaded with trees, and the quaint old town. In the cemetery repose the historian Niebuhr, Bunsen, Schumann and also Schiller's wife.

Near Bonn we went over the supposed site of Cæsar's famous bridge and a short distance above the city on the opposite bank is the romantic Seven Mountains country. Here overlooking the Rhine are the ruins of Drachenfels, which I once climbed with difficulty to find little or nothing left but the wide view, celebrated in Childe Harold. Here at her home Roland met and loved Hildegunde, daughter of the lord of the Seven Mountains. After he went away she heard a rumor of her lover's death at Roncesvalles, and she took the veil at Nonnenwerth on an island higher up the stream. Roland, however, came back, but only to find her beyond recall, and, as the best he could do, built a castle there on the Rhine overlooking the cloister, and lived disconsolate until at last her death induced his own.

Further on the same right-hand side is the modern and beautiful Apollinaris church, built by Zwirner, (who finished the Cologne cathedral) and containing the head of St. Apollinaris of Ravenna. This head when it was on the way by river to Cologne with the bones of the Magi stopped the boat and indicated that it preferred to remain on this spot, and therefore here they built it a church. In this neighborhood is the Apollinaris spring whose water is famous the world over. The spring is leased to an English syndicate, who send to America alone almost a million bottles a month.

As our boat went on up the river, making only short stops, we admired Andernach with its walls, bastion and tower lying picturesquely on the right, and beyond at Coblenz saw the bridge of boats, which opened to let the steamer through. Near there fell and was buried the famous French general Marceau in 1796, and opposite this city is the famous fortress of Ehrenbreitstein, the Rhenish Gibraltar, approached from the river by an inclined plane. It is said that this castle cannot be starved in less than ten years, and cannot be stormed at all. Stolzenfels higher up the river, also on the right, is a restored and handsome castle belonging to the emperor. Not far beyond this is the octagonal Königsstuhl near the confines of the Rhenish electorates of Cologne, Mainz, Treves and Palatinate, often the place of meeting of the electors to choose the German emperors. Then on the other bank came Sterrenberg and Liebenstein with their legend of two brothers, one noble and brave, the other selfish and faithless, even to the wife to whom both had paid court. Conrad, who had gone away in order to let his brother win her, now wished to avenge Hildegarde's wrongs, but she reconciled the brothers, and then retired to a convent below the castles. From the steamer we saw next majestic Rheinfels beyond on the right, the most extensive ruin on the river, and soon we curved around the famous Lorelei Rock. Here sat the enchantress and to lure sailors to their destruction sang as she combed her golden hair. Her echo still reverberates there, but huge as the rock looms up in the bend of the river, 430 feet above the water, with long slanting strata, at its foot has now been blasted a safe channel, and the saucy steamers below and the noisy railway piercing the mountain itself have driven Lorelei away from her haunts, and her German cliff by a bit of poetic injustice even pictures Napoleon's profile to imaginative eyes. Near here our patriotism was stirred by seeing the stars and stripes floating proudly from a tower of the castle of Schönburg. The Americans on the steamer, strangers to each other but moved by a common impulse, rushed to the side, waved hats and handkerchiefs and cheered lustily the emblem of our own united country, thus seen in the midst of mediæval castles. Above near the queer Noah's Ark looking castle of Pfalz on an island, formerly convenient for collecting blackmail on river commerce, revengeful Blücher crossed into France after Napoleon's defeat at Leipzig, and since that time there have been no more castles on the Rhine blown up by the French. Then came Rheinstein, perched on a projecting spur on the same side, picturesque and still in use.

At the Mouse Tower in the river below Bingen legend says that retributive mice ate the cruel archbishop who once burned the poor in a famine because he said they consumed the corn like mice. It is a signal station now

RHEINFELS CASTLE, ON THE RHINE.

and at this point the river widens into Bingen Bay. By Bingen, sacred to Mrs. Hemans' soldier of the legion, a channel has been blasted for the river commerce. Opposite on the left amid rich Rudesheim vines, planted originally by Charlemagne and the most prized of all, stands facing west the majestic national monument of Germania by Schilling, its base 111 feet high, the figure visible for miles in all directions. It was designed to commemorate the decisive war of 1870-1 which both crushed France, her ancient enemy, and united Germany into one empire.

We look back to the Rhine trip with much pleasure. Possibly the Hudson is by nature more imposing, but it has ugly ice warehouses instead of romantic castles and wild woods instead of carefully terraced vineyards, and is not for the present at least so attractive. Before the Hanseatic League built up foreign trade, the principal commerce of Europe was on the Rhine, and it was early the seat of civilization. For this reason rather than for the views these castles were built, some to oppress, but some to protect traffic. The river trade is still large, and besides passenger steamers we passed many strong tugs towing heavily laden barges.

At Biebrich below Mainz we got off the steamer on the east bank near dark and as the 'bus was not available the agent exchanged that ticket for a carriage to Wiesbaden. We were driven there in fine style, clattering over good roads, people flocking out to see who it was that was making so much noise in the world, and at last we were set down at the little Hotel Einhorn.

At Wiesbaden we spent a quiet Sunday. During the day we wandered about the city, quaint in its old parts, beautiful in the new, and in an elegant hall drank the hot, muddy water from the spring for which the place is famous. In the afternoon we rambled through the flower gardens and colonnades, visited the beautiful parlors, library and reading rooms of the Cursaal, and after supper there spent the evening listening to familiar music by a splendid band.

CHAPTER III.

HEIDELBERG TO WEIMAR: THE LUTHER AND GOETHE COUNTRY.

TO get to Heidelberg from Wiesbaden we passed by rail through Mainz and Worms on the upper Rhine. I wanted to go to Strasburg to see again its ancient houses, the noble monument of Saxe descending into the open tomb, the wonderful clock in the cathedral transept, and the spire, long unfinished, which the Germans during their short occupation have completed. But time forbade.

At Mainz we drove through the town, saw the palace of the old electors facing on the present drill ground, and visited the cathedral which has been so often burned. Land must have been very valuable in these crowded old German towns before they were extended by removal of the walls. At Aachen the cathedral even now is touched by secular buildings, at Cologne it was so until a few years ago, and here at Mainz the cathedral is all but completely surrounded by houses built solidly up to it and above them towers its roof. The chief if not the only entrance is by a narrow court between two houses. There is therefore no satisfactory external view of the church, but within the effect is good. Here at Mainz

Gutenberg about 1440-50 invented printing, issuing as the first book a Bible, and in a square near the Cathedral Thorwaldsen has a noble statue of him. For some reason we picture all great men as statuesque. We do not think of Gutenberg, Fust and Schöffer except as loving co-workers in a great invention, and yet we know that Fust went to law with Gutenberg and by legal process ejected him from control of the printing office.

Further on at Worms Luther in 1521, with the safe-conduct granted by the Emperor Charles V., faced the imperial diet or congress and defended his doctrines, concluding, " Here I stand, I cannot act otherwise, God help me. Amen." The diet condemned him, but the safe-conduct held until his Saxon friends captured and immured him in the Wartburg. Worms in the Reformation wars was burned more than once, and the episcopal palace, where the diet sat, has perished. Near its site stands now a large statue of the man who thus made the place famous.

About noon our train arrived in narrow Heidelberg on the Neckar, and we took the street cars up its Hauptstrasse to the incline railway, and then this last to the castle 330 feet above the river. The most familiar picture of the castle is a side view from the east, but this alone gives an inadequate idea of its extent. It is built around a square court, the main front facing northward towards the Neckar. The cliff is precipitous as seen from the promenade in front, and so too on the east, and on the south and west sides are abysmal moats. The schloss is on a projecting spur and since the days of artillery can be commanded from the higher portion of the mountain behind, but when built in the thirteenth century and for long afterwards was impregnable. En-

THE COURT OF HEIDELBERG CASTLE.

tering over the bridge and under the great Watch Tower at the south-west corner of the castle, we found ourselves in the court surrounded by palatial but ruined buildings overgrown with ivy. Near the entrance is a covered well, the handsome structure to the right is that of Elector Otto Heinrich of the sixteenth century, and that before us, constituting the front of the castle, was built by Elector Frederick V., who married Elizabeth, daughter of James I. of England. This Frederick, count palatine, was the Calvinist "Winter King" whose rule in Bohemia was cut short at White Hill near Prague in one of the early battles of the Thirty Years' War. This was in 1620, the year of the founding in America of Puritan New England. The war also cost Frederick his hereditary dominion, the Palatinate, a Rhenish electorate of which Bacharach had once been the capital, but of which Heidelberg was from the erection of this schloss. The castle was not much injured in this war, but Frederick was driven out of the country and his electoral right transferred to Bavaria, although at its conclusion a vote was given to the count palatine again. When the Protestant line died out in 1685 Louis XIV. claimed the principality, and the unprovoked harrying of the Palatinate by Melac under the orders of the Grand Monarque is one of the great crimes of history. The French were compelled to withdraw after a few years, but they then burned or blew up all they could of this noble structure. Four towers still mark the corners. The south-eastern one had walls 21 feet thick, and although half of this was precipitated by the explosion bodily into the moat the rest remains standing now. Next towards the river comes the familiar Octagonal Tower over the arsenal, and its summit, reached by winding steps, commands a magnificent landscape. Otto Heinrich's three story building, of which it is a part, was in fine Renaissance style, and Frederick's four-story one adjoining, the castle front, is still in fair preservation. Below this last is the promenade with wide view of town and valley, and beneath in a cellar is the Heidelberg Tun of 49,000 gallons capacity, on top of which is a platform formerly used for dancing. The Thick Tower at the north-west corner of the castle is connected with Frederick's main structure by his Elizabeth Building, and on the west side of the court face other substantial but less interesting ruins. The elector moved his residence to Mannheim in the last century and from the beginning of this the Palatinate has been broken up and the electoral power extinguished.

We took dinner at the restaurant Molkencur higher up the mountain, reached by the same incline railway, and we enjoyed between showers splendid views. Across the Neckar about where we now gazed I once had climbed a hill and looked at the ivied castle and the mountain upon which we now stood. Below was the swift river, and one of the usual ugly ram-like steamboats came along, keeping in the channel by taking up a chain from the bottom and passing it back over the boat. We had noticed this performance also in the Rhine by Coblenz. To the west of the surrounding mountains was a vast plain dotted with fields, houses and woods, intersected by tree bordered roads and the silver Neckar, and bounded on the west by a sharp line followed by a hazy one, marking the Rhine bed. In returning to the road I had passed by the otherwise uninteresting Hirsch Inn where the students fight duels.

On this present visit we descended to the town from

dinner, and, although after bank hours, drew our first money on the letter of credit from Brown Brothers of New York. Without stopping for more than a few minutes to see the buildings of the University, founded in 1386 and the oldest in the limits of the empire, we took the evening train northwardly for Frankfort on the Main. The ride was in part after dark and as we could see nothing we were glad to get to our comfortable hotel at Frankfort.

The name of Frankfort, and the suburb called Sachsenhausen from a colony of conquered Saxons, take us back to the time of Charlemagne. Still a flourishing Prussian city, and in this century the capital of the German Confederation, Frankfort has been in the past, however, of much greater importance as the place of election of the emperors. Charlemagne was made emperor at Rome when he was crowned, and so long as his descendants showed his qualities in any degree no special election was necessary. But after the weak successors of this Frank permanently divided his empire in 888, the imperial branch was soon superseded by Henry the Fowler of the very Saxon tribes whom Charlemagne had subdued and annexed a century and a half before. Otho I. after him in 962 re-established the empire on a firm German basis, besides reforming the corrupt court of Rome itself. German Kings, now to be Roman Emperors, were always theoretically elective. The dukes of the four races making up the German kingdom, the Franks, Suabians, Saxons and Bavarians, held the four great offices of the imperial household, those of cupbearer, chamberlain, marshal and seneschal, and the pastors of the three greatest sees beyond the Alps,—Mainz, Treves and Cologne,—were arch-chancellors of

Germany, Gaul and Burgundy. With the growth of feudalism these officials, assuming to represent the German races and the German church, gradually came themselves to elect the German ruler. With the independence of the Franks and extinction of the Suabian duchy, Bohemia and Brandenburg were substituted for them by Charles IV's celebrated Golden Bull of 1356, and later changes brought in the count palatine. The number seven was for a long time preserved, but the electors were nine at last, Hanover being the latest addition. The clerical members of the college suffered no change until Napoleon extinguished the electorates of Treves and Cologne when he made these principalities part of France.

The Golden Bull likewise fixed Frankfort as the regular meeting place of the electors and thus it continued until the empire ceased. We saw the dingy looking, many gabled Römer building where the election was held. There the emperor dined with the electors, and at its windows he showed himself to the enthusiastic crowd in the open Römerberg without, while the fountain in their midst ran wine. In his autobiography Goethe describes the election festivities as he saw them while a boy. In the imposing Frankfort cathedral under the central tower, itself like the high imperial crown of Charlemagne, the ruler was crowned by the electoral archbishop of Mainz. When the empire was a force as well as a title the proceedings at Frankfort were but the selection of the German king as emperor elect; this made him king of the Romans, but he was not Roman Emperor until crowned by the Pope at Rome. From the accession of the Hapsburgs in 1273 the imperial power as such was small, and therefore few emperors took the trouble to be crowned at Rome. Gradually even the necessity for it was lost sight of, and we, like the Archdukes of Austria themselves, generally think of the old Empire as Austrian or German, and forget that it was a continuation of the Roman Empire.

We took an interesting drive around the city in the morning. Old Frankfort has narrow, crooked streets, and one of them was Judengasse, the Jewish quarter, formerly locked up at night. There lived the first Rothschild, with his red shield sign. His banking sagacity placed a son at Paris, another at London, a third at Vienna, a fourth at St. Petersburg, and they have raised the family name to a high place in the world. The newer streets like the broad Zeil are handsome, and the wide zigzag promenades on the site of the old fortifications are pleasant and much frequented. Near one angle we visited the Bethmann collection of art, the gem of which is Ariadne seated on a panther, the six years' labor of Dannecker of Stuttgart. The attendant drew aside a curtain and showed us the group on a revolving pedestal. It is in a recess lighted from above, and the red curtains give the woman a realistic flesh tint. In the old town we saw the high house in which Goethe was born and brought up, with its old-fashioned projecting eaves. Not far off is the Goethe Platz and statue, and the statue of his friend Schiller is also near at hand, while a group of Gutenberg and his two assistants recalls that Frankfort too was an early seat of printing along with Mainz, Strasburg and Venice.

There was an electric exposition near the railroad station which dazzled us the night of our arrival. At this was demonstrated the practicability of bringing an electric current from a distant waterfall to run the machinery. Without stopping, however, to see much of the exposition, we took the train before noon for a ten hours' journey to Leipzig. The Frankfort station and car sheds where we got on are the most extensive and imposing that we saw in Europe. This city of 150,000 is growing rapidly and its central position makes it an important commercial point.

On this trip to Leipzig we saw a good deal of German railroad travel. Their trains are possibly more comfortable than the Belgian, but railroad arrangements are pretty much alike all over Europe. Some cars are better ventilated or cleaner than others, some have an automatic handle in each compartment for stopping the train in an emergency, and the railroad laws posted in the cars of different lines vary somewhat, but in a general way travelling is the same. The little cars—coaches or wagons as they call them—seemed odd to us. They are like small box cars without platforms, but the sides are broken by four or five doors, each with a window to its right and left, marking the four or five compartments running clear across the car, and making each car look as if it had so many coach bodies cemented together under one roof and on one floor. The compartments open on a board outside running the length of the car, used as a step, and on this the guard passes to collect fares while the train is in motion, for there is no passage way through as with us. Outside, each compartment is locked or at least closed with a large latch, opened at stations. Within, the compartment has two seats facing each other, each accommodating five persons. Half therefore ride backwards when all places are taken. There is no water aboard, and this, like the primitive toilet rooms, must be sought at the stations during the long stops. There are generally three classes of compartments, differing only in fares and in the upholstery. All three, marked on the doors with Roman numbers, are frequently in the same train, perhaps two kinds in the same car, but some special trains, however, run only first or first and second class. I have even travelled fourth class in Prussia, and had to stand up in a regular box car and hold on to ropes. The usual class travelled is third, but on our trip we used second as more comfortable and less crowded. The old saying is that only fools and Americans travel first class. One disagreeable feature of continental cars is that smoking is allowed in all except those marked otherwise, and even in non-smokers by consent.

In our compartment from Frankfort to Weimar was a German with two little boys, and through his English, which was not as perfect as he imagined, and my German, which was even worse, we carried on a pleasant conversation. I was interested at the frankness of his views as to the restless young emperor. "The emperor," he said, "is a young man of some promise, but he, like all others, has to learn his trade. As it has to be at our expense, we sincerely hope that he will refrain from unnecessary mistakes." We found him and all Germans, however, devoted to the Vaterland, the empire and its great founders.

Further on we passed Eisenach, Erfurt and Weimar without having time to stop, but I could not but recall pleasant visits to these places and Wittenberg while I was studying at Leipzig.

At Eisenach itself there is not a great deal of interest except the plain, long house where Bach was born, and on an open place the house where Luther as a boy chorister at school lived with Frau Ursula Cotta. This house had stories projecting each a little over the one below, and the entry was quaintly carved. Luther's birthplace was Eisleben near Halle, and there while on a visit in 1546 he died. By Eisenach is the Wartburg, covering the summit of a hill, visible for miles in all directions, and itself commanding an equally extensive view. I reached it from Eisenach after a forty minutes' climb in the rain. This long rambling Romanesque castle, dating back to the eleventh century, is made up of a number of parts, the rooms near the entrance being those connected with Luther. His friend Frederick the Wise, elector of Saxony, had him brought here for safety after he had left Worms under the ban of the empire. In this castle, habited as a knight and known as Junker Georg, he worked almost a year on his translation of the Bible, so important from a religious standpoint, and also as fixing the German language by thus giving it a universally used literary classic. His New Testament appeared in 1522. The whole castle is interesting and long before Luther contests of Minnesingers in the middle ages had made it famous. The first room usually shown is the rather sumptuous chapel where Luther preached, a sword of Bernhard of Weimar now hanging by the pulpit, and then I saw the plain room where he lived and worked. There were shown Luther's arm-chair, a foot-stool which was the vertebra of some large animal, his table, book-case, canopied bed, and portraits of his father and mother and of himself. In the wall is the hole marking where the inkstand struck which he threw at the Devil. He was better satisfied that he hit Satan than any one has been since.

Further on towards Leipzig is Erfurt, where some

years before he had retired in sadness from the wickedness of the world into an Augustinian monastery. Brother Martin's cell has been destroyed by fire. From there he was called by the elector to be professor of philosophy at the great Saxon university of Wittenberg.

Wittenberg is now a little Prussian town of some 14,000 people, midway between Leipzig and Berlin, but then it was the residence of the elector of Saxony, probably the most powerful prince of the empire. Thence Luther visited Rome, where he saw much to shock him, and at Wittenberg in 1517 he began the Reformation by opposing the Dominican Tetzel's sale of indulgences. Four years later was the open breach with Rome and excommunication. Then came Worms, the Wartburg, publication of the translated Bible, his marriage to Katharina Von Bora, and that life of piety and polemics which has changed the history of the world.

Luther's house at Wittenberg is at the entrance of the Collegienstrasse, right by the dismantled fortifications, over which it can be plainly seen from the oak, outside the gate, which marks the spot where he burned Leo X's bull of excommunication. The house is in the court of the old Augustinian monastery and was given him as a residence by the elector. It is a gabled building with dormer windows, a tower in the middle of the front containing the entrance stairway. In Luther's room is still shown his black German stove, cast from the designs of his friend Cranach, shaped like a church and having on it the evangelists and undraped female figures representing music and other arts. His much worn table has a removable lid and within are pigeon holes. At the window is a curious *tête-à-tête* seat, two chairs facing each other in one piece, and on the wall in a gilt frame is his many colored coat of arms,—a black cross over a red heart, with a rose on a blue ground. In the next room is his common cup of tin and wood, the wooden beads used by Katharina when a nun, and a large cut of Luther by Hans Luft, Wittenberg's first printer and the publisher of Luther's translation of the Bible. In an adjoining hall is a two story pulpit from which Luther lectured.

Not far away is Melanchthon's house near the site of the old university, which in our century has been incorporated with that of Halle. Over the door of a house in the Mittelstrasse I noticed the intensely sectarian inscription,—"Gottes Wort und Luther's Schrift des Babst und Calvini Gift," meaning that God's word and Luther's writings are poison to the pope and Calvin. At the termination of this street, just before getting to the market place with its quaint Rathhaus and stiff statues of Wittenberg's two great reformers, is the Stadtkirche, a double towered Gothic church where Luther often preached and in which he in 1552 administered the communion in both kinds, for the first time since the days of Huss. At the further end of the town is the castle and the handsome castle church to whose wooden doors Luther in 1517 affixed his famous 95 Theses. The original doors were destroyed during a bombardment, but Frederick William IV. has substituted metal ones on which is the Latin text, thus made imperishable. Within, the church is plain and narrow and there was little to detain me except the wooden slabs in the middle marking the graves of Luther and Melanchthon. The adjacent castle was the electoral residence down to 1542, but is now the barracks of the garrison.

Wittenberg is not on the route to Leipzig from Frankfort, but Weimar is, the home of another great German,

The Grand Duke Charles Augustus invited Goethe there, gave him an official position, and in the large but plain yellow house also furnished him the poet lived the fifty-six years preceding his death in 1832. Goethe induced Schiller also to come here. They were fast friends, and even in death they are hardly divided, for their great oaken coffins, covered with offerings, lie side by side amid the ducal dead in the dark Princes' Vault in the cemetery. Goethe's house was occupied by a grandson of his at the time of my visit and so was not shown, but I went over Schiller's house, climbing up the narrow stairs to his working rooms on the third floor. Amongst other relics were his table and single bed and several portraits. Wieland also lived at Weimar and near his plain little house is Rietschel's fine group of Goethe handing a wreath to Schiller.

Schiller was a lovable character and a brilliant man, but Goethe and Luther I think the greatest of Germans. Luther was a man essentially of one idea and carried it through despite pope and emperor. Goethe had not the same vigor, but was a broader, more fully rounded character. Luther created his age, while Goethe was the crown of his.

Rachel, however, had not reminiscences of an earlier visit to help her, and after the shades of night cut off the views and confined us to looking at some bold girls who were in our compartment we became headachy and tired out. There was no water and the yearnings for supper too made the last hours of this long ride very uncomfortable. Even the familiar names of stations near Leipzig did not take the place of a good meal, the more especially as when we did come in sight of the lights of Leipzig we seemed to spend a half hour going all around the city before reaching the station.

CHAPTER IV.

LEIPZIG: ITS UNIVERSITY AND ITS BATTLE FIELDS.

ABOUT 9 P.M. our train rolled into the station at Leipzig, and, tired out with travel, we took a carriage for Müller's Hotel. We rattled over the same cobble stones that had ten years before tried alike my patience and my shoes, and were greeted at the hotel side door by the same genial Herr whose perpetual white shirt and full dress had won my heart in auld lang syne.

A nice room on the third floor and good meals, all at six marks a day for each of us, were soon arranged for, and we retired to sleep, I to dream that I was a student of philosophy here again, at No. 5 Schletter Strasse, dritte treppe.

The next day we began with a visit to the post office, where we received the first letter from home written after our departure. The post office is at the east end of the old city, facing on the Augustus Platz, a large open place bounded north by the handsome new theatre, east by the post office and other buildings, south by the Museum, and west by the main University buildings. Here the street cars centre, and after visiting the Museum we took rides on them about the city, which I found larger and much improved.

When I was at the University this Museum was my first real introduction to art, and I have always looked back to it with affection. Returning now after ten years it seemed smaller, perhaps by contrast, although in fact enlarged since 1880; but the familiar pictures beamed a welcome back again, and I found the collections as worthy of admiration as formerly. The gem of all to me is the despondent Napoleon at Fontainebleau, by Delaroche, pictured as thinking of his abdication; but paintings by Calame and others, the crayon landscapes by Preller of the Wanderings of Ulysses, of which the completed paintings are at Weimar, Thorwaldsen's marble Ganymede, and many other works also well repay study. William Sohn's painting, The Consultation, (a mother and daughter with a lawyer,) detained me long, because of the striking resemblance of the kind attorney to my father, who had died in the interval between my two visits abroad.

Leipzig was originally an irregular square, about half a mile long on each side. It was bounded west by the small Pleisse River into which the Parthe empties from the east a little north of the old city, and into which flowed the Elster River from the west at the north-west corner of the fortifications. These walls were dismantled after the fall of Napoleon and their site is occupied by beautiful promenades and drives all around the old city, frequently ornamented with statues of distinguished Germans, and south of the Museum the walks expand into a valuable botanical garden. Within the old mediæval city four or five irregular streets run north and south, while but two—Grimmäische Strasse and the Brühl—run east and west. But there is also a network of passages or arcades through the blocks from street to street, many with shops or booths at the sides. In the centre of the city is the city hall—Rathhaus—facing on the Markt Platz in front and the Naschmarkt in the rear. The Rathhaus was built in 1556 and like the other high antiquated buildings about the square is black with age, in winter its towers and peaks jutting picturesquely up out of the snow on the roof. I instinctively went to where the Fleischergasse comes into the Markt to see if Del Vecchio's picture store was still there, before which I used to stand so much and admire the photographs and other pictures exhibited in the window. The store still exists. I remember one time a picture there of a baby show with the inscription in English, "We come all the way from Chicago," and the staid Germans crowded the sidewalks and gazed solemnly at the collection of laughing or crying baby faces. Near the Markt is Auerbach's Keller, where you now get a good meal of oysters, wine, etc., but no bier at all, and where formerly Mephistopheles induced Faust to partake of a more remarkable feast, drawing wine and fire from the tables. The legend is given in the old mural paintings of the place, and Goethe's signature, a lock of his hair and other mementos are also exhibited. In the Markt I found that they had erected in 1888 a fine war monument. The main figure is Germania, and below are William I. and equestrian statues of Frederick William, King Albert of Saxony, Von Moltke and Bismarck. This old part of Leipzig, with quaint tiled houses overhanging the narrow crooked streets, the big horses with pointed collars, drawing high wagons, the serious but good-natured people, the huge pumps, the old stores, the Brühl with its fur shops, the women driving little wagons drawn by strong dogs, the numerous children, the peddlers' cries, the newsgirls,—all make up an interesting picture familiar and dear to one who has lived in the city. The three Leipzig fairs are not kept up as they were before the time of railroads, yet on these occasions still every platz is filled with booths displaying goods of all kinds, and the Polish Jews in the Brühl, with beards, long coats and high hats, realized my idea of Shylock. At the south-west corner of the promenades is the old fortress, the Pleissenburg, now a garrison. In the low court back of it the soldiers drill, and the instruction is incessant and thorough. In this building Luther and Dr. Eck had their famous disputation. Not far from it is the Thomas Kirche, plain outside, like most other Leipzig Protestant churches, while inside it is furnished beautifully. Bach was organist at the Thomas Schule near by for over a quarter of a century previous to his death in 1750.

The original city is surrounded by five new quarters, each as large as old Leipzig. These suburbs are built of brick and plaster, in the handsome, if monotonous, Renaissance style, have flowers in the windows or on the porches, and stretch for great distances in regular squares, along numerous well paved streets. Off to the southwest is the new Gewandhaus, where the celebrated concerts are given. Mendelssohn conducted them in the second third of this century, but their origin antedates him almost a hundred years. Not far off is the celebrated Conservatory of Music, and near by is the block given up to the Imperial Supreme Court buildings, now in course of erection. Although an empire, Germany is made up of a number of semi-independent and jealous states, so that centralization is not perfect. To this it is due that the Supreme Court sits at Leipzig and not at Berlin. As a student I saw its opening October 1, 1879, under President Simson, in a building facing the park back of the new theatre, and I attended several of its rather prosy succeeding sessions. In the newer parts of the city are the great printing houses. Although a city of but two hundred and fifty thousand, Leipzig has the unquestioned supremacy in all Germany of the printing trade. The Tauchnitz edition of English and American authors is published here and much of the music on American pianos and organs comes from Leipzig. All the great German publishing houses have headquarters here.

Besides the city promenades Leipzig has to the northwest the large Rosenthal for drives and walks, well wooded and much frequented. This and other pleasant parks of meadow, water and woodland, are all judiciously arranged, and in spring they offer extensive and inviting walks, of which we students regularly availed ourselves. Further out in every direction are historic villages connected with the city by excellent roads lined with lindens or poplars, and we used to enjoy rambles also through wide meadows or along the banks of the interminable network of creeks that they dignify with the name of rivers. The many pretty girls remind one of Ovid's allusion to the number in Rome—*Quot caelum stellas, tot habet tua Roma puellas.* There seem to be no end of children, and all live in the streets. Girls in the spring are absorbed in jumping rope and playing with little hollow rubber balls, the boys in whipping tops,—something I had only read of before,—and all the year round the children have street games of some kind, many unknown to us Americans.

We went to see Frau Paetzel, in whose flat I had lived eleven years before, for university students have no dormitories. We entered the common hall, for it was not necessary to ring at the street door in the daytime, and ascended the common stairway to the desired floor, the third. Die gnädige Frau, as I used to call her, answered the bell in person, immediately recognized me and gave us a hearty welcome. As it was all in German, Rachel was much embarrassed, for her stock in trade was limited to Ja, Nein and my invariable inquiry at hotels, Alles eingeschlossen? Frau Paetzel in her frank way soon intimated that my own German had deteriorated since I left her influence. Still, our conversing at all showed I was not as bad off as once when I called on my friend Schmidt in Leipzig and asked the girl who came, "Wohnt Herr Schmidt da?" I had to repeat the question several times, and at last the maid laughed, shook her head, and said, "I spik not English." On our present visit to my old landlady the idea seized me of using the universal language of music, and I asked Rachel to play "Ripples of the Alabama" and other familiar airs. But I suspect that the instrument had not been tuned since little Martha had worried me with her practicing years ago, and I am not positive how far the music helped. For Rachel's sake—principally—I declined a pressing invitation to take dinner with the family and all the neighbors and after a glass of wine with the Frau and Herr we left.

My beautiful room near the landing looked natural with its blue walls, tall white porcelain stove in the corner, windows with lace curtains, and the single bed whose coverings fit so well that when I got underneath they regularly became all untucked. German bedclothes consist mainly of a feather mattress, which lies on top of one instead of underneath. In the stove I used to kindle a little fire and after that began to burn I would shut it up, smoke and all, and it radiated heat for hours. I had a good, plain lamp, but the "German" student's lamp so common at home does not seem to be much known in Germany.

This room was beautifully furnished and cost, attendance included, eighteen marks a month. Every morning before I got up a girl brought in my breakfast of bread, butter, soft boiled egg and coffee, for which I paid seven and a half marks extra. Dinner I took at a neighboring restaurant and at night a roll and glass of milk at a milch-halle around the corner finished up my meals. Bier I generally took at dinner only, but occasionally went of an evening with German friends to a garden, and like them spent an hour over a dull newspaper and a 25 pfennig glass of the favorite Bairisch bier. When men drink together they say "Prosit," a Latin health, and a stranger entering at meal time would say, "Mahlzeit," an abbreviation of a wish for a pleasant meal. I noticed less of this on my second visit. I remember that on the wall at my restaurant was a motto, "Even Dr. Luther says WATER does no good." But Dr. Luther spoke of baptism, and this wit applied the quotation as pointing to bier.

Whenever we called a waiter in Germany who was busy he would say, "Kommen gleich," "Coming immediately," and whenever we asked after a dish that had been ordered some time we learned that it too was "Kommen gleich." That expression stuck in Rachel's memory, and now we use it of every person or thing that moves slowly.

In the summer of 1879 as the winner at Princeton College of the John C. Green Mental Science fellowship, bestowed by the hand of venerable James McCosh, I came to Leipzig to continue the study of philosophy and take a course in Roman law. I spent some months perfecting myself in German under the tuition of a Dr. Asher, to whom his friend Schopenhauer had bequeathed his spectacles,—and Dr. Asher certainly looked at everything through pessimistic glasses. I was aided about as much by attending the Nikolai Kirche and listening to a distinct but tautological preacher. On October 16th I matriculated. This consisted in going to five different rooms, dealing with six persons, writing my name and address on cards and in big books, and then in hearing a speech from the rector, Herr Dr. Stobbe, and shaking hands with him. Forty of us entered on that day and of these seventeen wore glasses, and I found the same proportion of eyeglasses to hold all through the course.

The lecture rooms I attended were all in the dingy court back of the Augusteum, which fronts on the Augustus Platz opposite the post office. Many of the scientific departments, however, are in the suburbs of the city. The University Library of 350,000 volumes I find has now been transferred from its old dark quarters to a noble building near the new Supreme Court. I hope it is better managed. In my time they did not, as at Princeton, permit access to the shelves, but I had on one day to give a list to men at a counter of what I wanted, and come back the next to find out if the books were in, and the custodians, to my own knowledge, made frequent mistakes.

In the lecture rooms the young men selected their own seats and put cards upon them. The long benches and desks were plain and each man provided his own pen and bottle of ink. The professor entered twelve minutes after the stroke of the hour and lectured standing, reading from his notes or not, according to his individual preference. The students have no recitations and take down as much or little of the lecture as they choose, folding a page almost in the middle to give margin for their notes. The French sarcasm that the German professors have forgotten the invention of printing has much point. A book and recitations are far better than oral lectures. The lecturer leaves as near after the stroke of the hour as he can finish a sentence and then always receives liberal applause from stamping feet. The students eat and smoke freely in the room before and after the lecture, but during its delivery are very quiet and attentive.

In my first semester or term I heard Wundt on the history of philosophy, Fricker on applied ethics and Hermann on the philosophy of history. Wundt was one of their famous men and had been the magnet that drew me to Leipzig. He was a man under fifty, with short, black whiskers, wore glasses, and, while no doubt perfectly at home on the rostrum, nervously wriggled about while lecturing. He put everything very clearly, however, and his large room was always packed with auditors. His fame rests chiefly on studies in physiological psychology, so called, the border land between mind and brain, but I was not fortunate enough to hear him directly on this subject. King Albert of Saxony was in Leipzig at some exhibition and I saw him when one day he attended Wundt's lecture. He listened closely. Wundt bowed when he finished and the boys respectfully stood up as the king went out. Albert seemed to be a kind faced man and assumed no state beyond having one soldier as a guard and sitting off to himself in a red cushioned chair placed on a strip of carpet.

The second semester I heard Wundt four afternoons a

week on psychology proper. Along with these lectures I read Lotze's famous and interesting but somewhat extravagant Mikrokosmos,—regarded as conservative in Germany,—Kant's great Kritik, Fisher's History of Philosophy, besides much of Goethe and Schiller and other works more in the line of literature. In this semester I heard also the celebrated Windscheid lecture every morning on the Institutes of Justinian. Windscheid was an old man, thin but erect, with light gray beard on the lower part of his face. He spoke distinctly when quoting Latin but at other times often mouthed his words, particularly when he would shrug his shoulders and express disagreement with an author, and also when he had occasion, which was often, to characterize anything as "ausserordentlich,"—extraordinary. He quoted the *corpus juris* with great facility. He gave each student at the beginning a printed analysis of the course, with references to authorities. For clearness I have hardly seen his equal. He proceeded slowly, and yet, by avoiding much detail, covered a great deal of ground in a short time. The hour was always up before I knew it, such was the fascination the man and the subject exercised over me. Along with these lectures I read Scheurl's admirable book on the *Institutiones Justiniani*, and used Heuman's lexicon to the *corpus juris*, giving citations and biographical and historical matter of great value. The Germans, like the Greeks in their day, think everything not of their own country worthless, although they do give Americans credit for making greater practical use of many *German* inventions. So that it was with some surprise that I heard Windscheid speak of Gibbon's Decline and Fall of the Roman Empire as an extraordinary and unequalled work. Wundt is remarkably well read and I have also heard him refer to Mill, Spencer and Bain as valuable authorities. Hermann also referred to a book by Flint of Edinburgh as one of the best on the philosophy of history. A great many English and Americans now go to the German universities and possibly these institutions are themselves thus somewhat liberalized. In fact the authorities encourage American students to come, and sometimes aid them in completing the course in two instead of three years. As I had no aim, however, beyond general education, I remained but one year, the life of the Princeton fellowship. While in Leipzig I heard several of the other university celebrities also. I saw Hankel perform a number of simple electric experiments to the noisy delight of his class, heard Luthardt, the great and conservative Lutheran theologian, saw the venerable Delitsch lecture on Isaiah, and heard Curtius on Plato, when he amusingly scored the scholars who are more Platonist than Plato himself and have discovered that but one dialogue or two are genuine. On other occasions I heard also the judicious Heinze on Plato, and old Drobisch on Logic. Drobisch did not use glasses and spoke faintly but distinctly. Many of those professors have died in the few years' interval since I was a student, but even in scholastic Germany some of them have not been since surpassed, and perhaps not even equalled.

The only recitation is on the public final examinations for degree. These are strict. When I left they gave me but a certificate of attendance, as I had not completed the course. An interesting and amusing feature of student life is what they call " Privatissime,"—when a professor receives the students at his room, perhaps on the top floor of a building, or they meet at some other place, and informally discuss the study. The students and professor sit about a table and drink bier, while the boys quiz their teacher. The several professors I met from time to time struck me very pleasantly. They were all cordial and communicative, talking without reserve. The students have societies of all sorts, some for essays and debate, many for musical purposes. Different societies wear differently colored caps, but all make a feature of drinking bier. It is very common to see students with great cuts across the face from their secret sword duels in the depths of the Rosenthal or elsewhere, although there is much less of this than formerly. They are very proud of these scars.

Leipzig has had many famous citizens, such as Leibnitz and Wagner, both of whom were born here, Goethe, Schiller, Bach, Schumann, Gellert and others, as the many memorial tablets indicate. Goethe was a student and his quarters are still shown. Schiller lived and wrote for a while in a vine covered cottage at Gohlis in the environs.

Leipzig's plains in past times have been the site of at least three famous battles,—Breitenfeld and Lützen in the Thirty Years' War, and of Napoleon's defeat in 1813, and I visited them all.

Breitenfeld is an estate and village a few miles north of Leipzig. One day in harvest time in July 1880 I walked to the battle field alone, a friend going but a little way and then turning back from fear of rain. The country was flat, and the grain, almost ripe, waved on every hand. Starting at two I was at the simple monument, a stone cube surrounded by railing amid some pines, about half past three. South-east was Wiederitsch, the centre of Tilly's line in 1631, and north-east were the spires of several little villages, where the first engagement took place. There Pappenheim's cavalry was put to flight and by this Gustavus was enabled to turn here at Breitenfeld Tilly's left wing and rout his army. Leipzig's towers are in full sight and between me and the city swept around a black cloud with its rain and lightning.

Coming back I walked with an old peasant until I struck the high pike, shaded with trees, at Lindenthal. He said Breitenfeld was the biggest estate in the neighborhood. He thought I was a native, much to my satisfaction. Amongst other rural scenes I saw people binding sheaves. They twist a straw rope, lay the grain in it, and tie, using a stick to help. Men cut the grain with a cradle-scythe or a vehicle with windmill arms such as I have seen in New Jersey, and the women seem to do much of the binding. This reminds me that a country girl a few days later near Lützen called out to me to know if I did not want to marry? I respectfully declined.

I also visited with friends the even more important field of Lützen. Leipzig is in the north-west corner of Saxony, and on this excursion I saw the Prussian boundary marked by a straight clearing of probably fifty feet wide in which are heaps of stones at regular intervals. A party of us one Saturday took the train at 9:55 A.M. from Leipzig to Markränstadt, arriving at 10:18. We walked thence an hour and a half along the high road, watching the peasants cut and bind the ripe grain, and then came to the battle field of Lützen. Here in 1632, after his conquest of Germany, complete until checked near Nuremberg by Wallenstein, Gustavus Adolphus met this general for the first time in an open battle field. Wallenstein had been recalled from his proud retirement and put in command as a matter of necessity by his imperial master. Wallenstein had the larger army, drawn up on the west of the road, occupying, however, the opposite ditch also with outposts. He had a few cannon before his centre of infantry, and his right wing was cavalry. One infantry square was towards Lützen and he had a strong battery there on the hill. His weak cavalry left wing was where the Flossgraben intersects the road. This ditch curved around towards Lützen behind Gustavus. Gustavus with twenty thousand men, of whom ten thousand were cavalry, occupied the field on the other side of the road. His Swedes were similarly arranged, their centre being twelve sections of infantry under Kniphausen, and his wings of cavalry with a sprinkling of foot. Their largest array of cannon was by Lützen, but the rest of their one hundred pieces were divided evenly. Gustavus Adolphus commanded his right wing and soon broke the enemy's left and went to lead his own yielding left, commanded by Bernhard, while the two centres were fighting with varying fortunes. He fell, but exactly where is unknown. His death, however, inspired his army anew and Wallenstein was defeated everywhere. The re-inforcements under Pappenheim were also defeated and that general mortally wounded. Gustavus' body was discovered at last to the east of the road, under a heap of dead, naked and mutilated from the hoofs of cavalry charge and counter-charge. A Gothic cast-iron canopy near a boulder now marks where it was found, but it was taken finally to Stockholm for interment. Pappenheim died in the Pleissenburg at Leipzig. Wallenstein was assassinated not long afterwards by some of his attendants, while he was himself plotting treason with the Protestants. Lützen was like the Goetterdaemmerung.

Napoleon almost two centuries later also won a battle near Lützen, but this, with the victories of Dresden and Bautzen, is forgotten in the greater interest of the Battle of the Nations at Leipzig a few days later.

Leipzig itself has many monuments commemorative of this great battle of October 16-19, 1813, when Napoleon met his first great defeat, a struggle which was the turning-point in his career. He had made the disastrous retreat from Russia, re-organized his army, and was in Saxony to crush the rising of the German nation in this their war of independence. In three great battles he conquered, but Austria turned against him and even Saxony was wavering. The allies were endeavoring to surround him, and he characteristically marched to encounter their main body.

Two miles south-east of the city from a little knoll he directed during the first day his one hundred and fifty thousand men, their centre being at Probstheida, almost a mile further from Leipzig, as they fought double that number of allied Prussians, Austrians and Russians. Where he stood the Germans have now erected a monument, "Napoleonstein," a short stone shaft surmounted by his cocked hat and field glass in bronze. The inscription says, "Here Napoleon I. watched the fighting in the Battle of the Nations." The French, not successful in routing the forces opposed to them, at last retired into the city and at 11 A.M. on October 19 a Prussian battalion stormed the eastern gate. Napoleon, fearing that his rear might be covered by another allied army approaching from the north, soon afterwards retreated towards the west. The main army passed over the Elster bridge at the north-west corner of the old walls, and then by some fatal mistake the stone bridge was prematurely

WHERE NAPOLEON STOOD ON THE FIELD OF LEIPZIG.

blown up. Many French were drowned trying to swim the swollen stream, and 25,000 were captured on the Leipzig side. Among the drowned was the gallant Pole Poniatowski, to whom a monument has been erected where he perished. The total loss of life in this great battle is said to have been 100,000.

Among the many German holidays is Sedan day, September 2d, and I attended its celebration in 1879 on the battle field of Leipzig. I stood at the Napoleonstein and from there viewed the immense assembly, heard the Wacht am Rhein from thousands of German throats, and listened to patriotic speeches telling how, since Napoleon III. surrendered at Sedan and their Kaiser had been crowned at Versailles, the Rhine, touched by France at no point, is now the German Rhine in a truer and grander sense than was dreamed possible in the life of Napoleon I. As I returned to town the Napoleonstein was hid from view by the smoke of the bonfire and as I looked back in the moonshine the windmill at Probstheida flung its arms peacefully around where once had been the thickest of the great battle for German freedom.

CHAPTER V.

DRESDEN: ITS COLLECTIONS AND HISTORY.

DRESDEN is famous for its china and its picture gallery, but it is important in many other respects too. It is an old-fashioned town on the left bank of the Elbe, here crossed by several bridges to the new city, and, while in general like Leipzig, has even handsomer suburbs. Its population is 250,000, including a large English and American colony. Along the river below the old bridge are the court theatre and handsome carved stone picture gallery about an open square, and above the bridge is the Brühl terrace, much frequented for river views.

The centre of interest is the picture gallery, one of the four greatest of the world, the others being the Pitti and Uffizi at Florence, and the Louvre at Paris. The Vatican, Munich and London collections are very fine but hardly rival the four just named.

We spent day after day at the Dresden galleries, taking dinner at a restaurant near by on the river bank and going back again for the rest of the time. Here at Dresden I had made some study of art and possibly will find occasion in connection with Florence, the home of painting, sculpture and architecture, to give a short sketch of the subject. I will content myself now with describing some of the pictures that impressed us most in Dresden.

The building is a handsome three story Renaissance structure built by Semper in this century. Semper is considered the finest German architect of recent times and built also the court theatre. The Museum has, however, too monotonous a façade, and towers or a high dome would improve it. Adjoining are the Zwinger colonnades and pavilions, in an over ornamented Renaissance style called Rococo from its curves and shell ornamentation. The Zwinger encloses pleasant gardens. The collection dates mainly from Augustus III., whose splendid court in the eighteenth century almost equalled that of Versailles.

On the ground floor are sculptures, on the second the main collection of pictures, and on the third good modern paintings, and of the thousands of pictures some cannot be forgotten. The gem of all is the Sistine Madonna of Raphael, named from the convent at Piacenza, for which it was painted. The shrinking beauty of the young, girlish mother, her large soft eyes, which seem to avoid your gaze, the bright sharp eyes and firm mouth of the Child, the clouds of angel heads on which she stands as the curtains in the painting are withdrawn, the chubby cherubs below with red and green wings, and Saints Sixtus and Barbara at the sides, make up the most bewitching production of all human art. It stands in a corner room, well lighted, and the velvet seats are always filled with reverent spectators, who instinctively talk in whispers and enter and leave on tip-toe. A corresponding room at the other end of the building is occupied by what is now said to be a copy and not the original of Holbein's fine Madonna, standing with the Child under a canopy, but of a sturdy German type and in the midst of a German family. All between are large rooms hung with paintings and opening on one side into others not so large containing mainly the smaller French, Dutch and Flemish pictures. Correggio's Holy Night, representing the Mother and the Magi gazing on the Child from whom comes the light which shows them to us, is in a room near the Sistine Madonna, but has now become rather indistinct. Not far off is Battoni's Magdalene lying beside a skull and intently reading, a beautiful production, whether copy, as now set up, or an original, and Correggio's Magdalene, more exposed, but much like the other. Carlo Dolce's St. Cecilia listening to the heavenly choir is a picture of beauty and rapture, and Guido Reni's Ecce Homo, of which there are several copies, prays almost audibly in the gathering darkness. In one of the cabinets is Titian's Tribute Money, where the contrast is masterly of the open-faced but Jewish Christ and the sharp, brown Rabbi handing him the penny. Very different is his proud and voluptuous nude Venus, said to be a copy, in which Cupid is crowning her and a young man with his back turned is reading aloud. Palma Vecchio is represented by his Three Graces and by recumbent Venus taking Cupid's arrow. There is much there, too, of Paul Veronese, and the Sleeping Venus of Giorgione has one of the most beautiful faces and figures possible. Caravaggio has Card Players, and Card Sharpers with an accomplice behind the victim revealing his hand. Rubens with Snyders paints a vigorous Boar Hunt, and alone Neptune Stilling the Tempest, Love's Garden and the Judgment of Paris, but the women of the last two are fat and clumsy, and his Diana returning from the chase is much more attractive. The beautiful, recumbent Danae in the Shower of Gold, haughty Charles I., and Children of Charles I., are said to be copies and not original Van Dycks, but they are very good, and there are many fine animal scenes by Jordaens, Snyders and Teniers. Of the Dutch school Rembrandt has a number of fine pictures, one being a portrait of an Old Man, and another himself laughing with glass in hand and wife Saskia on his knee, sometimes called Wine, Woman and Song. Her back is towards us but she turns her face. There also are many pictures of the later Dutch school,—house interiors, still life, hunts, landscapes and curious studies of candle-light seen through fingers. In the same room with his Madonna are Holbein's picture of the goldsmith Mortet and a small but careful Crucifixion by Dürer. The two Cranachs are represented by a number of their rather stiff pictures, and there are many splendid views—generally not large—by Claude Lorraine. Macaulay's continuous praise of Claude is just. Everything by him is distinct without being sharp, his water the green and white of nature, his clouds perfect, and the pictures in all respects gracefully and carefully filled. Nicolas Poussin, too, has a number of paintings and there are courtly rural scenes by Watteau. Among the original pencil drawings were many by Raphael, Leonardo, Rubens and others, all showing the marvellous effect of a few strokes by a master hand, those by Leonardo and Raphael being particularly soft.

Among the modern paintings are Angelica Kaufman's pure Vestal Virgin, Hübner's girl listening to boy piping (the Golden Age), Munkacsy's large and realistic Crucifixion, Vautier's Wedding Dance, Hoff's touching picture of Bad News,—a letter read to old people, Dispute of Eck and Luther, and Hofman's Adulteress before Jesus. In this last the beautiful penitent has sunk on her knees, and, as a rabbi shows the book of the law to the gentle Saviour, an old woman can hardly be kept from striking while a young mother hurries her child away from so infamous a presence. On the ground floor, besides the casts, which extend over into the Zwinger, is an attractive collection of miniatures and crayons, and among them is Liotard's well known Chocolate Girl and his Beautiful Lyonnaise.

Near the Museum is the court Catholic church, for, while the established church is Protestant, the royal family is Catholic. There on Sunday we heard superb music, vocal and instrumental, to which people crowded in, many, however, leaving the services immediately afterwards, as I used to notice was also common at Leipzig. The voices were those of little boys, who, when not singing, could not help even in the public choir loft laughing and playing like other children. On a previous visit I saw King Albert and Queen Carola in a balcony above the altar and without attendants. This and others near look like stage boxes with movable glass fronts, and communicate by a bridge with a barnlike palace adjacent. Their majesties knelt most of the time and on that cold day blew their noses freely like us common mortals. The king was gray and had a subdued and anxious face. Both were plainly dressed, he in a military uniform, she in black with gray hat and short veil. When they rose to leave he stood aside until she went out, and then followed her. The church is oval and the nave projects high above the passage around it, which at the sides widens into aisles, where sit the non-Catholics and the overflow of the congregation in the nave. Over the altar is a dim Ascension by Raphael Mengs, but it is not now highly regarded. Externally, this church, so prominent an object in Dresden views, is Baroque,—a degraded Renaissance style of the last part of the eighteenth century. It has statues on all the parapets and the tower or steeple, like many others in Germany, culminates in something like an inverted turnip. Under this church are the royal tombs.

In the palace is what is called the Green Vault, from the color of the walls of one room, containing the most valuable collection of jewelry, crystal, bronzes, ivory carving and stones in the world. In the first room after the entry, where one pays a mark for a ticket, are many bronzes, principally of groups, such as the Rape of the Sabines, in the next a Dutch frigate with full spread sails, all of ivory and about one and one half feet high, and a Fall of the Angels, much smaller, but remarkable because cut out of one piece, and in another room is Dinglinger's Court of Aurungzebe, made of one hundred and fifty-two movable gold and ivory figures of men and beasts. In one room was a great deal of rock crystal, in others clocks, one with fine chimes, the Polish regalia, and priceless gems and jewels. Among these was the largest onyx known, an oval disk seven inches long, of the same red-blue color as the favorite Bairisch bier, also the one green diamond of the world, $5\frac{1}{3}$ ounces in weight, and a lady's bow of six hundred and sixty-two diamonds. The living rooms of the palace I did not see, but they are very handsome. A busy street passes under the building at one place, and the king thus dwells very close to the life of his people.

Further on in the Neumarkt, opposite the Hotel Bismarck, where we staid, is a handsome building called the Museum Johanneum, devoted to historical and porcelain collections. In one or more of the rooms armor was fitted to stuffed figures on horseback holding long thick spears in rest. Some of these suits were merely for display, and, being decorated with gold and silver, were very handsome. A good deal came from Nuremberg, that mediæval home of metal workers. The historic suits of Gustavus Adolphus and the Elector Maurice were much like the others, and the blood stained scarf of Maurice and fatal flattened bullet are also shown. The armor consisted usually, besides the helmet, of a collar, movable shoulder pieces, elbow joints, gauntlets, breastplate coming to an edge or point over the abdomen, hip pieces, and perhaps also sometimes greaves and foot coverings. Shields were apparently not much used, but chain shirts of small links were plentiful. Among the weapons there were, besides all the usual articles, rapiers with two blades, two edged swords, and I noticed also a dagger in two pieces made to spring apart in opposite directions after entering the flesh and thus cut a terrible wound. Of the historic relics we noticed Henry IV's twisted hunting horn, the long pistols of Charles XII. with ivory handles, all flint locks, and the marshal's batons of Tilly and Pappenheim. Swords of Peter the Great bore his name, and we saw also his three-cornered hat and some of his working tools. One of the most interesting articles is the long Cashmere tent of the Grand Vizier Kara Mustapha and in it the triangular Turkish flag, all captured by John Sobieski when he chivalrously came in 1683 and rescued Vienna. In this tent is also the glistening armor of that noble Polish king, made of scales, on each of which is a little cross, and on the front a larger Maltese cross. Among the later curiosities was the velvet saddle of Napoleon, used at the battle of Dresden, the stirrups made of rings. Napoleon's leg was unprotected, but the older saddles generally had guards before and behind. Napoleon's high boots worn on that occasion have thin soles, and the right one was apparently taken off in such a hurry as to rip the heel, while in peaceful contrast in the same collection we saw his white coronation slippers. Among the recent additions to the collection were two captured mitrailleuses. One of brass had twenty-five tubes, and near the back was "N" under a crown.

The porcelain collection on the floor above was also interesting. It begins with the big Chinese and Japanese jars ornamented with unearthly designs in blue, but the later work was more attractive. Japanese coloring was perhaps superior, while Chinese figures of men, lions, birds and other animals were stiff but forcible. Rachel admired most of all the cups and saucers, so neat in design and execution. The yellow dragon china made for the personal use of the Chinese emperor is rather rare than beautiful, and the tall Dragoon Vase given by Frederick William I. of Prussia to Augustus the Strong in exchange for a regiment of soldiers possessed little attraction beyond its history. Porcelain in China goes back to the seventh century but western china begins with the invention by Böttcher in 1709 at Dresden. It was at first red and then later white, was sometimes polished and always neat and often beautiful. The ornamentation by *genre* figures, garlands and heads was natural at that time, and established Rococo as the classic style for china. Painting and gilding came later, and in this the French excelled. The manufacture was early moved from Dresden to Meissen, where it still remains, and there during their occupation of Saxony in the Seven Years' War the Prussians learned the secret, which they have since used in Berlin to great advantage. We saw also numerous porcelain busts, figures and groups, meant for ornaments, one being a large Neptune Fountain. In the collection, too, is fayence and much rough Italian majolica with rude and often obscene pictures, and also English and foreign china and pottery of all descriptions.

We often went to Brühl Terrace near by above the Elbe bank. It was laid out as a garden by the minister of that name in the eighteenth century. The steps approaching it have on the sides at top and foot Schilling's gilded sandstone groups of Night, Morning, Noon and Evening, which are excellent, and the terrace, planted with trees and adorned with statuary, is a pleasant and much frequented resort. The old Elbe bridge is to the left, the growing Neustadt opposite, and below in the river the steam barges go up the stream by taking a chain from the channel, as we had seen also in the Rhine and in the Neckar. In the cemetery of the Neustadt is the Dance of Death, a wall relief dating back to 1534 and very curious in design. There are twenty-seven figures, representing skeleton Death as leading on king, priest, peasant and others.

Outside Dresden is buried Rietschel, the celebrated sculptor, who died here in 1861. A Rietschel museum is shown in the city, containing casts of his Weber, Lessing, Luther and Goethe-Schiller monuments, with many of the original little plaster models which he made as "sketches." He would make three or four for each statue before obtaining a pose that suited him. A commanding bronze Luther, cast from his original statue for Worms, stands in the Neumarkt. On the Brühl Terrace there is a bronze monument to Rietschel by Schilling, on which is the master's bust and below at the corners are three youths, personifying the three stages of designing, modelling and sculpturing.

It is evident that Saxony, to amass the treasures now found at its handsome capital, must have been once much more wealthy and important than the little existing kingdom of two million inhabitants. The Saxon tribes which colonized Britain and as a Saxon duchy furnished emperors to the old empire, have, however, no racial connection with the present kingdom of Saxony. Their centre was the River Weser, and Westphalia, Hanover and Brunswick mark the general territorial limits of the original Saxons. They then conquered eastwardly, and Brandenburg was one outpost, the Wittenberg country another. The present territories of the Saxon kingdom and the Saxon duchies of Gotha and Weimar were really Thuringian and became Saxon in name in 1423, when Frederick, landgrave of Thuringia and margrave of Meissen, was granted the Wittenberg lands and the old dignity of Saxon elector. So that the name Saxon has travelled east until the true Saxons are left behind under other names, and aliens in blood enjoy the name and the kingly title into which Napoleon changed the electoral dignity. Saxony really has no right to its name.

Primogeniture did not obtain in this country and the continuous subdivisions produced the numerous principalities which we now find. In the fifteenth century came the division into the Ernestine or Wittenberg line, and the Albertine or Meissen line. Elector Frederick the Wise, Luther's friend, was of the former and under him Saxony was the most important member of the empire. In the later wars the other line was imperialist and thus through the Emperor Charles V. acquired the Wittenberg title and territories, and left to the Ernestines only the small Weimar and Gotha principalities. But by turning against the emperor, Elector Maurice of the Albertine branch forced Charles V. to the peace of Passau in 1552 and ended the long Reformation wars by securing religious freedom. By similarly changing sides in the Thirty Years' War, however, Saxony suffered from the armies of both Gustavus and Wallenstein, and at its end her influence was much lessened. Augustus the Strong (1694–1733) was also king of Poland, and Saxony suffered much again from his Polish wars with Charles XII. He was Carlyle's "Augustus the Physically Strong," father of 354 children and amongst others of the French general Marshal Saxe. Augustus III. his son was under the influence of Count Brühl, who adorned the capital but brought on the disastrous wars with Prussia. Frederick the Great in the Seven Years' War ruled from Dresden as if he was the king, while the nominal king was hiding in Poland. Then came Napoleon's domination of Saxony, in revenge for which on his fall Prussia obtained from the Congress of Vienna her present Saxon province, the most fertile in the Prussian state and almost equal in extent to what was left unpartitioned as the kingdom of Saxony. She sided with Austria against Prussia in 1866, and was mulcted heavily in money for it, but, as an integral and loyal member of the new empire, Saxony, now a constitutional state, is at last again enjoying peace and prosperity. Frederick the Wise in the sixteenth century declined election as emperor, but had the Saxon electors enforced primogeniture and avoided the *ignis fatuus* of ruling as kings of Poland, the magnificent country they had at the Reformation would have brought the imperial title to them more permanently than it did to the old Saxon dukes. Their strong electoral territories would have become the nucleus for a centralized Protestant empire, and the work of 1870 done four centuries earlier. Austria would not have become dominant and Brandenburg would have remained a subordinate part of a great Saxon state.

CHAPTER VI.

CARLSBAD, NUREMBERG AND MUNICH.

WE left Dresden one day at noon for Carlsbad in Bohemia, and had a pleasant trip by rail up the Elbe valley through the highlands called the "Saxon Switzerland," a wild country affording many splendid views. From the train, however, we saw little except the high wooded Elbe cliffs with slides cut for shooting the timber down to the water. We passed under the fortress of Königstein, the one perfect stronghold in Saxony, more than once the resort of the royal family in times of disturbance, and all along were the peaks whence I once had views embracing the railroad on which we now travelled.

On that earlier trip a party of us Leipzig students one morning left Dresden on the train for Poetzscha, to spend a few days tramping over the mountains. The country was level at first and well cultivated, but the banks of the Elbe grew steeper and wilder and its valley narrower as we advanced. From Poetzscha we were ferried over on our arrival about 12:50 P.M. to Wehlen for eight pfennigs by the ingenious method of keeping the oar rudder of the small boat at such an angle to the swift current that the boat, attached to a trembling wire fixed in the middle of the river, there a hundred feet deep, just drifted over.

The more interesting part of this miniature Switzerland lies north of the Elbe, and we spent two days tramping over well kept roads and paths and enjoying fine views from its heights. Our first day was taken up in climbing to the Bastei, a mountain peak, and in thence descending to Schandau on the river. The route was at first up a wild, steep gorge called Tscherre Grund, where we saw a great natural fireplace and chimney, named the Devil's Kitchen, and passed through the Felsenthor, a doorway formed by the fall of a large rock into the narrow pass. The Bastei stands 605 feet sheer above the Elbe, and commands a wide and beautiful view. South in a bend of the river is craggy Lilienstein, across the Elbe the fortress Königstein, east the Papstein group, and away to the south the long, wooded Schneeberg, covered with new snow. The Brand is of greater height, and from its summit we had a grand panorama spread out before us, the dark mountain peaks rising from pine valleys or from green fields in all directions. The descent was in part over an enormous number of steps, and so tired us that we thoroughly enjoyed our night's rest at Schandau, despite the discomfort of our quarters there.

The next day we saw "the Falls," induced by pulling a rope, and stopped by the same means—to accumulate for the next inquisitive traveller. We told the innkeeper that his bier was better than his water, and soon left. Next came a fine view from the summit of the Kuhstall, an imposing natural archway, but the best of all was from a pavilion on the Grosse Winterberg, where we dined. Ravines, mountains, minarets and plateaus were all before us as we stood there 1,600 feet above the sea, and they made up a memorable picture. After leaving this we tried to get to Prebischthor, and made the amusing mistake of thinking the cleared boundary between Saxony and Bohemia was the path, and followed it some time before noticing that it went straight, over hill and precipice. Perhaps even a surer sign that it was not a road was the absence of guide-posts, musicians, and clamorous guides, so common elsewhere. Finally we found our way to Herrnskretschen, were ferried across the river to the railroad station, and went back by rail to Dresden, worn out but well pleased with our excursion through Saxon Switzerland.

On the later trip up the Elbe valley Rachel and I ascended it without stopping until we crossed through the break in the Erzgebirge range into Bohemia. Rachel was asleep most of the way, exhausted from sight-seeing, but I enjoyed the company of an old German and his wife who were going to Carlsbad for the summer, and found them pleasant and well-informed people. We entered Bohemia by the route pursued by Frederick the Great in one of his campaigns, but we had no battle of Kolin to fight, and, beyond the nuisance of lugging our big satchels to and from the baggage room for a hurried customs examination, and puzzling ourselves over change in florins and kreutzers when we paid for lunch, we had no trouble on our invasion of the country.

After a while we arrived at the station for Carlsbad, but the little town was some miles off down a deep descent, and could be reached only in carriages, which, however, were plentiful. This famous watering place is spread out on one or two streets along the banks of a half dry creek. It is made up of hotels and narrow, crowded houses, many perched on the sides of the high hills that bound the valley on either side. After loitering around and eying the hotels, we took dinner and then spent some time wandering about. In a handsome glass hall, where people gather to talk and read, is the small hot geyser called Sprudel, that throws its water intermittently as high as the ceiling, and is the chief attraction of the resort. There are, however, a number of other springs and halls all along near the shallow stream ; and Bohemia, moreover, is famous for a number of mineral springs besides those at Carlsbad.

The Bohemians or Czechs are neither German nor Hun, but Slavs like the Russians. The country was originally an independent elective kingdom, but for three centuries has been claimed as an hereditary possession by the sovereigns of Austria. Bohemia became Protestant when Huss was burned at Constance in 1415 in violation of his safe-conduct, and under one-eyed Ziska the Bohemians in revenge ravaged all Saxony and central Germany. Their action later in choosing as king Protestant Frederick, the Rhenish elector palatine, against the will of Catholic Austria, began the Thirty Years' War, in the course of which the Protestants were expatriated, the land catholicized, and national feeling all but crushed. The celebrated Wallenstein was a Bohemian, but served on the Catholic side. Since then, until the European disturbances of 1848, the country has been an integral, if dissatisfied, member of the Austrian empire, but a number of concessions have been made to Bohemia by Austria in this past half century. An intelligent Czech, in whose company a part of the above tramp in the Saxon Switzerland was taken, expressed the general Bohemian feeling when he said that the only hope for Austria is in federal union. He told us that there were then thirteen hundred students at Prague, and that the Czech and German divisions were very hostile to each other.

From Carlsbad we continued our journey towards Munich, spending the night near the Bavarian border, and next morning we were back amid familiar marks and pfennigs again. Our travel all through Bavaria was pleasant. There were many railroad officials, especially north of Munich, and we found them very obliging. Our numerous questions tested them thoroughly.

We did not go to Nuremberg in old Franconia, but I recall this German Chester as one of the quaintest towns imaginable. It was a free imperial city in the middle ages and ruled a large territory. It was an inventive place, and from it come watches, gun-locks, air-guns, and, strange to say, here means of punishment were studied to such an extent as to make cruelty one of the fine arts. It was also famous as the home of the early poet Hans Sachs, and of the great painter Dürer, both of whom are buried in its cemetery. The walls are still almost intact, and the many gabled houses and narrow streets still defy the march of modern "improvements."

After passing through the thick walls, at some places apparently double, one finds himself in the town, built on both sides of the river Pegnitz. St. Lawrence's church contains many carvings by Dürer, and a tall pyx elaborately wrought by Krafft, another celebrated artist, while in St. Sebald's is the iron sarcophagus of that saint surmounted by a fine Gothic canopy, the thirteen years' work of Peter Vischer and his sons in the sixteenth century, after training in Italy under Ghiberti.

In the citadel is a curious collection of old instruments

of torture. Drunken men were exhibited to public ridicule in hollow posts, the head showing through an iron cage at the top; and there were many devices for the punishment of feminine unchastity. To use the rack they tied the prisoner to a ladder and his feet or hands to a wheel, and then turned the wheel and pulled the limbs, it may be, from their sockets. I saw also thumb-screws, iron boots, between which and the leg pegs were driven until the flesh was torn and perhaps the bone broken; long pincers to pull out the tongue, a spiked chair, and the more merciful long-bladed sword. In the old castle were other instruments, such as a spiked cradle for grown people, and the famous Iron Virgin. The Virgin I think was mainly of wood. It was a hollow figure large enough to enclose a man, and as its front closed in on a criminal spikes ran through his eyes and breasts, and the bloody Virgin dropped her prey through a trap door. I saw also the plain seats of the judges and the cow bells rung when sentence was pronounced, as in Goethe's Götz.

Rachel did not see Nuremberg but she passed over the Danube between that city and Munich, and was much disappointed to see a narrow tawny stream instead of the beautiful blue Danube we read and sing about.

But Munich, a handsome city of 250,000 people, was as much above our expectations as the river had been below. We went to the post office first and received one lone letter, and then walked to the middle of an adjacent open square to look at a statue and the flat royal palace facing it. A soldier marched up and ordered us away. We had just got off the train and I dare say looked disreputable and like anarchists.

From here runs east to the river Isar the magnificent

Maximilian Strasse, flanked by splendid modern buildings, and indeed a fine bridge extends this wide thoroughfare across the river, while beginning in the centre of the city almost perpendicular to this street beautiful Ludwig Strasse extends northwardly until it terminates at a handsome triumphal arch. Since artistic Ludwig 1. began to reign in 1825 Munich has been beautified until it is among the best-built cities in the world. His ambitious architect Klenze gave the city no original style, but his modification of classic and Renaissance models presents impressive structures. The imposing buildings are given plenty of room and thus show off to great advantage. The Glyptothek, old and new Pinacothek, the Propylæa copied from the approach to the Athenian Acropolis, and other public buildings are surrounded by large grounds, and in public places about the city are handsome fountains, some pouring out water in the shape of lilies. The parks, too, are numerous and attractive, one being laid off by Rumford. Count Rumford, by the way, was a great scientist, and proposed to cut down army estimates in a novel but effective manner. He is said to have told the elector that if the soldiers were given less to eat and made to chew longer they would be better off, as they would digest their food more perfectly, and the commissariat at the same time would be much less expensive !

The city is well paved, the streets with stone, the sidewalks with square glazed bricks. Munich, like Frankfort, Leipzig and other cities, has a belt horse car line, called the Ringbahn, and it was a very convenient way of seeing the place itself and getting to the different points of interest.

Among these the picture galleries, called the old and

new Pinacotheks, are possibly the most famous. The old contains the old masters, the new the more recent paintings. The buildings themselves are not without merit. The old Pinacothek is of brick, but, as it is without the white lines between the bricks which we permit in America, the effect is very good, presenting a uniform reddish surface that is pleasing to the eye. Porches are closed in by glass projections which rather remind one of a greenhouse and detract from the general appearance, but neither Rachel nor I could recall a brick building that looked as imposing. The new Pinacothek has external frescoes by the great artist Kaulbach, but these have already been sadly marred by the weather.

The old Pinacothek within is arranged something like the Dresden collection, the larger pictures in the large connecting central rooms, and the smaller ones in smaller rooms adjacent. Many masters which had become familiar at Dresden were also represented here. In these collections we often noticed that a painter was apt to have the same type in all his pictures. Paul Veronese, (1530–1588,) for instance, has the same kind of woman always,—an aristocratic and modern type. His Woman Taken in Adultery looks like a scandal in high life. His Cleopatra is anything but Egyptian. It is only in recent times that artists have taken to correct costuming. The anachronism of transferring modern or mediæval dress to ancient scenes, even to the Crucifixion, is common to almost all the older painters. We are more critical and more accurate now-a-days, but if we forget these incidental defects and look at the motives of the painter and the emotions displayed, we find that we have more to learn from these old pictures than their authors could learn from us. Albrecht Dürer (1471–1528) has several excellent pictures. His Mark and St. John I liked much. The splendid vigor given John is rather unsuited to his traditional character, but probably Dürer does this son of thunder only justice. Raphael Mengs (1729–1779) has a picture of himself with palette; he looks a trifle thin and has the blackness of face caused by shaving close like a priest. Near by the Swiss Angelica Kaufman (1741–1807) has a pleasing picture of herself with crayon in hand, and is like her own Dresden Sibyl. A large room is filled with a splendid Rubens collection and an adjoining smaller one with smaller pictures by the same painter, less finished and colored. His Fall of the Angels is vigorous and gives human bodies in almost every position. How fond he was of female figures! He was thereby led, curiously enough, to make his Resurrection and his Last Judgment, too, almost exclusively of women. The large Last Judgment has some beautiful figures, some modesty incarnate, although he seems generally to know more of its opposite. Snyders (1579–1657) has some good animal pieces, such as tigers, and Van Dyck (1599–1641) has two sacred pictures well contrasting. One is Mary with the infant Jesus sleeping on her breast, she looking away, pondering her and His destinies, and the other the Descent from the Cross, where Mary weeps over her dead Son. We had not thought of Van Dyck's painting anything but portraits. Murillo (1618–1682) also appeared in a new light, but in the contrary direction. His pictures of a little ragged boy dropping something into his mouth while his envious companion looks on, of another little fellow eating off the end of a grape bunch which he holds up while looking at his friend out of the corner of his eyes, of two little ragamuffins throwing dice on a stone, near which a yet smaller boy stands contentedly munching,—all were clearly Spanish and excellent. These were in one end room together. Claude Lorraine (1600–1682) has some beautiful views with the sea in the background, Poussin (1594–1665) fine landscapes among the smaller pictures, and seemed to succeed best where he brought in a castle or something of the sort, while Salvator Rosa, (1615–1673,) on the other hand, does best with rocks. Barroccio (1528–1612) had a picture of Christ telling Mary Magdalene not to touch him, and her face was a marvel of love and puzzled uncertainty. Guido Reni (1575–1642) had several pictures, but I liked best the ecstacy of his Mary Ascending to Heaven.

Thus we ended the big pictures and then turned back through the smaller side rooms. Dolce (1616–1686) is said to have been of a very tender, sweet disposition, and his pictures show it. Nothing can be purer or sweeter than some of his heads, for example the Magdalene he has here. Of course there are no end of Dutch paintings of still life, *genre*, and candle light effects. Van der Werff (1659–1722) has a whole room of women in Scripture scenes, pictures with a beautiful glaze, but often Van der Werff—and even Rubens occasionally—brings in a fat, expressionless face. Gerard Dow (1613–1674) paints *genre*, so David Teniers the Younger, (1610–1685,) who has an animal concert, with cats singing from notes on the table, monkeys fiddling on the floor, and an owl perched gravely on the music book. Dürer has a portrait of himself at twenty-eight (A.D. 1500) so benevolent, the hair in such beautiful ringlets, that we took it at first for a picture of Christ. Holbein has a picture of himself in 1530, young, independent and almost stubborn. Van Dyck has many portraits, all fine looking, but with a uniform Dutchy cast, and Ribera has several emaciated old men, of whom one is the repenting Peter. We watched with interest the copyists, so common in all galleries. They first crayoned off the outlines, next set to work painting in grayish tints, and only then at last put on the right colors. They did good work, too.

In the new Pinacothek the large pictures in the central saloons first attracted us. There was Piloty's Wallenstein, as he lies pale and dead on the floor before an astronomer; the same painter's German prisoners scornfully passing before the Roman Emperor in a triumphal procession, hooted at by the Roman women and children; and Hess's fine painting of Napoleon at Austerlitz. The smaller pictures in side rooms pleased us also, particularly those of Alpine scenes and Italian and Greek peasant life. A series of fine wall paintings by Rottmann in an end room, lighted from above, of sites of ancient Greece as they now lie desolate, raised sad thoughts. The Greeks did not dream that "Barbarians" of whose existence they knew not would ever paint the tombs of Greek civilization.

The interesting Glyptothek has a fine ancient collection, in which are the archaic Ægina marbles, groups from the pediments of the great Doric temple on that island. Ægina was the centre of art before Athens came into prominence in the fifth century B.C., and the acquisition of this treasure in 1812 by Ludwig as crown prince was the beginning of Munich's artistic life. The Ægina warriors are under life size. Their hair is unnatural, and all the fighting or dying have a queer satiric smile, but these figures represent a great step forward in ancient art.

Munich has a number of handsome churches. In St.

Michael's is buried Eugene Beauharnais, Josephine's son, and Ludwigskirche has a passable Last Judgment by Cornelius, who flourished in Munich. The roof of this church seemed to be of variegated slate or tile and not of the common red tile of almost all others. In these countries the churches are open until late in the afternoon and some one is always praying in them. Inside with their shrines and pictures and gilt, the Catholic churches have the same type everywhere. In the basilica of St. Boniface are beautiful wall paintings, and the rows of pillars in the nave are monoliths of Bavarian marble. At Munich they use their own stone, and use it well.

I began one day by walking out of town to the statue of Bavaria and her lion before the simple but imposing Doric colonnade called the Hall of Fame, where on brackets are the busts of celebrated Bavarians. The wall behind was a dark red, and the ceiling, the frieze, etc., were colored as the Greeks used to do. It looked much better than one would think. The bronze statue, the work of the celebrated Schwanthaler, stands sixty feet high on a pedestal of twenty feet and is very imposing. The whole structure is on a hill by the meadows south-west of the city and visible far and near.

Bavaria is an art centre and has had a long history. It was a "march" or frontier province in Carolingian times, whose "margrave" (march count) had to watch and resist the Huns. In after centuries the more eastern realm of Austria (Oesterreich) had this duty and Bavaria became a duchy. By aiding the Emperor against the Winter King, it obtained the count palatine's electoral dignity. The country was devastated in the Thirty Years' War and in Frederick's wars, and, while uniformly and unpatriotically favoring France, received no substantial benefit therefrom until Napoleon made the elector a king. It aided Prussia, however, against the third Napoleon, and, though remaining a kingdom, became a part of the new empire, with many independent privileges as to post, telegraph and army which are accorded to no other state. We noticed that Bavarian soldiers dress in a lighter blue and their helmets also differ from the Prussian. Bavarians south of Nuremberg did not strike me as being so industrious as the northern Germans, but in art their supremacy in this century seems unquestionable.

Our plans, however, now called us from art to the realm of nature as exhibited in Swiss scenery, and one forenoon we took the train through the Bavarian lake country for Lake Constance.

The trip was a long one and the views at first tame, but the monotony was relieved somewhat by the performances of a bridal couple who occupied the other end of our compartment. Rachel and I had now been married so long as to watch the pair with some surprise and much amusement. We were very glad to arrive at Lindau on Lake Constance and walk aboard the steamboat at the pier.

CHAPTER VII.

CONSTANCE AND NORTH SWITZERLAND.

SWITZERLAND is the little mountainous country in which the Rhine, the Rhone and the Po take their rise, and, while the people along these head waters speak German, French and Italian respectively, they are all intensely Swiss. The part on the Italian side of the Alps is, however, not considerable, and is really but a conquest dating back to the middle ages. The main Swiss country cannot be understood without a good map. It may be divided geographically, however, into two almost equal northern and southern parts, separated by the Bernese Alps and their continuations. South or south-east of these are the valleys of the Rhone and the upper Rhine, with their tributaries. North or north-west of the Bernese Alps are the many lakes fed by mountain snows, emptying into rivers which flow westwardly out through level country to join the central Aare River, and the Aare then in turn pours its waters into the Rhine below the falls. These lakes and streams are in valleys, of which the country is a network, separated themselves by mountains over many of which are passes. West Switzerland is comparatively level, and even in central and southern Switzerland it is only the highest Alpine peaks and ranges that carry eternal snow. Of these the greatest are in the Bernese Oberland and in the vast Alps that separate the country from Italy. Our northern division and the southern from Lake Geneva up to the water shed between the Rhone and Rhine valleys make up the Switzerland generally travelled. Of late the Grisons, the large south-eastern canton about the upper Rhine, is coming more and more into notice and the strange names of its Engadine mountains are more familiar, but our own route was along the older track,—from Constance and Schaffhausen to Zurich, then Lucerne, next over the Brünnig Pass to Interlaken to see the Bernese Alps, and then by Berne to Geneva, thus embracing the larger half of the country. From Geneva we went up the Rhone valley to the Simplon Pass and then travelled southwardly over the Alps from Switzerland into Italy.

The western part of Switzerland is French in both the divisions we made above, but from about Berne east it is all German, and this comprises two thirds of the country. On Lake Constance we were in German Switzerland and so continued until we turned south-west from Berne many days later.

Lake Constance is bounded east by Austrian Tyrol, south by Switzerland, and north by Germany. The eastern end of the lake is surrounded by mountains, among which the snow clad Sentis stood up prominently, but as we steamed on over the green water the scenery became more tame, and in the cold at dark we were not unwilling to seek the cabin. This body of water is thirteen hundred feet above the sea and over eight hundred feet deep. On its shores is not much of interest except Constance, our destination, but not far from its southern bank is famous St. Gall, a suppressed Benedictine abbey, founded in the seventh century by the Irish monk St. Gallus at the time when England had become Saxon and pagan, and the Irish were the great orthodox missionaries of western Europe.

At Constance we were again in Germany. We wanted to spend the night at the Hotel Barbarossa, where the defeated Frederick in 1183 concluded a manly peace with his revolted Lombard towns. So we tramped up cobble stone streets and were directed to a high, dark house, entered the driveway which goes through to the courtyard within, and on this entry, as usual in old German buildings, the house-door opens. We climbed some winding steps before we found anybody and then it was a maid with a waiter of bier for uproarious guests in the dining room, and she told us that the hotel was full. We had our suspicions that the guests were also, and beat a retreat. Not far off was where in 1415 Frederick, burggrave of Nuremberg, was invested with the march of Brandenburg and thus became the ancestor of kings of Prussia and the new German emperors; but a hotel was more our search and we at last found refuge at a similar lodging house, Badischer Hof, where, although tired out, we had to climb two flights of steps to the room assigned us, the only one left. This experience was the beginning of our hotel troubles. All over Switzerland we found hotels crowded, while all over Italy we found them empty.

Next morning we drove around. The oaken Kaufhaus still stands where the Cardinals of the Council of Constance met, and behind the carved doors of the cathedral sat the great assembly itself whose labors in 1414–1418 healed the Great Schism which had for a quarter of a century produced but popes and anti-popes.

This council is yet more memorable for its condemnation of John Huss for heresy. In the middle of the cathedral is the place where Huss stood and it is said to be always dry although the rest of the pavement may be damp. Near this church we saw the Insel-Hotel, made in part of the Dominican monastery where Huss was confined, and then we drove out past the Protestant Church to a newly planted grove a half mile off, the scene of his execution. The spot is marked by a huge boulder overgrown with ivy and enclosed by an iron fence. Here Huss was burned and later Jerome of Prague also.

Then we took the boat and the trip down the green Rhine to Schaffhausen was delightful despite showers which drove us sometimes into the stuffy little eating cabin. The swift river was bordered on the south by wooded hills and romantic seats of the Bonapartes and other modern great, while mediæval ruins, so common on the lower Rhine, were here infrequent. Very interesting was the way the boat was handled. At least once the funnel was lowered for a bridge. The steamer made landings with great ease, and the men calculated a rope throw to the inch. Finally at Schaffhausen the boat turned completely around and shot back to its landing like a flash.

At Schaffhausen we had a good dinner, and were interested to learn that Schiller's Lay of the Bell was suggested by the inscription on the cathedral bell, *Vivos voco, mortuos plango, fulgura frango.* Leaving our satchels and bundles, as usual, in the railroad cloak room for Gepaeck at ten centimes apiece, we took a carriage for the Rhine falls and return for four francs seventy centimes, and the drive along the cliff above the

WHERE HUSS AND JEROME WERE BURNED.

river, commanding its rapids, was very pleasant despite the shower coming back. We remained some time on the gallery of the island restaurant Schlösschen Wörth admiring the scene. The river above is several hundred feet wide, and at its falls is divided into two parts by a high projecting rock, on which is a small pavilion. The twin cataracts thus made are fifty to sixty feet in fall, but, while the green and foaming water is imposing, especially on a nearer view, it disappointed us, fresh from the grandeurs of Niagara.

The railroad from Schaffhausen crosses on a bridge just above the falls and over this we soon rolled, getting a few minutes later a farewell view of them. I did not revisit Basel, with the red sandstone cathedral famous for its curious carving and as the last resting place of Erasmus, but we went on southward to Zurich, where we arrived in two hours and dismounted at the handsome central station. We made our way across the river Limmat to the excellent Hotel Central, where we were given a good room over the murmuring river. At Zurich began the painful experience, repeated all through Switzerland, of regularly going to the post office and finding no mail from the dear ones at home, who, as we now know, wrote regularly but whose letters in some manner never came to hand. The comfort, yes, the necessity of hearing from home grew as time and distance increased, and our journey was partly spoiled by the total depravity of the postal authorities.

The most famous view about Zurich is from the neighboring Uetliberg, but the evening we set apart for this was rainy and we perforce rested content with the beautiful lake scene, with snow mountains beyond, enjoyed from the High Promenade by the cemetery.

Zurich has fine parks and quays by the lake and a few good streets, but it is in general old-fashioned and quaint, like most of the Swiss cities that we saw, with narrow, winding streets overhung by dark houses, and its shops hardly amounting in dignity to stores. It is a great manufacturing point, due in part to the many and swift streams running through it, and is the great educational centre of the country. Lavater, Pestalozzi, Bodmer, Gessner, and other educators lived and worked there.

Zurich was a typical mediæval town, long ruled for the emperor by a lady abbess and an aristocracy, until after the Hohenstaufen emperors the industrial classes became strong and under dictator Brun in 1336 revolutionized the constitution and became dominant themselves. Up to this time Zurich had been a free city, whose ties to the empire were lightly regarded, and the prosperous but now isolated community finally joined in 1351 the league of the forest cantons.

The minster or cathedral dates back to Charlemagne, who often resided in Zurich, and this was the church centuries later of the intrepid reformer Zwingli. The Reformation in Switzerland was independent of that in Germany and much more thorough. Zurich was then a leading city of the confederation and the market for the forest cantons at the other end of the long, narrow lake. There had of old been hostility between them, leading to the building of a wooden bridge across the lake at Rapperswyl for obtaining provisions from other markets than Zurich. In our own day a handsome railway viaduct has taken the place of this historic structure. Zwingli had been pastor at Glarus until his attacks on the Swiss practice of sending out mercenary troops in the pay of France and the Italian states made him unpopular and he took refuge A.D. 1516 in the rich and famous Benedictine monastery of Einsiedeln near the south end of the lake. There the miracles of the famous image of the Virgin and the corruptions of the clergy caused him to preach reform. On being called in 1519 to the minster at Zurich his field was widened. His earnest efforts gradually reformed the whole community, and in 1523-1524 it became truly a primitive Christian state. He was a statesman as well as a theologian, and, as the reformed doctrines took hold in adjacent cantons, Zurich became with Berne the head of reformed Switzerland. The religious dissensions of the cantons were as acute as those of the German states and led also to wars, in one of which Zwingli in 1531 fell in battle against the conservative and Catholic forest cantons, and his body was barbarously quartered and burned.

We saw on a quay by the Reuss his bronze statue and not far off the Rathhaus. On its top floor are sundry interesting collections, chief of which to us were the relics from the ancient lake dwellings in the vicinity, consisting of flints, pottery, stone pestles, stone knives, weapons, cloth, trinkets, bones of animals, antlers and even fruits, burned grain and bread. These lake dwellers were pre-historic Celts or of even some earlier race and many settlements have been found in Lake Zurich at low water and in other parts of Switzerland. Their houses were on piles out in the lakes for protection against animals or enemies, and in some places show much neatness and evidence of civilization. Little, however, is even yet known on this interesting subject.

The railroad trip one evening from Zurich to Lucerne gave good views, but was uneventful. On our arrival at

Lucerne we could not get in even the "unpretending" hotels, so that we had to follow the advice of the fair landlady of the Couronne and get a room in a third story flat in the old town, overlooking the river Reuss. This was a most delightful apartment, giving us also the run of the family parlor with its German and French pictures and books. The view from the windows was pleasant. Not far above us in the river was the rude tower which as a light-house (*lucerna*) is said to have given the name to the city. Away to our left was the lake and its side bays, further on the Rigi mountain group with its flat summit, and to the right the jagged, sierra-like Pilatus. Across the river was the smaller quarter of the city.

We were over Sunday in this great tourist centre and went to the Scottish church on a hill near the old walls and heard a good sermon. These missions pretty much support themselves and do a great deal of good to travellers, who are so apt when away from home, particularly in Europe, to forget all their religious ties and duties. I can go on record as to the benefit an American sermon in Florence did me twelve years ago.

Lucerne is a city of about twenty thousand people and except for the scenery and as a convenient and favorite starting point for tourists is in every way of less importance than Zurich. On a side path in the outskirts is a wild place, however, with two great attractions. As we passed shops of wood carving and other Swiss articles so common everywhere, we came in sight of a perpendicular cliff down which trickles water into a large pool at its base, overhung by trees, and carved in the side of the stone as in a niche is the Lion of Lucerne, Thorwaldsen's monument to the Swiss guard massacred by the Versailles mob while defending Louis XVI. The lion has broken the fatal spear which transfixed him and though dying still protects with one paw a shield bearing the Bourbon lily. Passing to the left from this great work we entered the Glacier Garden and its unique array of deep spiral holes and the round stones which caused them. There are thirty-two holes within a space not over one hundred yards square. We passed among them by paths and over several large ones by bridges, the largest being thirty feet deep and twenty-six feet in diameter. This region, like much else of Switzerland, was once under glaciers, and the streams of water from these moved loose stones, causing them in turn to grind holes in the rock beneath. Some of the holes intersect and make it difficult to identify the spirals. A few of the stones were full of shells, one we noticed with a fossil palm leaf, and a number were scratched, no doubt by the glacier as it slowly passed above.

We took a steamer excursion one day the length of the mountain-bordered lake and found it full of interest. Near Lucerne the lake is a cross and then after passing through a narrow neck it becomes a carpenter's square joined to the long arm of the cross. The trip to Fluelen at the further end consumed about two and a half hours. The mountains were wild, their upper heights bare and the lower slopes timbered and dotted with occasional dwellings, but there was no snow visible except in the arm near Fluelen. Along this branch of the lake, called Lake Uri, is the railroad to the St. Gotthard tunnel into Italy, and sometimes above, sometimes below it on the eastern side runs a picturesque public highway, the Axen Strasse, in many places passing through galleries blasted in the rock. Shortly after making the bend in Lake Uri we saw on our right a little clearing half way up the mountain and were told it was the Rütli. Here, where three springs providentially came up to commemorate the event, on November 7, 1307, thirty-three men of the cantons Schwyz, Uri and Unterwalden, which border on this part of the lake, met and pledged themselves to drive out their imperial Hapsburg oppressors, and here often before had also met the three first conspirators from these adjoining forest cantons and planned the revolution. The Hohenstaufen had given the cantons charters rendering them independent of Zurich and Einsiedeln, and to these emperors they had been loyal, even in the wars against the Lombard cities. But the Hapsburgs desired to annex Schwyz to their family domains and the cruelty of their rapacious representatives caused revolts.

From Fluelen I once walked to Altdorf, where I found a plaster statue representing Tell after he had hit the apple and holding up the second arrow with which he would have shot the governor Gessler had his first killed the boy, whose statue is two hundred feet away. Further on at Bürglen I had a pleasant view from a church on the site of Tell's house. At Altdorf a restaurant keeper asked me to come in. I asked if Tell had taken his meals there? He said yes. But, said I, your house is but a few years old. "True, mein herr, I forgot that, but this is the place where he would have dined had he lived to see so pleasant a restaurant." On this I went in and had a good dinner.

On our return up the lake we saw again opposite Rütli Tell's familiar big windowed chapel. They had loosed him in a storm to row them to land, but he escaped, leaving them to their fate, and the chapel is on the flat rock where he jumped from Gessler's boat. Gessler got to shore, but not long after Tell met him again and sped an arrow through his heart.

However true these stories may or may not be, the three forest cantons were the first Confederates or Eidgenossen. They gradually made themselves free and at Morgarten in 1315 defeated the Hapsburgs in a famous battle, which marked out for the future the predominance of infantry over the noble cavalry. From that time they became as independent but allied states the nucleus of a growing Confederation. Pastoral Unterwalden was less aggressive than craggy Uri, while Schwyz as the most active has even given the name to the present country. Lucerne joined the league in 1332, Zurich 1351, Glarus and Zug the next year, and powerful Berne in 1353 completed the League of the Eight Cantons, which remained unchanged for over a century.

At Vitznau on the lake we took the inclined railway up the Rigi. A heavy steam motor pulls the passenger car, both built at an angle, and we instinctively held on to the seats. I cannot think it perfectly safe, especially as they allow two trains on the track at once in sight of each other. There was no check available that I could imagine if a cog broke or the engine in any way got beyond control, but I believe they have had no accidents. A cog wheel under the motor works down into a rack rail between the tracks and thus regularly and even at considerable speed we curved around the mountains and upwards, sometimes crossing bridges over yawning chasms, outdoing Longfellow's youth with a less strange device. As we went on a beautiful sunset colored the mountains and lighted up the blue lake stretched out before us, its four western arms becoming more and more distinct as we ascended. We went clear to the top, called

Rigi Kulm, but arrived too late for much of a view, and found it cold and windy. We were almost frozen as we followed the path some hundred yards down to a cheaper hotel at Rigi Staffel, where we had engaged quarters as we came up. The next morning was cloudy and we again had no view. Our trip was thus almost fruitless, and we descended disgusted. On a previous visit, however, I witnessed a beautiful sunrise. On that occasion I staid also at Staffel, and about four A.M. was awakened and climbed hastily to the Kulm in hopes of a sunrise to repay for the misty sunset of the day before. I was not disappointed. First came a white streak, then a red, and then the daylight spread, revealing to the north and east plains and mountains. The sun next came up, at first an oval disc, renewed the tints above him and colored the opposite horizon over Pilatus, and on that mountain fell the shadow of Rigi. Full of interest was the gradual differentiation of the plains far below to the north, the clouds hanging like solid smoke over the lakes, the gradual penetration of light into the Lowerz lake to the east, embosomed in mountains, and the indistinctness of the peaks between me and the sun from the very overbrightness behind them. The white Alps to the south were not visible from mist. Soon the sun himself went permanently under clouds and Rigi's shadow disappeared from Pilatus. On the Rigi too I first heard the Alpine horn. It is a long tube fixed to the ground near a ravine and its beautiful echo music begins whenever the man in charge sees a traveller who looks as if he has a heart and pocket too.

We had a quick trip back to Lucerne, got our things from the hotel, and just made the train for Meiringen. To travel from the Lucerne region south to that of Interlaken, as from any valley in central Switzerland to another, one has to go over a mountain pass. In this instance the ascent over the Brünnig Pass is not so steep as to prevent using the common style of railroad track except near the top and on descending into the vale, where we had rack and pinion like the Rigibahn. Not far from Lucerne we saw the three-mile incline railway up Pilatus. This had not long been in operation and is very steep, the angle being almost forty-five degrees. I would not care to risk my life on it, although they claim to have greater safeguards than the Rigi in that the motor cogs work from below in teeth hanging vertically under the edges of a central T shaped rail. The view from Pilatus is more extensive because the mountain is higher, but the summit is oftener in clouds and the weather always uncertain. Pontius Pilate drowned himself in despair in a lake at the top, and when his wraith tries to wash from his hands the sacred blood he spilled, outraged nature moans and storms. The mountain is the local barometer for Lucerne. If its head is clear in the morning, the weather is doubtful, but if it be shrouded in clouds until noon and then clears, the afternoon will be fine.

The views *en route* to Meiringen were less grand than from the Rigi, although good, and those of the vale of Meiringen and of Lake Brienz were very pleasing. The railroad has been built in the last twelve years. On a former occasion I could not get a seat in the diligence and so spent two days walking over the pass. We had next a short boat passage to Interlaken over Lake Brienz, on the way seeing Giessbach falls, and finally at our destination put up at the Hotel Interlaken. This was good in every respect, even to the number of stairs we had to climb. Interlaken is made up of attractive shops with fine wood carving and other Swiss articles, and of hotels, many of which are palatial and have beautiful grounds.

The next day we took the train to Grindelwald to get a better view of the great Alps of central Switzerland, the Jungfrau, Mönch and Eiger of the Bernese group, beyound whose impassable heights of snow lies the Rhone valley, into which we were finally to come after a long detour westward to Berne and Geneva. Interlaken lies between two lakes in an east and west valley, and from the south comes another vale, itself the union of yet two others opening from the south and south-east. In the south-eastern branch is Grindelwald, below the vast and snowy Eiger. The village is scattered along in front of two rather dirty looking glaciers, which curve down from behind some peaks and melt into streams of water, which probably are making glacier gardens under the green ice in our own day. I once climbed over the pass to Grindelwald from the southern valley I mentioned, that of Lauterbrunnen, where the small brook Staubbach falls nine hundred and eighty feet and becomes a mere swaying veil of spray before it reaches the ground. On this trip from Lauterbrunnen the Jungfrau with deep snows and glaciers, the peaks bare stone, stood opposite in the south until I reached the Little Scheideck. The huge mass of snow was blinding and as I walked I saw several impressive avalanches sweep majestically on and fall as dust over three successive precipices, with noise like thunder. I was glad that there was a safe valley between us. From the Scheideck, a water shed, I climbed the Lauberhorn to the north and had a magnificent view ; to the west and north was the Lütschine valley with Interlaken and its mountains beyond, east the Grindelwald valley with little squares of wheat on the slopes, the high Wetterhorn and Screckhorn by it, and then, connecting them with the Jungfrau, the precipitous Eiger and snowy Mönch. West of the concave Jungfrau were the Silberhorn, Breithorn and other white peaks, and all around on the west, north and east were smaller mountains. The view was much finer than from the Rigi because nearer the great snow heights.

 On that trip I did not return to Interlaken and go around west to the Rhone valley, but climbed over the pass to Meiringen and went southwardly to the Rhone glacier. To effect this I left Grindelwald at 6:30 o'clock one morning and commenced climbing the Grosse Scheideck Pass. The sun was just beginning to touch the lower grass-grown mountains like the Lauberhorn, whence I had been driven the day before by a hailstorm, and it now produced a soft and pleasing impression. From a meadow I had a fine view of the green Rosenlaui glacier, with bare mountains above the pines. Further on in descending to the vale of Meiringen with its pleasant waterfalls and distant view, I sprained my ankle and could hardly drag myself up to Guttanen. On the way I saw the industrious cheese carriers in abundance. One Saturday I spent from 6:30 A.M. to 1:30 P.M. climbing the bare upper Haslithal valley, where but a few houses exist. Granite prevails, pines become stunted and finally cease, while daisies and rhododendra flourish. The view was always wild and sometimes imposing, as at the double cataract of Handeck, two hundred feet in fall, the foaming Aare River dancing over rocks hundreds of feet right below the path. The summit is called the Grimsel Pass and there above the clouds in 1799 was a battle in which the French defeated the Austrians. Over that desolate place I passed and in descending the zigzag road was lost in admiration of the huge Rhone glacier, whose melting ice supplies the head waters of the great French river. Thence I took the diligence down the Rhone valley towards Zermatt and Chamouny.

But that was years ago, in August, 1880. Now we went back by rail from Grindelwald to Interlaken and one morning started off westward in a two-story car for Lake Thun, had a pleasant boat trip on that blue sheet of water, commanding fine Alpine views, and then an uneventful railroad journey over lowlands to Berne.

CHAPTER VIII.

BERNE AND FRENCH SWITZERLAND.

BERNE is the capital of Switzerland and has had a long, eventful history. It has been a powerful and aggressive state, always oligarchic in its tendencies, and thus often compared with Venice, despite their opposite geographical surroundings. It was founded in August, 1191, in the next century became independent of the empire, gradually acquired a great deal of subject territory, including the Bernese Oberland which we had just visited, and since it joined the Confederation has always been a leading member. The legislative assemblies meet here twice a year, their proceeding being in both French and German.

We had but a few hours after dinner to spend seeing this quaint city. It is on a precipitous peninsula surrounded on three sides by the river Aare, here much larger than where I had seen it near its source. The main street of Berne runs east from the railway station a mile, but under several different names. At one place it is crossed by a portal, once a city gate, with a remarkable clock. Bruin is the patron saint of Berne and just before this clock strikes a number of miniature bears parade before a seated figure near it. Many streets have covered passage ways instead of sidewalks, and from a bench on one we saw soldiers pass to join in celebrating the city's seven hundredth anniversary. The main street at its eastern extremity crosses the Aare by the fine Nydeck bridge, and on the other side of the river is a bear pit maintained at the expense of the city. The view from this bridge of the river far below is impressive. On our return we went off to the left to see the distant Bernese Alps from the cathedral terrace, but a heavy rain cut off all views and drove us into a shop. No carriages were near and we had to pick our way back to the main street in the rain and there take the car to the station.

The glimpse we had of the cathedral, inside and out, made us wish for more time here, but we could not stay. We were still several days behind in our plans, despite the change in route at Lucerne by which we gave up the trip from Altdorf to the Rhone glacier. So we went aboard a train and kept on towards Lausanne, and, as usual in Switzerland, were in a very comfortable car. In French Switzerland we found the cars somewhat on the American plan in that they had a passage way through the middle and seats on the sides, but these faced each other and so some people rode backwards. The second class cars are quite comfortable, and even have lavatory conveniences aboard.

Not long before we reached the Lausanne we passed through a tunnel and came out on our first view of Lake Geneva. The large sheet of blue water, dotted with steamers and boats with lateen sails, the sloping shores revealing vineyards and handsome villas, to the east the high peaks, on the top of many of them snow, and lower down wreaths of clouds, all colored by a glorious sunset, made up together a vision of beauty which we have never seen equalled.

Lausanne is on a ridge high above the lake and very uneven,—one is going up or down hill all the time. It is broken in two by a valley between the castle height and the cathedral hill, but a handsome bridge connects the two quarters. In the lower level between we found a hotel, which we remember for the lake view from its terrace and also because they charged us extra for soap. Attendance and light, that is to say a candle, always add a franc or two, but soap we had generally enjoyed without extra charge. We had learned the trick of taking the candle along that we paid for and so avoiding charge for *bougie* at the next stop, and so now we put the soap in the satchel too. After a hasty view of the magnificent cathedral, where in 1536 a disputation in which Calvin took part resulted in winning this Canton Vaud for the reformed faith, we went down the incline railway to the lake at the boat station Ouchy, a separate town, and here, where Byron wrote his Prisoner of Chillon, we went aboard a steamer for Geneva.

Two hours over the beautiful blue waters brought us to that city and we went to Hotel de la Poste, which proved to be rather unsatisfactory as to meals *à la carte*. We remember the steak, for one thing, with peculiar horror.

Geneva is the handsomest and probably the largest of the Swiss cities, Zurich being next in size. Its position is somewhat like Zurich, Lucerne, and even Constance and Basel, in that it lies on both sides of a river into which a lake contracts to discharge towards the western streams. The Rhone, however, like Lake Geneva, is a beautiful blue, while all the other lakes we noticed except Lake Thun are green, and this difference has never been satisfactorily accounted for. The city extends along the river and lake, bordered by promenades, quays and parks. The river is swift but in some places shallow and full of floating wash houses with women hard at work, and the long connecting bridges are substantial, the Pont du Mont Blanc, the one nearest the lake, being very handsome. From the adjacent Quai du Mont Blanc that high round-topped peak and group are visible although fifty miles away, and sunlight and sunset coloring stay on it after the city is in twilight. Mont Blanc is the highest mountain in Europe, being fifteen thousand seven hundred and thirty feet, while the Jungfrau is thirteen thousand six hundred and seventy feet and Monte Rosa on the Italian line fifteen thousand two hundred and seventeen feet high.

On this quay is the handsome monument to the eccentric ex-duke Charles II. of Brunswick, who died here in exile and bequeathed his property to the city, and behind the Mont Blanc bridge is a pleasant little island in the river with a seated statue of the " self-torturing sophist, wild Rousseau." The city has had many other famous residents, including Calvin, Beza, Knox, Voltaire, Hume, Gibbon, Mme. de Staël, Sismondi and others, and it has produced many scientists, particularly botanists and geologists. In 1536 the austere John Calvin, a refugee from Paris, came here and aided Farel, the fiery Protestant preacher, and, despite a temporary banishment, obtained the strongest possible hold on the community, it being both political and religious. His method of church and social government was by the Consistoire, made up of half as many ministers as elders, and their rule, almost inquisitorial, suppressed vice and made of

CALVIN'S CHURCH AT GENEVA.

gay Geneva a model community whose influence was world-wide. His reformation was as much more thorough-going than Zwingli's as that was than Luther's, although his teaching as to the communion was mediate between theirs. Luther in his dispute with Zwingli said dogmatically that the words, " This is my body," were to be taken literally, and his consubstantiation was very nearly the Catholic doctrine of the Real Presence of Christ in the emblems, while Zwingli claimed that the words were figurative and the act but an instructive memorial. Calvin said that Christ was present spiritually to such as communed aright and that He could be spiritually discerned. Calvin was almost a Protestant Pope while alive, and as the interpreter of Paul and Augustine and their teachings as to predestination was the founder of great churches, and even after his death in 1564 he powerfully influenced the doctrine of others which did not accept his method of church government. The Church of Scotland was built by his disciple John Knox, Holland followed him, and the Presbyterians of the United States look to Calvin as the greatest of all expositors of the Bible. He was an untiring worker. His greatest book, Christianæ Religionis Institutio, was published at Basel in 1535. The stern man loved Geneva as his own soul. He preached in the cathedral, a stone church with handsome Corinthian portico, the interior an imposing transition between Romanesque and Gothic, and his chair stands under the pulpit. We heard a magnificent organ concert there one night, the vast building lighted only by a few little lamps which hardly lessened the gloom. Calvin's grave is outside of the city, but exactly where is not known, as he wished it to be unmarked. He lived near his church in a plain house, and not far away in Grand Rue was born in 1712 Jean Jacques Rousseau, the son of a watchmaker. We visited the Calvinium, said to contain memorials of Calvin, but there was nothing to be seen of his except some books and I believe a chair. There was a good relief of Jerusalem and other interesting things, but they did not relate to Calvin.

Geneva from Calvin's time long had no theatres. Voltaire chuckled greatly over getting the strict city fathers out to his villa at Ferney and treating them to a performance of one of his plays. Now the Geneva theatre is as handsome as the cathedral and the fine square on which it faces far outdoes the cramped hilly surroundings of Calvin's church. On this square is also a handsome museum presented by the Rath family to the city in honor of the Russian general of that name, who was born in Geneva. Near is a botanic garden, and above on the hills is the University, with valuable scientific collections. In the old hilly cité not far from there I noticed Paradise Street, Purgatory Street, and Hell Street,—a curious survival of old nomenclature.

Geneva was once subject to Savoy and the history of its struggles with the counts and dukes of that country is interesting. The bulk of the patriotic citizens were for a league with powerful Berne of the Swiss Eidgenossen, of which the French pronunciation made *Huguenots*. It was only in Calvin's time that the bishop was driven out and the state became truly independent, for ambitious Berne had only aided Geneva for her own purposes, and would if uncontrolled have annexed this canton as she had Vaud. The last attempt of the Savoyards to capture the city was by escalade December 12, 1602, (still celebrated as a holiday,) at a place in the old walls near the river now marked by a fountain. Under Napoleon the city was a part of France, but after his fall it became the twenty-second canton of the Swiss Confederation.

We had a long steam tramway ride in the eastern suburbs but I remember even more pleasantly a walk I had on a former occasion past the fine Rothschild chateau to Ferney. At this village, which is over the French border, I saw an ugly bust of the "patriarch" Voltaire and since then I believe he has been honored with a bronze statue. My tramp out consumed about an hour and I spent the night at the little Voltaire Inn, from whence I was all but driven, however, by the odorous Swiss cheese set before me. I had never seen liquid cheese before, and have avoided it ever since. In the outskirts of the village is Voltaire's church with the ambitious inscription, "Deo erexit Voltaire." It is of stone, low and squatty, with a small clock tower and cross on top,—the last, however, hardly Voltaire's. His adjacent long, white chateau looks cool and pleasant. It is of French Renaissance style with mansard roof, has three entrances from the front, and, with its fine shrubbery, is kept in beautiful order by its owner, M. Lambert. Voltaire lived here the last twelve years of his adventurous life, spending his vast means in helping the poor and aiding political and religious offenders. He wished to be near the border so as to escape if his satires should happen to hurt those in power at Paris.

From Geneva one morning we took the boat to Villeneuve at the other end of the lake. The trip consumed between four and five hours, pleasantly spent in watching the exhibitions of a contortionist, in listening to a good string band, which, like the other exhibitor, took up frequent collections. We especially enjoyed the beautiful scenery. The lake is a crescent forty-five miles long, with its horns pointing southwardly. It is at one place, off Ouchy, ten hundred and fifteen feet deep, but generally much less. On the south side are the abrupt mountains of France, which there touches the lake almost its full length, while on the north are gentler slopes with beautiful villas and vines and foliage. On that side at Coppet was the residence of the Genevan banker Neckar, celebrated perhaps more as the father of Mme. De Staël than as finance minister of Louis XVI. Further east is the chateau of Prangins, formerly the property of Joseph Bonaparte, and then of Prince Jerome, who died lately. At Paris a few weeks later we saw it advertised for sale, but we made no offer, as it did not suit us in several respects.

Familiar Lausanne we then passed, soon were opposite Vevey and Clarens, immortalized by Rousseau, and we hurried through dinner to get on deck and see the gloomy but not imposing red roofed Castle of Chillon. It was once on an island but the shallow channel under its bridge has been filled by time. It dates back at least to Louis le Debonaire in 830, and the celebrated Count Peter of Savoy in the thirteenth century put it in its present condition. Every one remembers here Byron's Prisoner of Chillon, but, as in so much familiar poetry of his, we cannot look for the exact historical truth. When he wrote it it was intended as a fable, and he did not know the story of one great victim, Bonivard, a friend of Geneva and an enemy of the Savoyards, who was imprisoned here by the duke from 1530 until rescued six years later by the Bernese. Bonivard may have been chained to one of the massive pillars in the dark dungeon and the sad floor trod until his very steps left their trace in the worn stone pavement, but he had no brothers there to die before his eyes, the dungeon is well lighted, it is not below the level of the sea, and the smiling little isle was not planted then. The only way to read the poem is as an idyl and not as history. Imprisonment in this gloomy place, hearing only the waves beat on the thick stone walls, is, however, a sufficiently sad fate in itself. Bonivard on his return to Geneva tried to make up in gaiety for some of the years thus lost, and fell more than once under the displeasure of Calvin and the judgment of the Consistoire. At the east end of the lake we noticed, by the way, that the river, which issues at Geneva a blue stream, is where it comes in very muddy and not blue, as Byron has it in the poem. Its deposits are gradually extending a marsh out into the lake.

From Villeneuve we went by rail up the Rhone valley to Brieg, the river being now on one side, now on the other of the track, passing interesting places, and having often fine views of mountains, side valleys and cascades. At St. Maurice the Theban legion under its commander of that name suffered martyrdom in A.D. 302, but we had already found them buried at Cologne. As we waited at the station for a train we saw before us a hermitage perched picturesquely half way up a cliff, reached only by a path cut in the rock.

Martigny further on is the usual stopping place for travellers to Chamouny, and from here I made that trip some years ago. I started early up the zigzag road, at seven I believe, and resisting all seductions of ugly young girls with fine grapes, plums and pears, temptations common enough, I climbed on, having beautiful views of the great valley clear up to Sion. Near the Col de Forclaz

Pass I left the road for the Col de Balme bridle path and just before reaching the steep zigzag overtook a guide, a young man on horseback, and one on foot. I soon made the acquaintance of the one afoot and we went on together. A rain storm overtook us near the summit but afterwards we obtained a view of the Mont Blanc group of snow-clad mountains, with an occasional glacier projecting into the valley. About five, after being caught several times in the rain while descending, we arrived at a hotel near Chamouny, and there stopped. The next morning my new friend and I started about seven, climbed the Montanvert opposite and on top had a good view of the Mer de Glace as it lay before us, bending around from behind peaks to the right, and below us sinking as a frozen waterfall, much broken as it came over a sharp incline. We did not appreciate its size until we saw the little people on it. Our economical plan for crossing without a guide was to follow a party who had one, and so we did. The uneven surface was as if made up of frozen waves. These were easy to climb and the melty ice was not slippery, but it was not pleasant to see around us fissures of all sizes and holes that apparently had no bottom. The party ahead became alarmed and after a while turned back, leaving us without a guide. I then undertook to pilot, as my bump of locality is well developed, and I got along all right until we approached the shore, where the ice was rough and broken. A man directed us from land, however, to some steps in the ice, and we finally found our way over the moraine of rocks and dirt and climbed a narrow and steep path that runs along the frozen river.

The next day my friend left and I climbed the Flégère alone. From this mountain Mont Blanc is seen to advantage, its rounded peak and companion group standing prominent to the right of the town, letting down near Chamouny the huge, broken Glacier des Bossons, while to my other hand was the Mer de Glace, surrounded by its needle peaks, more pointed than those so common in the Saxon highlands. The amount of the Mer de Glace which actually goes over the final cliff is very small, red stone being visible on one side. The upper part of Mont Blanc is precipitous, its needles bare of snow. The ice is in some places smooth, in others cracked and broken in every direction as if by an avalanche or earthquake. The lower half of the group is covered with the green of pines and shrubbery and grass, and its easier slopes melt insensibly into the valley. Occasionally I saw a châlet of logs, and storehouses resting on pillars and round stones to keep out rats. Mont Blanc is on the line between France and Italy. It was first ascended in 1786 and has been often since. There are regular guides who take you up in three days, but the trip is sometimes dangerous and the view always unsatisfactory.

But Rachel and I did not stop at Martigny to make an excursion to Chamouny nor did we branch off there to follow the St. Bernard route into Italy. Keeping on up the Rhone valley, we passed the two castled hills of Sion, the capital of the canton Valais, which extends all the way up to the Rhone glacier. Sion's bishop was much courted in the middle ages, for he could direct the mercenary troops of Switzerland in any direction. Above Sion are terraced vineyards, and here too in the Rhone valley we saw many cases of goitre, but the disease seems to distress strangers much more than the unfortunates themselves. Swiss costumes are picturesque. About here the black hats with brush-like edge of the women and the blouses of the men worn outside their pantaloons are noticeable, and the way children salute by kissing the hand is very attractive. French is common up to Visp but from there German prevails.

From Visp there is now a railroad to Zermatt, but on my earlier visit I had to foot it up this side valley, a distance of perhaps twenty-five miles. A steep climb from Zermatt up the Riffelberg brought me to Gorner Grat and the view of Monte Rosa, the Matterhorn and that vast field of glaciers, the grandest view in Switzerland. It was a bad day, however, and rain and sleet and volumes of mist obscuring everything soon drove me down.

Not far above Visp is Brieg, the starting point of the Simplon route over into Italy, and there we stopped, almost in sight of the Rhone glacier and Furca Pass, by which I had once come over from Canton Uri and the head waters of the Rhine.

CHAPTER IX.

THE SIMPLON PASS AND ITALIAN LAKES.

IT was a choice at Brieg between crowded hotels, and our choice unfortunately gave us a cold though good dinner at second table and a room over the hotel stable. Fleas had been rare heretofore but from here on we had them with us always.

Early in the morning we were called, had a breakfast of eggs and coffee, and left the hotel, fully disgusted with the big prices and poor service. Switzerland was overrun with tourists. On account of the strained relations then existing with Italy, few Americans went there that summer, and the hotel keepers in Switzerland knew that they would necessarily get crowds, regardless of how they treated them. At the post office, which runs the diligences, we found them hitching up two ponderous stage coaches. The night before I had been balked by finding that but one coach was contemplated, and, as applicants ahead of us had secured the *coupé* in front under the driver and the seats on top, we were then assigned to the *intérieur*, which gives a poor view; but now we were enabled to get seats on top of the second coach by paying extra. This place is at the rear and they call it the *banquette*. On our coach it was unusually large, consisting of four seats facing each other and having a buggy top behind, which could be raised in bad weather. After the numerous pieces of baggage had been put on the coaches, strapped safely in front of the *banquette*, and we had with more or less grace climbed up a ladder and got into our places, we started off in fine style, the driver in front cracking vigorously his long whip and another man musically blowing a horn. Our party of four in the *banquette* was made up besides ourselves of a silent young man, I think a Frenchman, and a most entertaining and travelled elderly Englishman, of whom we were to see a great deal for several days.

The forty-one miles over to Domo D'Ossola were made inside of ten hours, including a rest at the Hospice on the summit of the pass and half an hour for dinner at Simplon half way down the other side. The view at first presented no unusual features as we zigzagged up the mountain side above decrepit Brieg and commanded the valley of the Rhone. The clouds hung over the Aletschhorn and Finsteraarhorn across the valley and only occasionally through rifts could we see their snowy robes. We were almost opposite Lauterbrunnen and due south from Grindelwald, twenty miles away on the other side of the great Bernese Jungfrau group, of which the mountains just named are the rear peaks. I do not know whether adventurous travellers have climbed over this group or not. The Jungfrau has frequently been ascended, but certainly not often the whole of this great barrier between the Rhone valley and the Bernese Oberland.

The Simplon road was constructed by Napoleon 1800–1806 to avoid the necessity for such another feat as his passage of the Great St. Bernard in 1800 with 30,000 men. The route finally terminates at Milan, where it is spanned by a triumphal arch, and the road is one of Napoleon's best monuments. It winds up around the edge of mountains, bordered with stones and a strong railing on the brink of precipices, and in places is blasted out of the solid rock. Often one can climb from one level to another in a few minutes and have to wait half an hour for the diligence to wind up to the point thus gained. Where avalanches are common it passes through tunnels with windows, and the masses of snow and ice harmlessly thunder overhead and fall thousands of feet below. The road up to the Hospice in general overhung the deep valley of the Saltine stream, once making a long detour to the left to cross a side valley near its head. We had now left the Rhone and the views were only of bleak mountains, pine covered slopes and perhaps pleasant valleys below us, bare or snowy summits towering above. Sometimes we would see a little clearing on the mountain side and in the middle a cottage, its wide eaves projecting and roof boards held on by weighty stones instead of nails. The owners are often hunters or herdsmen and absent much of the day. Such homestead entries surely cannot cost much. As we ascended, the temperature became continually colder and our thick buggy robe from Leipzig aided nicely in keeping warm all four of us. Every few miles is a refuge, a stone house for travellers in time of storm. Our English acquaintance had a friend who was confined in one of the upper refuges for two or three weeks and lost his health from exposure. Not far from the top is the Kaltwasser gallery, a tunnel over which now in summer poured water from the blinding Kaltwasser glacier above, a part of Monte Leone, the snowy group which is here the crown of the Alps. The highest point of the pass is 6590 feet, and a short distance off, and but twenty feet lower, is the plain stone Hospice with high steps ascending to it. All was bare around except for daisies, bluebells and rhododendra. Napoleon erected this large building to take the place of the smaller Old Hospice further down, and in it is his portrait. The institution is now owned and managed by the St. Bernard brethren, a branch from the higher but less frequented hospice on the St. Bernard pass. These noble men devote themselves without remuneration to the rescue of travellers, living a life of hardship and want in order to aid others, and early lose their own health and retire to the valleys to die. The great tawny dogs walked around before us, taking now their short summer vacation. I went over this pass once in April. The snow was then as high as the top of the diligence, and although it was cleared away from the road, it stood in walls on either side. The dogs then were on the alert and sniffing the air. Now after a short halt we went on and at Simplon, two thousand feet lower, we had an excellent dinner about noon at a reasonable price.

The descent was much more rapid, of course, and the scenery perhaps more picturesque. The brawling Diveria, our first Italian stream, accompanied the road, and soon we found ourselves in the gloomy Gondo Ravine, where perpendicular walls of stone towered on either hand two thousand feet above us. At one point the road seemed shut in by a rock, but there was a tunnel, out of which we came beside a waterfall. This gorge is perhaps the most impressive part of the trip.

A granite column near here marks the Italian boundary, and at Iselle the suspicious-looking custom-house officials thoroughly went through the baggage. Rachel had a wooden darning ball which they examined with great care, shaking their heads and bouncing the suspected article on the floor, but tobacco and wines are their especial objects, as we had opportunity on several occasions to notice. At this place I met with a painful accident. In descending from the *banquette*, as the stage leaned over to one side I had to catch the wheel to keep myself from falling. I happened to grasp the tire and it was so hot from its long journey that it burned its painful width across my hand. Fortunately we had vaseline along and I was made as comfortable as circumstances admitted, but it was a number of days before I could use the hand again.

On account of this accident the rest of the trip was less enjoyable, but we went down at a rapid pace, finding the climate vastly changed and trying by discarding shawls and hoisting umbrellas to become acclimated. The trees and flowers all became more tropical and reminded us of our own southern home, and about four P.M. we reached Domo D'Ossola and left the great diligence for a rather primitive railroad train, which, however, brought us safely down a valley to the station for Pallanza. We there got in a 'bus and had a pleasant trip to Lake Maggiore, I keeping the western sun out by holding my umbrella outside of the rear of the 'bus, much to the surprise and amusement of the natives. At the town we changed to a vehicle lighted by electricity and were finally landed at the Grand Hotel.

This is beautifully situated on the lake, lighted by electricity, complete in all its arrangements, and reasonable in its charges. It was the best hotel by far of all our travels and here we spent most delightfully several days, not a little of our enjoyment due to discovering that the cook could prepare American ham and eggs. The hotel is near where a western bay joins Lake Maggiore midway its length and a few feet off is one of the islands that adds so much picturesqueness to the view. Opposite across the lake is a high mountain from behind which the sun rises, and north and south stretches green Lake Maggiore, its sloping wooded banks dotted with villages and the handsome gardens of hotels and private residences. To the north appear snowy Alpine peaks in the distance which contrast strangely with the figs, olives, flowers and vines about us on the hilly shores.

One day we took a boat ride on these waters. We passed through the Borromean Islands near Pallanza, one inhabited by fishermen, and another the famous Isola Bella, occupied by an uncompleted chateau with ten terraces, or hanging gardens, filled with all the beautiful vegetation that Italy offers, her "waste more rich than other climes' fertility." About are statues and the general rococo ornamentation of the seventeenth century, fashionable when Count Borromeo converted the bare rock into this rather artificial Eden. Isola Madre is not unlike Isola Bella, and in fact the whole group is interesting. Further south above Arona is the colossal bronze statue of S. Carlo Borromeo, seventy feet tall and standing on a base almost as high. He was born here and has for his goodness been canonized by the people as well as by the pope. At Arona itself we took dinner with our English friend and were introduced by him to the famous and delightful Gorgonzola cheese.

After this good rest at our Grand Hotel and many chats and strolls with Mr. Holmes during our stay, we started one morning for Lake Como by way of Lugano.

We left the Maggiore steamer at Luino and entered a narrow gauge car, which whirled along a wild and wooded route, following the line between Italy and Switzerland, to Ponte Tresa. There we went aboard a small boat on Lake Lugano, but were kept down in the cabin much of the way by the rain. Rachel was annoyed by an impolite couple who spent much of their time looking at her. They were human pigs, any way. We first saw them at Brieg taking up four or five seats in the 'bus with umbrellas and sticks, which could have gone on the floor, and thus all but making several people walk that long road up to the hotels. Unable now to stand it longer, I took a chair and sat down in front of them, and stared at them myself until they left that part of the boat. We expressed our opinion of them fully to each other and were delighted later to learn that they understood English. I do not know what they thought of us, but I know that it could be nothing worse than we thought of them.

Lake Lugano somewhat resembles the letter S, with the town on the west side near the middle. We got on the boat near the southern extremity and navigated the whole length of the lake, and although the views when the rain permitted us to go outside were much the same, they were quite imposing. We all but circumnavigated a range, called Mte. Arbostora at the south end and at its north Mte. S. Salvatore, and just after turning to the north towards Lugano passed under the arches of the St. Gotthard railway as a train thundered across above us. We had seen this railroad coming down the east end of Lake Lucerne in many turns and tunnels, and, passing through Altdorf, it climbs the Reuss valley in numerous curves until at Andermatt it goes under the

Alps through a tunnel nine miles and a quarter long. It thence descends a valley here to Lugano, crosses down to Como and finally ends at Milan.

At Lugano we were in Switzerland again, in the Canton Ticino, and got from the post our spare satchel, shipped at the price of one franc from Geneva. We dined here and had a view of the railway up Mte. S. Salvatore, operated by a cable but re-inforced by rack and pinion too, whose incline near the top is as sixty to one hundred. This was worse than the trans-Alpine Switzerland and we had no desire to try it. From the Lugano pier we took a second steamer up to the north end of the lake, where at Porlezza we got on another narrow gauge railroad. Our train dashed at great speed along the edge of precipices and on bridges over deep chasms, all in a heavy downpour of rain that obscured the view and in places covered the track with water. It was an uncanny trip, but, as the road bed was rock, no harm came to us from the storm.

At last, as we arrived in sight of Lake Como and began to back down to its level, a great ray of sunlight came through the clouds and struck the water midway between the shores, and it then travelled up and down the lake, lighting everything with a beautiful blue. All the passengers crowded to that side of the car and gazed in rapt silence at the wondrous sight. It was as if a spirit walked the water.

The boat soon arrived at the landing and we crossed to Bellagio, near the point where the two arms of the lake separate. There at our pleasant little Hotel Florence we staid from this Saturday evening until Monday afternoon, enjoying the views and trying to resist buying more of the native carved olive wood than we could carry.

Lake Como is thirty miles long and at its widest part is 1930 feet deep, over a quarter of a mile, but Lake Maggiore at some places is 2800 feet. About half way its length Lake Como divides into two southern branches, of which the western, at the foot of which lies Como, is the more beautiful and better settled, while the banks of the eastern arm, called Lago di Lecco, are steeper and wilder and from it the waters of the lake empty into the river Adda, a tributary of the Po.

The sunsets and views on Lake Como have been famous since the days of Pliny and Virgil and we enjoyed them in all their glory even from our room windows. One day we rowed around the point and found that this promontory has been left in its natural state, although it is a part of the grounds of some hotel or residence away above the little town. On the eastern bank was the Milk stream, falling in white cascades a thousand feet down the side to the lake. Away north we could see the Alpine snows near St. Gotthard, while on the rippling blue water near us floated by a Maréchal Niel rose, which we secured and pressed as a souvenir. All along the western slopes were villas of the Milanese or foreigners, picturesque villages and landings, and on the quiet lake we saw occasional boats and steamers and other forms of life.

On the western shore across from Bellagio is the villa Carlotta, now the property of the Duke of Sachsen-Meiningen. The grounds are laid off in slopes and terraces, and the luxuriant flowers and trees of this clime make it a charming spot. One of its greatest curiosities is a magnolia tree, shown with great pride by the gardener, but which, though of fair diameter, is squatty and cannot compare with the beautiful magnolias of our home in Mobile. The villa possesses several artistic treasures. In one room is Lazzarini's thin Consul Napoleon and in another a frieze relief by Thorwaldsen of the Triumph of Alexander, Acquisti's group of Mars and Venus, and several pieces by Canova, of which the gem is Cupid stooping over to kiss the recumbent Psyche. There is a duplicate of this in the Louvre, but the marble of that is imperfect.

Monday after dinner we took the boat for Como. At some places the swift steamer landed and at others little boats came out to meet it. At several points the lake contracted. On both sides the villas became more numerous as we neared the southern end, and the views were always charming. Finally we landed at Como, and drove off to the railroad, getting farewell views of the beautiful lake from the top of our 'bus.

Como is a place of some interest itself as the birthplace of the younger Pliny and of Volta, and its famous Gothic cathedral is worthy of inspection, but here as often elsewhere we had to be content to lose sights of lesser importance in order to have time for the greater ones. So we took the train for Milan and travelled through in about two hours, passing on the way Monza, where is treasured the jewelled Lombard crown, spoken of as the iron crown because it contains a nail of the true cross. Despite what was before us it was with real regret that we now left nature and her haunts for human history and the abodes of men.

CHAPTER X.

MILAN AND ITALIAN HISTORY.

MILAN is apparently a flourishing and progressive modern city. Besides the cathedral it has among places of interest a fine picture gallery and The Last Supper painted by Leonardo da Vinci on the wall of the refectory of Sta. Maria delle Grazie, a monastery since suppressed and converted into barracks.

This refectory is a long way from the Duomo square, the centre of interest at Milan, but the good horse car went on a number of lanes and avenues and so we saw many novel street sights on the way. After arriving we paid our two lire, passed through a turn-stile, and were ushered into the old dining hall of the monks, for this is preserved inviolate now. Napoleon's irreverent horses were stabled in this room when the floor was higher and kicked off the legs of the Disciples sitting at table, but time is making even worse havoc. The painting is in oils and is fading out. So marked has been the change in even the ten or eleven years between my own visits, that it is evident Leonardo's masterpiece will before long be but a memory. It is said the artist could never venture fully to complete the Saviour's face, but the variations of the countenances from divine love to satanic hate are wonderful. The picture takes up the end of the room and had more copyists than any other we saw on our travels. The room was full of easels and copies were all about in the windows and corners.

In the great square the white marble Duomo now stands free from the profane touch of other structures, but the tall surrounding buildings dwarf the church despite its marble terrace. Leading through them from the cathedral square is the lofty sculptured passage or arcade Victor Emanuel, covered with glass and lined with tempting shops, itself one of the wonders of the continent. When lighted by electricity at night and thronged with well dressed and animated promenaders, this gallery, the largest in Europe, presents a sight not to be forgotten.

The Duomo, in Italian Gothic style, was begun by a Visconti in 1386, and is the third largest in Europe. Gothic architecture never took strong root in Italy on account of the native Romanesque and classic styles, and from their revival in the fifteenth century the Gothic lost much of the hold it had acquired. Even this beautiful church, the most perfect specimen, has more breadth in proportion to height in each part and as a whole than the northern Gothic. It has, indeed, a low central tower, but not the usual spires. Without and on the roof are multitudes of flying buttresses, arches and minarets, and there are said to be two thousand statues looking, as Ruskin says, like angels alighting. From the roof the most attractive part of the panorama is to the north, where Mont Blanc is visible among the Alps and distant Monte Rosa looms up the most distinct of all. Monte Rosa is so hid by other ranges from the Switzerland side that one has to go to Italy to command a good view, half Swiss though the mountain be.

Within the cathedral the effect is perfect. The nave is one hundred and fifty-seven feet high, the double side aisles somewhat lower, and with the transepts make the church cruciform. The arched ceiling seems to be stone tracery, and we were surprised to learn that it is merely skilful painting. The dim, religious light from the beautiful, stained glass windows, and the magnificent music add much to the impressiveness of the church. In the crypt before the high altar, visible also from above, is the tomb of S. Carlo Borromeo, who was Archbishop of Milan in the sixteenth century, deservedly loved and honored for his piety and goodness, particularly shown during a visit of the plague in 1576.

Milan is a flourishing place of four hundred thousand inhabitants, ranking in Italy second to Naples in size, and having many wide streets and imposing buildings and places. It was a cisalpine town before Rome had subdued Italy, a great centre under the earlier Roman Empire and under the German substitute for the Roman Empire, but it was razed by Barbarossa in 1162, and, while it was rebuilt and has always been an important place, its tangible antiquities do not go much beyond this destruction in the middle ages.

At Milan we thus first really touched Roman history and a short study of this subject will be found interesting and perhaps also useful in connection with the Italian journeys which follow.

Many incidents of Roman story are familiar to us, but a correct understanding of the history as a whole is rarely met with, and yet if, as Freeman says, all ancient history merges in that of Rome and all modern history starts from it, a philosophy of Roman history is eminently desirable. We generally cease our reading with the close of the republican period, and yet it was under the empire that the world became Roman. The republican times are the most interesting because of the free play and conflict of the developing human spirit, while under the empire it all crystallized into a vast administrative system, whose conflicts were but struggles of soldiers for power. But from first to last it was one historical development and should be studied as such.

Roman history, I think, has four grand divisions,—1, The Republic of Rome, 2, The Empire of Rome, 3, The Roman Empire, and 4, The Holy Roman Empire of the middle ages. The first two divisions deal with rule by the city of Rome, at first when the city was republican in form and then when it was under a master, but still in both cases concern domination by the local city. In the third and fourth divisions, on the other hand, the rule was that of a personal sovereign, for a while by Roman sovereigns over the ancient territories, and then by Frankish and German temporal sovereigns who recognized the Roman Pope as a co-ordinate, spiritual ruler. Thus Roman history continues all through the middle ages, the empire becoming always more shadowy, it is true, but lasting in form until Francis of Austria in 1806 resigned the dignity.

The development of the city as a state was in the republican period. As soon as the first Alban settlers had demonstrated against neighboring nations that the little outpost city on the seven wooded hills was something that would stand and settled down themselves into patrician pride, their plebeian retainers and the lower population strove for a share of the government which they had helped make something to be proud of. Their success gave them one of the two consuls and a tribune who could check any unfair legislation by the senate, and the happy close of this civil struggle was marked by the erection of the Temple of Concord in the Roman Forum. Rome had now become the head of the Latin League, and the Latins next struggled, but unsuccessfully, for a share in the government of the growing city, and yet they failed in a measure only. The third struggle was both civil and social. All Italy had now become subject and all Italy soon desired Roman rights, but besides this the rich in the city had become richer and the poor poorer. The Gracchi in their agrarian legislation sought to alleviate this friction. The rivalry of men brought the discontent to open war, and Marius and Sulla, to some extent for personal advantage, respectively headed the popular and senatorial sides. Julius Cæsar, the nephew of Marius, and Cneius Pompey inherited these respective traditions, but Cæsar prevailed and attempted to establish a monarchy as the permanent leveller of civil castes and the assurance of civil peace. Before these later struggles the wars of Rome had been directed to obtaining the supremacy in Italy and so far as her arms were displayed without those bounds it was for commercial power or to humble a dangerous neighbor, not to conquer for war's own sake. That was left for Sulla and those after him who desired for their own ends to dazzle the citizens at home with the glamor of military glory. Thus gradually was subdued Greece and Palestine and the Mediterranean made a Roman lake.

With Cæsar and his more lucky nephew, named Augustus by the senate, begins the second historical division, the Empire of Rome. Cæsar aimed as a dictator at superseding the other republican officials, and was assassinated. Augustus and his successors sought by securing the grant to themselves of the powers of these magistrates to preserve the republic in form, while in fact they were autocrats, for Imperator, whence we have "Emperor," means but a general. The early emperors sought to re-build the city so as to cause the people to forget republican days, and for this reason few of the old structures remain at Rome. Through the Julian emperors of Rome, the Italian Vespasian and his sons, and the provincial Antonine dynasty from Nerva and Trajan through Marcus Aurelius, and even under the anarchy of the next hundred years, relieved as it was by Septimius Severus and Alexander Severus, while there was a single head to the government, the state was still the city of Rome. Rome was not the capital, it was the state, and it was the right to vote at Rome and have the protection of the Roman law that was coveted and was gradually extended until Caracalla in A.D. 215 for purposes of taxation granted it to all the world. Men only gradually came to realize that world rule by one municipality was a failure. The residents and senators at Rome had to do all the electing, as a representative government had not yet been devised, but with their local limitations they were incompetent to select rulers for the world. In this period the external policy of the state changed sooner than the internal polity. The defensive growth of the republic had, as we have seen, from the time of the popular leaders become war for conquest, and this lasted with intermissions even through Trajan's Parthian war. But the state had now reached its growth and the better emperors felt that organization and not extension was henceforth the true policy.

From Diocletian's accession, A.D. 284 the empire at large and not the city was the thought of the rulers, and our third historical period then began. The government was administered no longer under the popular and municipal forms, for its weight and the ambition of the emperors had broken down the rule by the city of Rome. All men had substantially equal rights, but they were now protected by prefects and other imperial officers, and the military, not the senate, were the advisers of the prince. The world henceforth was not ruled by Rome or from Rome. The capital was where the emperor was. Diocletian's headquarters were here at Milan, (Mediolanum,) and Constantine went even further and built a New Rome on the Bosporus, and it was called after him. The momentous division of the empire into East and West, tentative at first and then permanent A.D. 395 under the sons of Theodosius, was but a clearer recognition of the formal needs of administration. It was now a universal, not a municipal state. Under the eastern emperor Justinian about 533 were formulated the Institutes, Pandects and Novellæ that digested the whole body of law, Roman in origin and still Roman in name, but universal now in application. The external politics of the empire, particularly of the now effete western branch, had long been defensive against the new races of the north, themselves pushed southward by pressure of Huns from central Asia. The city of Rome itself fell before the Herulian Odoacer in A.D. 476, and, while the Eastern Empire lasted a thousand years longer, in the Hegira A.D. 622 and the growth thence on of Islamism we see its doom. First came the gradual amputation of its provinces, whether its princes were active or feeble, and then, after the new and selfish nationalities of Europe had failed in the Crusades, came the capture of Constantinople itself by the Turks in A.D. 1453.

But strange to say the Roman Empire survived the destruction of both its capitals and lived on through what is our fourth historical period. Christianity, founded under Tiberius, had grown at first unobserved, and then despite bitter persecutions. The evil emperors let it grow because they cared nothing for their old state religion, while the reforming good emperors tried to crush out the new and inconsistent faith, driving its living adherents to dwell with its dead underground in catacombs. Constantine recognized the inherent divine growth of Christianity and made it the Roman state religion, while the removal of the seat of government left the bishops of Rome without a superior in that city and the troublous times of invasion that followed caused these able pontiffs to assume rights and powers which successfully protected Romans against barbarians, but which unfortunately gradually led later to the temporal rule and spiritual supremacy of the popes. At the same time the name of the Empire, the many surviving facts of Roman civilization, the disorders of the time, and the distance and external impotence of the eastern emperors, who now claimed universal dominion, caused a demand for the restoration of the old empire in some energetic western ruler. Pope Leo III. rose to the occasion and assumed as God's representative to crown on Christmas A.D. 800 the Frankish chief whom we call Charlemagne as Roman Emperor instead of the woman usurper who ruled at Constantinople. The universal emperor was to be God's vice-gerent in temporal matters, and the universal pontiff was in this Holy Roman Empire to be God's vice-gerent in spiritual affairs. This dream was handed on by Charles to the German Othos, Henries and Fredericks who followed him, and by Leo to the Alexanders, Hildebrands and Innocents, and is the key to the middle ages. The theory was impossible of realization at any time, but doubly so when the temporal and spiritual co-vice-gerents were always quarrelling as to the limits of their jurisdictions, producing the strife of the Ghibelline and Guelf parties in Italy, if not in Germany, from the coronation of any emperor at Rome until his death. Oftentimes the emperor was at Rome only to be crowned, some were never there at all, and those were the best rulers indeed who had least to do with their nominal possessions south of the Alps.

The intestine strife in Italy was in the twelfth century varied by the struggle of the Lombard cities like Milan for autonomy, against both pope and emperor, and then by the numerous wars of the Italian cities against each other, but this activity yielded during the following centuries in almost all cases to subjection to petty local princes. The extinction of freedom was veiled by the splendor of the arts of the Renaissance, but it was after all stagnation of what is best in man and death of all in the social system that is worth living for. North of the Alps the dream of a universal empire, despite the impulse given it by the re-discovery and study in the twelfth century of the Roman civil law, was outgrown as the new infusion into the old stocks and in some places races altogether new gradually grew up into the several nations of modern Europe as we know them now, although the imperial title lasted until extinguished by Napoleon and the glamour of the old name carried away even that iconoclast. If in the north the inevitable growth of race nationalities was the knell of the Roman Emperor, the struggle with France which led in 1309 to the transfer of the seat of papal government to Avignon for seventy years, the existence sometimes of rival popes, the corruption of the clergy, and finally, growing out of these, the Reformation of the sixteenth century and its wars were the knell of the Holy Pontiff in those countries which since have been in the van of human progress.

Modern history so far has been the growth and unification of races and the mutual strife of nationalities. What it will be has not been revealed. But it will be, we may hope, the upbuilding of free and enlightened individual character within these nations. Nature unassisted seems to aim at preservation of the type and race without caring for the individual, but surely intellect will modify and direct that law, as it has so many others, and preserve the national type under such form as will secure the best development of the individual. The end of government is protection of persons and property and perfecting of safeguards which permit individual competition and growth, not the assumption by the state of social functions and the direction of all human activity. If Roman and Italian history teach anything, it is that if the state controls from above the individual life stagnates below. That government is best which governs least.

Milan, a flourishing place from the time of the defeat of the invading Cimbri and Teutons by Marius, situate in the country where the nobility of the early empire resorted, itself the seat of empire under Diocletian, has seen all these variations of history. It saw the Lombard conquest of North Italy. At its church of St. Ambrogio the Lombard kings assumed their iron crown, and in that church repose the remains of St. Ambrose, the fearless archbishop who shut the doors on the Emperor Theodosius after his cruel massacre at Thessalonica. In the war of the Lombard towns for independence the Holy Roman Emperor Frederick Barbarossa entirely destroyed the city except this revered church, and after the success of the league over the emperor they rebuilt Milan and the emperor dwelt there himself an honored guest. It flourished under its dukes of the Visconti and Sforza families when republican freedom was dead, and finally became the prize sought at once by France and Spain, but remained with the Empire until Napoleon reconstructed the map of Europe. Lombardy afterwards lapsed again to Austria until Napoleon III. freed it and it became a part of the present kingdom of Italy.

This Italian kingdom itself presents a curious story. A Burgundian family has gradually worked its way southward, voluntarily leaving its former possessions behind as it goes in exchange for others which it wins of more value, until it now rules all Italy from Rome, while its original Savoy and Nice are left as integral parts of France.

But Milan with all the reflections to which it thus gave rise did not detain us long, for we had to press on to other places. We left one day at noon and went by rail to Venice without stopping. The trip was pleasant but had no particular incidents. At one time the road skirted Lake Garda, where it gave us beautiful lake and mountain scenery, while to the right there was in full view the monument built by Napoleon III. to commemorate his victory of Solferino, which liberated Lombardy from

Austrian sway. We then passed Verona Vicenza, and Padua, all once Venetian and with interesting histories and associations, and the mountains finally drew off, the country gradually became low and we were in sight of the Venetian lagune.

THE ARSENAL AT VENICE.

CHAPTER XI.

VENICE.

VENICE is reached from the main land by a pier or embankment through the lagune, and over this run all trains into the city. As one avoids or follows the pertinacious porters and reaches the door of the station, a novel sight meets the eye. Beyond the quay is the lively Grand Canal, with noisy gondoliers pushing their picturesque black gondolas to the marble steps, some belonging to hotels, some open to bargains to go anywhere, and across the Canal rise residences and gardens, touched, as we arrived, by the light of the setting sun. In this medley of movements, tongues and costumes, it was evident that Lord Byron had not the railroad station to look from when he said that Venice was dying before his eyes.

The porter of the hotel which we had selected called his gondolier and we stepped into the comfortable craft, and in a moment more were out in the stream, gliding quickly down the Canal towards the heart of Venice, the Piazza of S. Marco. The Grand Canal is shaped like an inverted S, the station at one end and the Doge's palace at the other, with the beautiful marble arch of the Rialto about midway between, but our gondolier took a short cut through the narrow intersecting canals. He stood at the stern and pushed the single oar, which rests on a curved stick affixed to the side, but propelled the boat at a good speed, guiding it skilfully, and before turning corners uttering a warning cry. Gondolas, like other vehicles in Italy, pass each other to the left, and we noticed too that rowers of all boats in Switzerland and Italy generally stand looking to the bow and push on their oars. At the gondola prow projects an indented piece of metal that gauges the height of the bridges, and if that does not go under, the cabin will not. It is ornamental but thus has also a use. The buildings, mainly of stone or marble, rise sheer from the water, each generally with its steps and posts to facilitate landing, and as Rogers has it the salt sea-weed clings to the marble of the palaces. The buildings are continuous, the trees few. Venice has no speculators in vacant lots, but it has an active insurance company "Venezia," whose signs are all over Italy.

Our Pension Anglaise was on the St. Mark side of the Grand Canal, five minutes' walk from that church. We had a room on the first floor, a balcony over the water, and, with excellent meals included, paid about $1.85 per day apiece. Opposite in full view was the beautiful dome of Sta. Maria della Salute, and a little further down the low Egyptian-like custom-house. One of the narrow passage ways that serve as streets terminated beside our hotel at a ferry and gondola station. The picturesque gondoliers amused us but their incessant talk finally became something of a nuisance.

The evening of our arrival we hired a gondola for a franc and a half per hour and took a turn about the harbor. Two large Adriatic steamers lay at anchor off the

Dogana and we rowed around one, and then landed at the Piazzetta near the great square Ducal Palace. Men with poles made a great show of helping moor the boat, all in order to claim a copper. Rachel was thirsty and so we went up to what looked like a portable soda water stand. She took aqua pura, but I tried with the water something the man had in a bottle. He put a few drops in my glass, and it tasted remarkably like paregoric. He charged for the pure water as well as for that he doctored.

We then walked up to the adjacent square of St. Mark's, passing on the way between two red pillars. I did not know that this was considered unlucky because public executions were had there formerly. However, no harm befell us, and we reached in a moment the well lighted Piazza S. Marco, crowded with promenaders listening to a military band. Here daily at two o'clock the numerous tame pigeons flock down from the surrounding buildings to be fed. The state cared for them in its palmy days but now they are dependent on private charity. The square is surrounded by a handsome high colonnade on three sides, the Procuratie, in which attractive shops display everything that may tempt travellers, from glassware and gold lions to photographs and coffee. The first impression of St. Mark's is not favorable. It is not a high structure at best, and, as its floor and entrance are not raised above the level of the piazza, the church looks somewhat squatty. Moreover the high buildings surrounding are elevated by a step or two, and they and the majestic bell tower or Campanile in front tend even more to dwarf the church.

The moon rose late during our visit and was always at first obscured by clouds, so that we saw only the

Grand Canal by its beams from our hotel balcony, but a calmer or more beautiful scene than the marble Salute church, the adjacent Dogana, and the dancing water about them, all bathed in moonlight, cannot be imagined. A band played regularly in the royal gardens near us, and every night serenaders went up and down the canal in boats hung with Chinese lanterns. These Venetian days and nights are like a dream of delight.

Not that all Venice is beautiful. It is, rather, quaint and strange. It is built on one hundred and seventeen small islands separated by one hundred and fifty shallow canals hardly wider than the lanes passing over them on bridges. The many streets, or rather passages, are hardly more than six to ten feet wide, but one can even go all over the city without noticing the water. The bridges over the canals all arch to permit passage of gondolas and have side parapets. The Grand Canal, which is two miles long and one to two hundred feet wide, has two bridges for foot passengers besides the free Rialto, and there is, in addition to these, a railroad bridge over the west end to reach the large freight docks. The Rialto is by all odds the largest of the Venetian bridges. It has shops on each side, and the Merceria, coming from St. Mark's, the most important street in Venice, passes over it. We could not see the water for the stores and but for the ascent could easily imagine that we were still on land. Outside the green blinds of the shops there is on each side a gangway across, and from the dirty marble balustrade we had good views as far as the curves of the canal admit. This is a busy quarter. On each bank to the east of the Rialto for some distance are quays, rather unusual in Venice, while on one side to the west is a longer quay and also the open market sheds and buildings. Vegetables and fruits are brought in barge-like boats from the many islands of the lagune, and we found fruit good and cheap.

The history of Venice is probably less generally known to English readers than that of any other great state, for the reason that Venice for many centuries came little in contact with northern countries. It postdates ancient Rome and at its greatest power was a maritime trading community like Phœnicia of old, with possessions on the Italian main land and near it, it is true, but its principal strongholds in Dalmatia, in Constantinople, in Greece, Cyprus, and other parts of the Levant, acquired to promote commerce rather than to gratify military ambition. Padua and Aquileia had been flourishing cities in Venetia when that was a province of the Roman Empire, and, on their destruction by Attila and other invading barbarians, many of the residents took refuge on the islands near the coast. The cluster of Rivoalto was finally adopted as the capital, and there gradually was built the city of Venice. It was impregnable against attack from land, and, as even after passing the fortifications on the long sand islands (*lidi*) which separate the shallow lagune from the deep sea, the approach to the city was possible only through narrow channels which could be obstructed, from the sea too Venice was practically safe. Its first doge was chosen by the people A.D. 697 and given unlimited power, but this constitution was gradually modified until the Great Council, which soon indirectly elected him, became really the head of the state, while from 1310 dates the Council of Ten, originally a criminal court selected from the Great Council, and which heard and tried secret accusations of treason. In 829 the body of St. Mark was secretly purchased by some Venetian ships from the monks having it in custody at Alexandria, then under Moslem rule, and brought in great pomp to Venice, and the saint and his lion thenceforward became the tutelary guardians of the country. The basilica bearing his name was built over his remains, which are said to rest beneath the high altar. In 1177 Pope Alexander III. was driven from the continent by Frederick Barbarossa and was welcomed at Venice, which espoused his cause and conquered off the Istrian coast the great fleet which acknowledged the emperor. In reward for this the pope gave the Venetians a ring and with it dominion over the Adriatic, and yearly for centuries afterwards the ceremony was observed by the doges of publicly dropping a ring into the sea from the deck of the Bucentaur, their ship of state, in token of the wedding of Venice and the Adriatic. Barbarossa was also defeated in a battle on land and finally came to Venice to make his peace with the pope. In the portico of St. Mark's the emperor kneeled and the pope put his foot firmly on the prostrate neck. A stone even now marks the spot.

From the crusade of 1204 in which the aged and blind doge Enrico Dandalo conquered Constantinople, Venice was long the first maritime power of Europe. Her eastern commerce and possessions gave an oriental bent to all her art, easily recognized in the bright color and voluptuous figures of her paintings, and in the Saracenic arches and tracery of her architecture, so unlike the Romanesque and Renaissance styles of the main land of Italy. The Levantine trade was long divided between Venice and Genoa, and rivalry caused almost unremitting warfare between these two naval states. At one time the Genoese captured Chioggia, a gateway to the Venetian lagune, but the release of Pisani from prison, to which the council had sent him for losing a battle, and the return of Carlo Zeno in 1380 from an expedition to the east, enabled the Venetians in their turn to besiege the Genoese at Chioggia and cause them to capitulate. This terminated the more active hostilities between the two powers. The gradual acquisition of continental dominion by Venice, due in part to the supposed necessity of having a "scientific frontier" to protect the capital from attack by the growing Italian principalities, and culminating in the first part of the fifteenth century in the forced annexation of the country from Padua to Verona and Vicenza, involved Venice in Italian wars, particularly with the Milanese dukes. In the period from the thirteenth to fifteenth centuries the ancient free cities of North Italy had gradually found refuge from factional outbreaks and rivalries in the rule of energetic families, such as the Visconti and afterwards the Sforza at Milan, Carrara at Padua, Medici at Florence, Bentivogli at Bologna, Gonzaga at Mantua, and Scala at Verona, while in Venice politics had taken a different turn, leading to the dominion of the Great Council, originally open to any citizen but gradually closed to all but certain aristocratic families. The height of Venetian power was from the time of the Crusades until the discovery and use of the passage of the east round the Cape of Good Hope gradually provided an easier route for trade and also developed the great marines of Spain, Portugal, Holland and England. At the same time the capture of Constantinople by the hostile Turks and the consequent gradual loss of the eastern markets and possessions co-operated to reduce the commercial importance of Venice. From the beginning of the sixteenth century Venice politically and commercially stood still, but her art attained in that century its greatest splendor under Palma Vecchio, Titian, Paolo Veronese and others. The league of Cambray of 1508 against her, the gradual losses to the Turks in the east, despite her great naval victory of Lepanto in 1572, and the struggles of France, Spain and Austria for the conquest of North Italy impaired the continental power of Venice. She gradually went into a decline, ending finally in her capture in 1797 by the French, when Napoleon thoroughly reformed and republicanized her government, but this was the first time that an invader's foot had trod her streets. Since Napoleon's fall Venice has been a part of the Austrian Empire, until incorporated with the present Italian Kingdom.

Such architecture as the times produced from the fall of Rome to the eleventh century was rude but substantial. St. Mark's, built of brick faced with marble, is an example of this Romanesque style, but the subsequent ornamentation is Oriental. It is in the form of an equilateral or Greek cross, with dome over the intersection of the nave and transept and others at the extremities of the arms. The façade is made up of a number of arches, and over the central one is the ancient bronze group of four horses. They are much travelled. Made in Rome under the empire to adorn some triumphal arch, they were taken to Constantinople by Constantine, brought by Dandalo to Venice, removed by Napoleon to Paris, and restored to Venice in 1815. Within the church is the entrance hall, infested by would-be guides and impertinent picture sellers, whom we had now learned to snub, and passing then behind a curtain we were in the dim interior. Around are hundreds of foreign marble columns of all colors, many archaic and sacred mosaics above, and a most uneven and rolling mosaic pavement beneath our feet. The high altar is at the back under a canopy. The church is not bright or beautiful, but an atmosphere of quaintness fills all the place.

Going next to the Campanile in front, we passed the porphyry block at the church corner from which the decrees of state were once proclaimed. The old square bell tower, standing entirely isolated, is of brick and rises three hundred and twenty-two feet high. The easy ascent within is by inclined planes, one on a side, four of them marking a story, and just below the top a few dark steps complete the ascent. From the top Galileo made his observations, and the general view, especially at sunset, is superb. We could trace the Grand Canal by the Casa Grande and other of its palaces, but the water is hid by the buildings. Venice is a long triangle, the shorter side and greater thickness to the west, tapering to the Arsenal at the east. The serpentine Grand Canal divides it into two irregular halves, the principal buildings being in the eastern or St. Mark division. South of the main city and separated from it by a canal, or rather an arm of the sea, is the narrow Giudecca, also an important if isolated part of Venice. All around the city is the lagune with the Venetian islands, among which are the cemetery and further off to the north Murano, famous for its glass. Far to the east is the sea, to the west the main land with its hills, and over all the rich Italian haze and color.

Adjoining St. Mark's is the open piazzetta, on which faces that singular pile, the Doge's Palace, built around a court. The exterior from the front or from the water makes an uneffaceable impression. On the ground floor it has a pointed arcade of heavy pillars without bases, above that a second yet handsomer gallery, and the high reddish façade above all, broken by a balcony and windows on each side, terminates in battlements. From between two red pillars in the upper gallery were read sentences of death, carried out between the two Oriental columns of the landing. One of these is crowned with the winged lion of St. Mark and the other by St. Theodore on a crocodile.

Entering by an archway near the church, we found two cisterns and around the palace court arcades. Opposite the entrance is the commanding Giant's Stairway, so named from Mars and Neptune at the top. The arrangement of the interior of the Doge's Palace is bewildering. As I understood it, on the first floor shown is the hall of the Great Council, the hall for the election of the doge by the forty chosen from that council, and the residence apartments of the doge himself,—the last now a museum. The whole of one end of the Great Council hall is taken up by Tintoretto's Paradise, an enormous oil painting, the largest in the world, and on the other walls are exploits of Doge Ziani against Barbarossa, and of Dandalo at Constantinople. For a frieze in this and the voting room are the portraits of one hundred and fifteen doges, but the place for Marino Faliero is painted out by a black curtain on which is recorded that he was decapitated for his crimes. This happened in 1355 when the conspiracy of this doge to overthrow the oligarchy and establish himself as an unfettered prince was discovered and punished by hanging the inferior plotters between the two columns and by beheading the doge on the Giant's Stairway, where he had taken the oath of office, and his head was then publicly exhibited from the gallery of the ducal palace.

On the floor above were the official apartments. By the stairway is the hole, formerly ornamented by a lion's mouth, into which secret accusations were cast for consideration of the Three Inquisitors, the executive committee of the black Council of Ten, instituted in the fifteenth century. The Three, the Ten and other officials had offices on this floor, and the rooms are very handsome. As in the apartments below, while most of the historical pictures are on the walls, many beautiful allegorical paintings are framed to the ceiling, and we had to strain our necks to see them. Plans are furnished, in the shape sometimes of paper fans, for the better study of the collections and are absolutely essential.

With a very practical view of matters of state, they had on the ground floor, beneath all these apartments of beauty, the Pozzi, the unlighted stone prison cells. We were shown by candle light where Marino Faliero was imprisoned, a bare cell with an opening in the wall for receiving food. In the passage way are three holes in the stone floor for the blood of beheaded victims to flow into a canal, and the bodies were thrown out into the water. The Piombi, or cells under the leads of the palace, were destroyed by Napoleon, who also walled up one of the two passages of the Bridge of Sighs leading across this canal from the prisons on the other side to the judgment halls in the Doge's Palace. We were told that few prisoners had ever passed through the present bridge, "a palace and a prison on each hand," but in this palace and in these prisons was the centre of Venetian secrecy, craft and cruelty, and the ghosts of the murdered dead will down at no man's bidding. Here in the Pozzi was confined the great general Carmagnuola in 1432, enticed home by fraud. He expiated his alleged treason at Cremona by decapitation between the Two Columns and was buried in the Frari church. In these cells, too, in 1406 perished by the bowstring Carrara, prince of Padua, and his two sons. Carrara had come to Venice under a safe conduct to treat for peace after the conquest of his country by the Venetians, and when treacherously thrown into prison with one son found another there, and together they fought the executioners in their cell until overpowered by numbers. If these prisons could tell the horrors of the secret rule of The Ten it would hardly be equalled in the world's history for perfidy and cruelty. Treachery was its vital breath and assassination its right hand.

At the eastern extremity of Venice is the Arsenal which built the fleets that conquered the Mediterranean from Genoa to Constantinople, and at which, as in Athens, in disastrous days when the state treasury was bankrupt, the liberality and patriotism of private citizens equipped ships for the public use. The spacious docks although quiet are not even now deserted. In front of the square red entrance towers of the Arsenal sit four stiff marble lions brought from Attica, and in the museum are many models of ships, from the high, gilded Bucentaur, burned by the French, down to modern screw propellers. I saw the huge triangular flag captured from the Turks at the battle of Lepanto, lifted the heavy visored helmet of Attila, and saw the iron one worn by his horse.

Of the many churches the most interesting are those of Giovanni and Paolo, near the north edge of the city, and the Frari, in the great bend south of the Grand

Canal. The former is spacious and lofty, containing the handsome tombs of doges and also monuments to other famous men, and in a fire here was destroyed Titian's celebrated painting of the Martyrdom of Peter. Across the Grand Canal and adjoining the great collection of Venetian archives is the large Frari church, much more attractive within than without. It, too, is the burial place of doges and eminent men. It is particularly famous for Titian's painting known as the Pesaro Madonna, representing a vision of the Mother and Child by the Pesaro family, for the large monument over the grave of Titian, erected by the Emperor Ferdinand I. in this century, which represents a triumphal arch decorated by reliefs of his more celebrated paintings; and there, too, is the incomparable mausoleum of Canova, erected after the great sculptor's death in 1822 from the design which he had made for Titian's monument. It represents a marble sepulchral pyramid, into the open door of which a veiled woman, bearing the cinerary urn, is about to enter. Behind her are several weeping figures, of exceeding grace, and on the other side of the door crouches St. Mark's winged lion. Beside the lion is seated a mourning genius, his extinguished torch inverted. Canova is buried, however, on the Venetian main land at Passagno, his native place, but his right hand is in a porphyry urn at the Academy, and beneath it is his chisel.

At the next steamboat landing below the Frari and on the same side is the Academy, where the prevailing characteristics are good drawing and bright colors. Among the most famous pictures are Titian's beautiful Assumption (Ascension) of the Virgin, and the Pieta or Entombment which he left unfinished at his death

1576, in his ninety-ninth year. The striking Entombment is in rude, bold and almost colorless strokes.

I returned from here in one of the swift little steamers which regularly ply the length of the Grand Canal at ten centessimi the trip. They go too fast for one to appreciate the palaces, and we therefore made the slower voyage by gondola several times.

One morning we regretfully loaded up one of these vehicles with satchels, bundles and ourselves in travelling costume, and directed our course to the station, making a farewell study of the Grand Canal as we went along. The buildings are generally in the Renaissance style, many with oriental arches or ornamentation, and some with gilt or paintings on the façades. In these lived the Foscari, Contarini, Pisani, Dandoli, Bembi, Manin and other noble families of Venice, and there staid also at times such noted foreigners as Lucretia Borgia, Byron, Wagner and Browning, and among them too are the mediæval warehouse buildings of the Germans and Turks, but many of them are now used for hotels or public purposes. Anxious to see Shylock at home, we went to the Ghetto or Jewish quarter, reached from the Grand Canal by a large cross artery near the station. We entered under an arched gateway and walked through. It looked like the rest of Venice. All about were dirty children, working women, and officious men who wanted to help land the gondola or act as guides,—for a consideration,—watching us with as much curiosity as we did them. One old woman carrying a bucket of water amused us by exclaiming "Bella, bella!" as she saw Rachel. Such is the avidity for small coin among the lower classes, however, that we were not certain but that pay was expected for even this deserved compliment. But we did not find a satisfactory Shylock.

Then came the bustle of the railroad and the fading away of the city as we crossed through the lagune to the main land. With a sigh as the straining eyes lost sight of Venice, we put our satchels in the large racks above our heads, settled back in the comfortable second class compartment to talk over our visit, and to study up for Florence.

On the way near Ferrara we went over the Po where it flows between embankments high above the adjacent country, and after passing Bologna were among the Apennines. There we had a most deafening and choking series of long tunnels, forty in three hours, I think, although the views which we did get between, especially from Pistoia on, were of pleasing valley scenery, almost as grateful to the bewildered eye as the Venetian waters.

CHAPTER XII.

FLORENCE AND ART.

WE arrived in Florence late on Saturday afternoon August 29th with only seven lire in pocket to last two people until banks opened on Monday. We had selected as our stopping place the small Hotel de Londres opposite the imposing but prison-like Palazzo Strozzi, and were chagrined to find, that, while we could get a comfortable room and morning coffee at four lire a day for each, our hotel did not open its regular restaurant until September 1st. The *portier*,—that important official who everywhere speaks all languages, knows everything, and is general outside manager of hotel business,—recommended a restaurant underneath, but we discovered that the prices there were so large as to admit of division between its proprietor and our *portier*, with fair profit to each. We therefore started out on Sunday to find a restaurant. After eying several we came across the best one of our travels. It was in a back street behind S. Maria Maggiore, and I think was named Restaurant National. There for two and a quarter lire we had a first-rate supper in a garden under electric light, with statues and inquisitive people about us, and a band in a gallery above affording delightful music. For breakfast the next day we took eggs, bread and butter at the hotel. After a luxurious dinner at our restaurant of soup, steak and potatoes, fruits and wine for three and a half lire, we had but one lira left, and so as a matter of necessity that night we made a supper of eggs, bread and butter again on our hotel credit. We were much relieved when I drew next day at Cook's Tourist Office near by my usual weekly six pounds in the shape of one hundred and fifty-two lire. After this Sunday of pecuniary anxiety and physical rest we could now begin sight-seeing again.

The Arno runs through Florence from south-east to north-west, dividing it into two unequal parts. The long Pitti Palace in *rustica* or undressed stone and the high Piazza Michael Angelo with its beautiful view are on the south side of the river, but all other principal objects of interest are in the older part to the north. There are a number of bridges across the deceptive Arno, of which the oldest is the Ponte Vecchio, the handsomest the San Spirito. The streets of the old quarter run perpendicularly to the Lungarno, a highway along the river bank, or as cross streets are roughly parallel with it. In every mediæval town the cathedral was the most important of all buildings, and as the chief place of interest and resort was near the centre. Here, too, the Duomo is near the heart of the city and the other attractions seem to radiate from it. North of it is S. Lorenzo and its chapels, off to the north-west near the station is Sta. Maria Novella, west in the suburbs is the pleasant Cascine, a park on the river, south-east is Sta. Croce with its famous tombs, and south near the river is the Piazza Signoria, on which face the castellated

Palazzo Vecchio, the Uffizi with its picture galleries, and the open Loggia dei Lanzi full of sculptures.

Florence dates back to a Roman settlement made by Sulla's soldiers. Rebuilt by Charlemagne, early in the middle ages its enterprise and commerce soon made it a place of note. The strife of papist Guelf and imperialist Ghibelline, who became feudal Neri and popular Bianchi after the old contest of pope and emperor died away, long divided the citizens, but Florence was essentially Guelf while that name meant anything. The civil dissension resulted for one thing in the perpetual banishment of her great citizen Dante, one of the Bianchi. The commercial standing of Florence is shown by the fact that her florin, first coined in 1252, became the standard for Europe and even now gives the name to coins in England and Austria. The guilds of tradesmen came in 1282 to rule the state through their respective priori or presidents, and soon established the executive office of *gonfaloniere di giustizia*, who became president of the priori, collectively known as the Signoria. Later came the rivalry of the middle class families who had become wealthy through trade and succeeded to the influence of the old nobility, which had died out in the mediæval wars. The Albizzi, the stern Capponi and the rich bankers Medici were now prominent. The Medici, coming in 1426 to the head of affairs, ruled off and on for three centuries, first as popular leaders and later as dukes, but with intervals of banishment. At first, however, they did not disturb the republican forms. Lorenzo the Magnificent died 1492, some months before Columbus started on his adventurous voyage, as Florence was enjoying a splendid age of art, which boasted of Leonardo, Michael Angelo, Raphael and others. Lorenzo in his lifetime surrounded himself by a circle of literary men and classical students, comprising Polizian, Ficino, Mirandola and the like, the pride of their age, while not long after him flourished the statesman Macchiavelli and the historian Guicciardini. Politically little power was left to the people, but the old spirit was only slumbering, and they revolted from Medicean timidity at the time of Charles VIII's invasion from France, and for a while enjoyed a republic again under their Gonfaloniere Soderini, and followed and then burned their prophet Savonarola, prior of S. Marco. This tragedy occurred before the Palazzo Vecchio, built 1298 by Arnolfo, enlarged by Savonarola himself, and always the seat of government In the time of the Medici popes Leo X. and Clement VII. Florence came more and more subject to that family, and as grand dukes of Tuscany from 1530 its members ruled until the line ran out two centuries later and Francis of Lorraine, husband of Maria Theresa, was by the Pragmatic Sanction awarded the crown. With some intermissions it remained with the Austrians until the struggle for Italian independence in this century. Lately Florence was temporarily the capital of Italy, for the Italian Parliament sat in the Palazzo Vecchio from 1865 to 1870, and during that time the city bankrupted itself in public works. Florence is still an important city and pleasant resort, but its energy has flagged and its grandeur is principally to be found in the remains of the past.

The narrow winding streets present interesting sights. There are many handsome buildings, mainly churches, but the most original works of Florentine architects are the fortress-like castles in rough stone. The tall square municipal building — Palazzo Vecchio in the

Piazza Signoria—has a tower three hundred and eight feet high, and the vast Pitti Palace, built by Brunelleschi for Pitti, who wished to outdo the splendor of the Medici, fell at last into possession of the Medici themselves and is now a royal residence. The palaces show how turbulent the times were to require such strongholds.

The cathedral square contains the Duomo, Campanile and Baptistery, and with these we reach specimens of Gothic architecture hardly equalled elsewhere in Italy. The Gothic is a style of large, high windows as well as arches, for the northern skies are not clear and all the light available is essential. In Italy the Gothic influences details, but the ground work of churches is still the old Roman basilica, with small windows and large blank wall spaces, because the bright Italian sun needed rather to be excluded than invited, and the Florence cathedral follows this obvious and proper departure from the northern style. Again, in the north the belfry steeples are at the front and with the portals make up one grand façade, while in Italy the separate bell tower (campanile) of Romanesque times is preserved, and the dome over the intersection of nave and transepts instead of the spire absorbs the attention of the architect. Greek styles laid stress on columns and horizontal lines, and so too the Roman except so far as the round arch came also into play, while the Romanesque emphasized the round arch, and the Byzantine the dome. All of these tendencies, domesticated in Italy, modified there the nature of the Gothic style, which in its purity soars heavenward with arch, buttress and spire.

The Florentine cathedral was almost two centuries in building, being designed and begun by Arnolfo in 1294 on the site of a church of Sta. Raparata, an old patron saint of the city, who once appeared with a lily and aided the Florentines in battle. Thence they derived the lily for their coat of arms. Giotto carried on the cathedral work after Arnolfo, building the graceful square campanile also. For a long time it was supposed the space was too great to vault, as up to that time only the ancient Pantheon excelled this diameter of one hundred and thirty-eight feet, but in the year 1418 Brunelleschi's competitive design was accepted and he began the construction of the great cupola, and it required fourteen years to complete the work. The handsome façade has been finished only in our own day.

Externally the panelled green, white and red marble of the cathedral and light four-story belfry produces a beautiful effect, but it must be confessed that the interior of the church is bare and disappointing. The Milan cathedral within looks far more imposing, while even the lower Dom at Cologne seems higher.

The adjacent campanile is two hundred and ninety-two feet, and Giotto, who built it in the fourteenth century, designed surmounting it with a spire one hundred feet higher. The windows, tracery and statues make up an artistic whole, contributed to by Giotto, Pisano, Donatello, Robbia and others. Charles V. said that the campanile was so beautiful that it ought to be kept in a glass case, and in our own day Ruskin pronounces it the only perfect combination of power and beauty.

The Baptistery opposite it dates from 1100 A.D., and is built possibly on the foundation of a temple of Mars and copied from the Pantheon. A beautiful, domed building itself, it is yet more famous in the history of sculpture for its three bronze doors covered with figures. That on the south by Andrea Pisano goes back to 1330 and the reliefs represent among other things scenes from the life of John the Baptist. Niccola Pisano at Pisa had before anyone else caught the inspiration of ancient statuary and by his pulpits and sculpture burst mediæval trammels, begun the Renaissance of art, and indeed fixed its course. Of his school was this Andrea, who had come to Florence to work with Giotto on the campanile. The other doors date from the first half of the fifteenth century and were the forty-nine years' work of Ghiberti. The one facing the cathedral is considered the finest of all, and pictures scenes from the Old Testament in varying relief, with the perfect perspective of painting itself. Michael Angelo considered this exquisite portal worthy of forming the entrance to Paradise.

Two unsuccessful competitors of Ghiberti for the completion of these gates became famous,—Brunelleschi as an architect, and Donatello, the sculptor. Contemporary with them was Lucca della Robbia, whose sculptures ornament parts of the cathedral and who has given his name to relief scenes in glazed earthenware and friezes in houses, churches and palaces throughout Italy. Sansovino sculptured the group of John baptizing Christ now above one of the Baptistery doors, and somewhat younger was Verrocchio, whose greatest title to fame was that he was the teacher of Leonardo and Michael Angelo, both of whom were great painters as well as great sculptors.

Ancient paintings may or may not have been in oils, a point upon which critics are divided, but except a few on the walls of provincial Pompeii none of any kind have survived. In the Eastern Empire despite iconoclasm sacred subjects continued to be painted, but it sank to be as lifeless an art as in Egypt under the rule of the old priests. Possibly through the Crusades, these eastern pictures may have contributed to the revival of art in Italy, but Cimabue just before the fourteenth century all but re-discovered painting at Assisi and Florence, and his Madonna, followed in a procession by acclaiming thousands, is still preserved in the interesting old Florentine church of Sta. Maria Novella, and, stiff as it seems to us, it marked a new era. At first art was but the handmaid of devotion, and church decoration was long the peculiar domain of painting. The Crucifixion, the Madonna and local saints painted on the walls or on wood or canvas to place above altars were its earliest subjects. Giotto, sculptor and painter, followed Cimabue, and then early in the fifteenth century Masolino and Masaccio worked with a greater freedom of design and touch on the frescoes of the Brancacci chapel, illustrating the legends of the Apostles in a way that marked a transition to an age which should treat art as a thing apart from religion, her sister, but honored for her own sake.

Gentle Fra Angelico (1387–1455) in his monastery of San Marco painted famous frescoes and Ghirlandajo was also well known at Florence in the fifteenth century, while art had become so diffused that at the same time Mantegna (1431–1506) flourished at Mantua, Bellini (1426–1516) at Venice, and Perugino, the master of the more famous Raphael, worked on pious themes at Perugia. Leonardo (1452–1519) was Tuscan and resided longer in Florence than at either Milan or Rome. He painted his cavalry battle for the Palazzo Vecchio at the same time that the younger Michael Angelo made for the same hall the picture of bathing Florentine soldiers surprised by Pisans. Both of these masterpieces have perished, but they drew many artists to Florence, Raphael, (1483–1520,) for one, and here he gradually changed his religious Umbrian style to one more human and modern. He was afterwards at Rome under the patronage of Leo X. and his wall paintings and some of his best easel pictures were painted there. He left scholars, among whom were Giulio Romano and Caravaggio. Contemporary at Florence were Bartolommeo and Andrea del Sarto and at Siena Sodoma.

The sack of Rome in 1527 by Charles V. dispersed its artists, while in north Italy art lasted longer. At Bologna was Bagnacavallo, at Parma Correggio, and at Venice, the home of color, after Bellini and Giorgione came the long-lived Titian, (1477–1576,) the greatest of her school, who painted serene madonnas and seductive Venuses with equal relish and facility. After Titian Venice produced only Tintoretto and Paul Veronese, and indeed art in all Italy retrograded. Yet on the main land it lived long, and even in the seventeenth century we find at Bologna the Caracci, Domenichino and Guido Reni, and at Florence that painter of lilies and sweet faces, Carlo Dolce, and at Naples the master of landscape, Salvator Rosa.

The fame and students of the works of the greater Italians soon naturalized art all over Europe, and each country now developed in turn some peculiarities of style. Transalpine art woke first in the Netherlands. In Flanders the brothers Van Eyck had indeed early invented oil painting, but the country found its most famous master centuries later in Rubens, (1577–1640,) the prolific painter of women as well as of famous altar pieces. Of his school were Jordaens and Teniers, who struck out further in the path of representing secular affairs and excelled in pictures of every-day life, called *genre*. Holland had been more successful than Flanders in revolt against bigoted Spain and her painting departed even further from the old ecclesiastical models in the direction of portraying common life. Rembrandt (1607–1669) was its greatest painter and contrasts superbly his principal figures with surrounding shade. Gerard Dow was his pupil and Ruysdael paints landscapes that seem almost unlike Holland, but later artists waste the same ingenuity and finish on still life and common objects worthy only of the walls of a restaurant.

In Germany Hans Holbein (1498–1554) at Augsburg was influenced from Italy and painted equally well madonnas and portraits, while earlier Albrecht Dürer (1471–1528) near by at busy Nuremberg represented religious subjects both before and after his life in Venice under Bellini. The Cranachs were friends of Luther, but from then until lately painting did not flourish in that war-distracted country. In Cornelius and Kaulbach of this century we must recognize fine academic artists, although they aspire to greater things than they can accomplish.

In France Poussin (1594–1665) was famous for landscapes, but he was surpassed by Claude Lorraine, (1600–1682,) who, however, lived mainly at Rome. After him graceful Watteau painted the *fêtes champêtres* of the Regency, and art died in rococo styles. A revival of classic painting in France dates from David at the beginning of this century. Present French art is occupied too much with sensuous female figures, but Millet's Angelus and the Vernets, Delaroche, Bonheur and yet others with good aims are not far in the past. Spain's brief artistic life produced Ribera, in the seventeenth century Velasquez, famous for his portraits, and Murillo, the painter of street sights.

Although the portraits by Kneller and Reynolds, Hogarth's cartoons, Landseer's animals, and later Turner's magnificent landscape coloring are familiar to us, English artists are not well represented in continental galleries, while American art is so far almost conspicuous by its absence.

At Florence one finds almost all schools, but principally, of course, those of Italy. We went first to the Uffizi gallery near the Piazza Signoria, on the top floor of the *offices* of the municipality,—whence the name. A long covered way across the Arno connects it with the famous collection on the top floor of the Pitti palace, and at both places we regretted that elevators had not come into more general use. The Uffizi building has little pretension to beauty. The collections are on two sides of a court or short street, the parts connected at the river end by a corridor of ancient sculpture. The east arm contains the main collection. The pictures are classified according to countries, except that a small octagonal room in the centre, the Tribune, has some of the principal treasures all together.

In the Tribune are fine pieces of ancient statuary,—a Satyr playing on cymbals, the Wrestlers, a Scythian grinding his knife to flay Marsyas, a young Apollo, and the Venus de Medici, found at Rome in the sixteenth century and brought to Florence in 1680, the most famous of all. She stands within a shield-shaped railing, the model figure and yet under the usual female size. Her attitude is as if frightened while bathing and she conceals herself with her hands as best she can, although very inadequately from the point towards which she looks, her wrists gracefully bent and her fingers daintily separated. Around the head is a fillet, her hair in a Grecian knot, but the hair and eyes are not now clean cut, probably from earth corrosion, and this gives her perhaps a somewhat sleepy look, redeemed partly by a pretty dimple in her chin. The marble is no longer white and the statue, broken in several places, has been patched, but so skilfully as to be hardly noticeable. The goddess breathes in stone and is so fascinating that one can hardly blame the poet Rogers for sitting day after day admiring the figure. One time they say a note was found in her hand addressed to him, requesting him to quit ogling her.

Raphael's Fornarina in the Tribune (his Roman mistress) is a sensuous but imposing Italian woman, and his St. John is a very youthful though handsome preacher, pointing to a cross. His Madonna Cardinellino looks with a dreamy smile down at little John girt in a skin, as he holds out to the infant Jesus on the other side of Mary's knee a goldfinch, which that solemn child strokes. Dürer's Adoration of the Magi is an early work, and the positions of some of his wise men were ridiculous; one was a carpet bagger. In a room left from the Tribune Sodoma has a fine St. Sebastian shot through by arrows and about receiving on his beautiful head the crown of martyrdom, and Caravaggio and Leonardo have each a horrible, snaky head of Medusa spouting blood.

In the western branch of the palace is a bust of Dante taken from his death mask of 1321, giving him, as might be expected, a very hooked nose and thin face. The Niobe group there is much more extensive than we had thought. Niobe herself and some of the other figures are over life size, and the noble and appealing look on her face and her attempt to shield her kneeling daughter from the arrows is very touching. The statues were found outside a gate at Rome and probably constituted the pediment of a temple of Apollo, but the actual arrangement of the group is entirely conjectural. It is said to be a copy of the original work by Praxiteles. On the Niobe side of the Uffizi was Titian's mild looking Flora, and in the famous gallery of self portraits near by was jaunty Rubens in his big hat, long bearded Da Vinci, and many others. Van Dyck in this collection was a dashing bright young fellow with moustache and goatee. Dolce was somewhat old and meek, with black moustache, and held a comic picture of a man with eyeglasses. Salvator Rosa was a clean-shaved, wild haired but good-natured man, and sickly Guido Reni had on a broad-brimmed hat. Del Sarto was fat and stern, his face clean shaved, while Titian was a kind, healthy gentleman with full beard. This collection upset many of our mental portraits of what the painters ought to resemble.

The Pitti gallery across the river contains some statuary and only about three hundred paintings, but many of these are "gems of purest ray" and the beautifully decorated rooms are a worthy setting. There are also in the saloons many fine mosaic tables, representing sometimes Roman ruins. The government has a mosaic manufactory in Florence, whose beautiful products are more fully exhibited near the Academy. Church decoration and sacred paintings were the great field of the old masters, and Raphael painted so many Madonnas that they have to be distinguished by some little peculiarity. The one in the Tribune is called "Cardinellino" from the goldfinch in it, one in the Pitti "Seggiola" from the chair, and so on. His Madonna del Granduca in the Pitti is the blonde he generally makes his Virgins and has the same softness and gentleness, but in some way all are sad and thoughtful. His Madonna della Seggiola, seated with Jesus in her arms and John at her knee, has a more oriental look than the others, and to my mind it ranks next to the Sistine Madonna. It is said to have been engraved more than any other picture whatever. His fat Leo X., and bearded, thoughtful Julius II. were excellently done, and not at all what we had expected these men would look like. Murillo's famed Madonna disappointed us in several respects; for one thing the chin is disproportionately small. Titian's Bella had a Jewish cast, an imposing bearing, and appeared well in her rich purple dress, but in herself did not strike me as beautiful at all,—she was "stylish" rather,—and he had a voluptuous looking Magdalene that did not appear very repentant. Guido's Cleopatra was not unlike Titian's Uffizi Flora. Both were well conditioned, but there was a lurking expression at least to Flora's face that reminded me of the mumps. We tried to find the secret of Salvator Rosa's landscapes. He almost always brings in rocks, sometimes shipping, and gives every play of light and shade in rocky crevice and on mossy surface. His background is a hazy, greenish blue in which things gradually become indistinct. Poussin is far inferior. His background does not haze off so nicely and his houses and castles are conventional. Rubens loved to draw the female form, but the women are generally somewhat too stout,—so of his Train of War, of his Venus and Mars in the Tribune, and so throughout all these collections. That came, I suppose, from his Flemish models. We were much struck by seeing good landscapes by such humanity painters as Rubens and Domenichino, excellent pictures, too. This is said, indeed, to have been Rubens' favorite branch of art. There are several beautiful pieces of modern statuary also in the Pitti of which the most famous is Canova's marble Venus, pressing a garment against her bosom, seeming to anticipate intrusion. It is a thing of grace, about life size, but the garment conceals too much of the form. Almost as fine is Consani's seated marble Fame, writing on a shield which she holds with her right hand.

These galleries have not many of Michael Angelo's paintings. I recall principally his three hag-like Fates, more famous than pleasing. But Florence contains some of the finest sculptures of this great genius. Michael Angelo was born at Arezzo 1475 and died 1563, the greatest architect, sculptor, and perhaps painter of his age. His house in Florence is still shown. With him the art of sculpture reaches its summit. In Florence at the Academy is his spirited and gigantic David, made of one block which had been partly used years before by another and abandoned as inadequate, and which even Leonardo da Vinci had refused to go on with. The youth stands erect in the rotunda, holding the long sling over his shoulder, an end in each hand. His head however, seemed, perhaps too large.

Even more famous are the unfinished figures on the tombs of two younger Medici in the New Sacristy of S. Lorenzo, carved in the fulness of Michael Angelo's fame and after his period of artistic activity at Rome. The interior of the Sacristy is of black and white marble in Corinthian style. To the right is the tomb of Julian, his alert figure above in a niche and under him lying on marble pallets on the sarcophagus are Night, personified by a middle-aged woman with crescent on her brow, Day, a man, like the woman in a very uncomfortable position and both surely meant only to prove Michael Angelo's knowledge of human muscles. Day is still in the rough, Night in general finished except a foot. Opposite is young Lorenzo sitting in thought, Il pensiero. Below him to the left is Dawn, a man half recumbent, and Twilight, a younger woman,—the woman as before more nearly completed. The allegory is hard to understand but the figures are magnificent. Near is the later Medicean Chapel for the ducal family, with make-believe sarcophagi on its four sides and corners, the tombs and walls being of richly colored marble. In the vault below by which one enters are the actual graves of these later Medici. In handsomely restored S. Lorenzo near by at the foot of the altar is the grave of Cosmo, who died 1464 " Pater Patriæ," as the inscription says.

In the Loggia dei Lanzi we saw among other works some later Florentine sculptures. This open Gothic colonnade, once a guard room, is itself a thing of beauty, and the statuary is a public school of art to all who pass on pleasure or business through the busy Piazza Signoria. There we saw an ancient Ajax supporting dying Achilles, and Donatello's bronze Judith slaying Holofernes, vigorous indeed if stiff. This was originally erected as a public warning in front of the Palazzo Vecchio on the expulsion of the Medici. There are also a number of other celebrated pieces of statuary, and amongst them a bronze Perseus holding up the dripping Medusa head, while the body is in a most remarkably and impossibly twisted state, the work 1553 of Benvenuto Cellini. Behind is Fedi's recent and beautiful group, the Rape of Polyxena,—in which with his left arm the warrior holds the maiden, with the sword strikes at the mother grasping for the girl, while at his foot lies a dead man cut on the head.

In the niches of the Uffizi portico are also recent statues, inside Cosmo and thoughtful Lorenzo, shaved clean but with long hair, while outside are Giotto in a monk's cowl, snub-nosed Michael Angelo, Petrarch in a mumps bandage, Boccaccio not dissimilar, Macchiavelli thin and meek, Leonardo with beard and long locks, our own Amerigo Vespucci, a fine looking, slim old gentleman with side whiskers. On the other side of the street stands bearded Benvenuto Cellini, besides many others.

We walked one day towards the end of our stay at Florence down past the Palazzo Vecchio eastwardly to the church of Santa Croce. In front of it is a favorite piazza with benches, and in the midst of this stands Dante's white marble monument by the sculptor Pazzi, placed here in 1865 on the six hundredth anniversary of the poet's birth. The sad faced Dante is drawing his robe around him very much as if like ourselves he was about to depart from Florence. He guards the approach to Santa Croce, which has an imposing Gothic façade of black and white marble, but the remainder of this modern Pantheon is of rough brick as yet unencrusted. Arnolfo designed the church for the Franciscans and Michael Angelo worked on its front. Within, its high nave is separated by columns from the aisles, and the whole interior has a rich effect. Along the side walls, which are also of black and white marble, are placed handsome monuments of celebrated men, the peculiar glory of the church, but after all they are much alike, being generally a marble sarcophagus, with bust on top and allegorical figures near. First on the right is Michael Angelo's tomb, of reddish marble on a white pedestal. By it sits on one side a woman personifying architecture, in the middle another with a chisel, to the left a third with an unfinished statue,—in that not unlike the great artist himself, who began so much that he never completed. Next is an empty white marble sarcophagus of Dante, to the left of which stands proudly a female with mural crown and star, and opposite her weeps another with wreath in hand—probably because Dante never was buried there and "sleeps afar" in Ancona. By Alfieri's, which has tragic masks at the corners, stands a similar woman with a crown, and on Macchiavelli's, elevated like all the others on a white marble base, sits a figure holding his medallion. Facing Michael Angelo's on the other side of the church is the not dissimilar tomb of Galileo, on which his half-length figure holds a small telescope in hand, and further on in the right aisle is the grave of Rossini, marked, however, only by his name on the floor. The church also contains carved pulpits, Donatello's Crucifix, and many other objects of artistic or historical interest, the chief being Giotto's wall painting, the principal basis for his fame as a painter, although this was largely a faint tradition until in our own century it was accidentally discovered that under the whitewash of the Medici chapel the unappreciative monks had concealed his animated frescoes from the lives of St. John and St. Francis and their rescue immediately followed.

The churches of Florence as of so many other Italian cities are among the most interesting monuments. But Florence is attractive in every way. Nowhere else did we find so much of interest crowded into so limited a space. History and romance, religion and art all lay claim to Florence, and the student and the pleasure seeker leave it with equal regret.

CHAPTER XIII.

ROME AND ITS RUINS.

AFTER a long and hot night ride from Florence we arrived about 2 A.M. September 1st at Rome, entered a 'bus and were jolted down hill the long way to the Pension Suisse. There was much trouble waking up the portier but finally we were let into a dark but handsome hotel and were shown into the "lift." This elevator, like most others in Italy, was very deliberate in its movements and managed from below, no boy going along. We were ushered into a nice room with unswept marble floor, and, although we protested later against the dirt and were given another room, it was not an improvement in this respect. Marble and dirt go together in this country.

We were curious to discover where we were in Rome, and were glad next morning to find ourselves centrally located on the Via Nazionale just round the corner from the Forum of Trajan. We had got out of the train at the handsome station near where the railroad pierces the east walls of the city, adjacent to the arched ruins of the Baths of Diocletian. There is but this one railroad station.

The Via Nazionale is probably the widest and hand-

THE ROMAN FORUM, FROM THE CAPITOLINE HILL.
ARCH OF SEPTIMIUS SEVERUS. TEMPLE OF SATURN. BASILICA JULIA.
(Comitium, Colosseum, Arch of Titus, and Temple of Castor and Pollux in the background.)

somest of the streets. It is well paved, bordered by new edifices, and has one of the very few street car lines of the city. It is new itself, for in 1880 this street did not exist. Now it runs direct from the railroad station to near the Forum of Trajan and there bending first to the north and then back to the west terminates a few hundred yards further on at the Piazza Venezia, where ends the Corso also one mile south from its beginning at the Porta del Popolo. The Corso (the ancient Via Flaminia) was formerly the great street of Rome, in many respects still is such, and here meets its younger rival almost at right angles.

Most of modern Rome was north of us, and most of the principal ancient ruins south, so that our pleasant little hotel formed a good starting point for sight seeing, the more especially as almost all the omnibus lines leave from the Piazza Venezia. Hacks also are abundant and cheap and may be found everywhere.

Ancient Rome was east of the Tiber and built upon the Palatine and six other hills surrounding it. The Palatine Hill was the first settled by the Latins, and in many respects must have been the centre of the public or at least of social life under the kings as well as under the emperors. There mythical Romulus built his wall, there the kings resided, and there the emperors erected their great palaces. The Sabine village was on the Quirinal Hill to the north, and on the amalgamation of these two settlements the valley between, the scene once of their battles, became the Roman Forum, the place of joint assembly for commerce and discussion. This site was marshy but was early drained by the first great sewer, the Cloaca Maxima, which is still in operation and empties into the Tiber. The Capitoline Hill at the north-west extremity of the Forum, really but a spur of the Quirinal and then approached only from the south, became the seat of government, with the citadel and temple of Jupiter as points of common resort. Between the Tiber on the west and these more northern hills is a level extent of territory, formerly without the walls and called the Campus Martius. This was at first uninhabited, but, as Rome grew, theatres, race courses, mausoleums, arches, and other public structures were erected there. It is now the most thickly built part of Rome, and the crowded mediæval houses are separated only by narrow and crooked lanes.

Rome was long bounded west by the muddy Tiber, to which navigable stream it owed its early commercial greatness, and the town, its very name showing it to be a settlement in the woods, was a Latin colony placed here to defend the confederation against the alien Tuscans on the other side of the river. The present Italian government seems to be trying to make the river navigable, for I have seen clumsy dredges at work near the mouth of the Cloaca. Near there was possibly the site of the Pons Sublicius, Rome's first bridge, so well defended by Horatius. The commerce on the Tiber must have been great in ancient times, but with the modern increase in size and draught of ships it has become insignificant, and, besides, the city is fourteen miles from the mouth of the river. There were in ancient times a number of bridges, but none are now pointed out among the remains of antiquity, except that by which we crossed to go to St. Peter's, the Pons Ælia, built by Hadrian to connect with Rome the imposing mausoleum which he erected for his dynasty.

Rome, a place of three hundred thousand people, is

a world in itself and we hardly knew how to plan our sight seeing. We found the city perfectly healthy in August, although the weather was so warm that we always came back to the hotel between twelve and one, took dinner, rested and did not venture out again until five o'clock, when the sun was lower and the shade better.

We first took an omnibus up the Corso to the handsome and hot Piazza del Popolo to see the obelisk, and our main feeling was one of surprise that Rome looked so much like other cities. On the left as we went north was the Piazza Colonna with the marble Doric column of Marcus Aurelius towering ninety-five feet high among modern stores and sights. This and the column of Trajan near our hotel are much alike and have spiral reliefs of battles running around from top to bottom. The former monument has the celebrated relief of Jupiter Pluvius showering down rain with his outstretched arms. Both columns now have statues of saints at the top, and this consecration has probably saved the monuments by deterring the mediæval faithful from stealing the marble to burn for lime, and their robber nobles from using it to erect palaces. These native Italians, as Raphael declared, destroyed far more than the earlier Barbarian invaders. Similar consecration has saved a number of temples and monuments, but, alas, was not extended to all.

On the first day and several times afterwards we went to the Roman Forum, it being near, possibly the most interesting spot in the city. Up to the beginning of this century it was covered twenty or more feet deep with rubbish from the surrounding hills, and was merely a grazing place for cattle. It was known as Campo Vaccino, Cow Pasture, but a few projecting columns identified the spot. Something was accomplished before the middle of the century but the most rapid progress in excavation has been effected since 1870, when the present Italian kingdom captured Rome from the popes. Even yet much remains unknown, but the general arrangement of the ground at the time of the destruction of the buildings can be made out. The best view of the Forum must always have been from the southern slope of the Capitoline Hill. Thence it stretched south-eastwardly between the Palatine and the spurs of the Quirinal and Esquiline until interrupted by the low Velian Hill, and in the same general valley beyond the Velian the view terminates in the imposing ruins of the Colosseum. The excavation now is several hundred yards wide, and probably a quarter of a mile long, its greater length descending south-east from the slopes where was the ancient record office, (tabularium,) whose massive stones and vaults even now form the foundation of the Capitoline buildings, to abreast the basilica of Constantine and arch of Titus, where the Velian Hill and the foundations of the temple of Venus and Roma terminated the Forum. The central spot, the true Forum, was the rectangular Comitium near the Capitoline Hill, an open place of assembly, with a rostrum for speakers at either end. This had a paved highway on all four sides, two branches in fact of the Via Sacra. The Via Sacra seems to have been a continuation of the Via Appia and Via Latina, which ran to Rome from the Alban country and other places south, if the Via Sacra be not indeed the combination of all the southern and eastern highways to Rome continued northwardly from their union near the Colosseum to the Capitoline Hill.

Not far from the Colosseum it passed under the arch of Titus, which has sculpture on the inside of its single arch showing in a procession captive Jews with the table of shew bread, trumpets and seven-branched candlestick, spoils brought by Titus A.D. 70 from his sack of Jerusalem. They say that good Jews even now will not go under this arch. The Via then descended past temples and entered the Forum under the arch of Augustus, now destroyed. It there divided, as we have seen, to embrace the Comitium, united and then went under the massive marble arch of Septimius Severus, with its separate passages for vehicles and foot travellers. Reaching now the temples on the slope of the Capitoline Hill, the Via Sacra turns at an angle to the left and climbs in front of these, and again turning to the right it must have ascended the Capitoline Hill and terminated at the venerated temple of Jupiter. It was thus bordered all the way by handsome temples and public structures; but the whole scene is now a wreck,—large pieces of basalt, worn into ruts by ancient wheels, make up what is left of the roadway, and marble pavements, brick foundations, and occasionally a marble pillar mark the sites of the buildings. It looks somewhat like part of an American town after a disastrous fire. The Comitium in ancient times was bounded on the Capitoline end by temples, that of Concord being where the Senate usually met, at the other end by the temple of Cæsar, built by Augustus. From the rostrum at this latter point Marc Antony pronounced the oration over the body of Cæsar after the assassination in the Senate Hall March 19th, A.D. 44, which so enthused the populace that they hastily made Cæsar's funeral pyre and burned his body in honor there in the Forum.

On the left of the Comitium coming down from the Capitoline was the underground Mamertine prison where Jugurtha was abandoned to starve in the cold, Catiline's followers killed, and Saint Peter imprisoned. It dates back to the earliest kings, and still exists under the church of S. Pietro in Carcere. The prison is in two stories. The upper chamber cut in the tufa rock is itself some twelve feet below the church level, and a round hole in the floor was originally the only communication between this upper room and the lower oval cell beneath, but we go down now by steps at the side. St. Peter once leaned or fell against the wall so heavily as to leave the print of his face, now behind a grating. This chamber is so low that the hand easily reaches the ceiling. In it was shown—of course by lamplight—the pillar where Peter and Paul were bound, near by the spring, there long before Peter, (although he is said to have miraculously caused it to well forth in order to baptize his jailer,) and not far away they show too the spot where in ancient times they strangled prisoners by tying them to the wall. At the other or stair end they erroneously showed also the Tarpeian Rock, and near it is a passage leading straight on, the guide said, to the Catacombs, but more reliable Baedeker says to the Lautumiæ stairs eighty yards away. Any way there is a strong draught from somewhere perceptible at the mouth of the tunnel. Next east of the prison is the Curia Hostilia or first senate house, and last the Basilica Æmilia. Opposite, on the right coming down from the capitol, is the temple of Saturn, its unfluted granite front columns still standing, from old the Roman Ærarium or treasury. Then beyond the cross street (Vicus Jugarius) was the extensive Basilica Julia, built by Julius Cæsar for the courts, but foundations of pillars and the marble pavement are all that remain, for here the mediæval Romans had their lime pits. Next on the same side of the Comitium but across the Cloaca Maxima and the Tuscan street (Vicus Tuscus) was, high above on a platform approached by eighteen steps, the temple of Castor and Pollux, of which three side pillars of beautiful Parian marble are yet in place.

Such was the Roman Forum, and on it from all the hills looked down handsome structures of the eternal city. But Rome outgrew its republican forum, and other fora, mainly for judicial purposes, were added on the north by the emperors from time to time. Julius and Augustus built one, Augustus another, Domitian perhaps a third, all connected ; but there are few traces of these, as they are covered by modern buildings and have not yet been excavated. Trajan determined to give easy access from the now well built up Campus Martius to the old forum, and he accordingly dug down the neck joining the Capitoline and Quirinal Hills and built for himself a grand forum in the valley thus created. His forum, however, during the middle ages was itself gradually buried and even now but a part has been again cleared,—the Basilica Ulpia with its granite pillars and his column towering 128 feet. The column indicates the depth of his excavations and as well depicts his Dacian victories, and beneath it were once buried Trajan's now scattered remains. In the sculptures on the column the Roman soldiers, I noticed, wear the sword on the right side.

The present Italian government lays bare something new from time to time as its means allow, and every new visit to Rome will teach us more of the architecture and life of that wonderful city, but Italy is anything but a prosperous country, and the process is necessarily slow. The private holders dispossessed must be compensated, in addition to the direct expense of digging, and the needs of modern commerce must also be respected in the selection of sites to be excavated.

The Palatine Hill is in process of recovery and much that has been accomplished is due to Napoleon III., who owned it for some time, beginning in 1861. While there is a wilderness of ruins and vast substructures, including at the north end the approaches of a large bridge which Caligula erected to connect his palace with the Capitoline Hill, and at the southern extremity the buildings of Septimius Severus, the discoveries are not at all well settled and do not at best rank in importance with those in the Forum. On the middle of the hill Augustus lived unpretendingly, and on the slopes were once the houses of Cicero, Catiline, Livia and others. The later emperors, however, covered the hill with their vast but useless palaces, and largely obliterated the unmortared tufa walls and buildings of the original Roma Quadrata of the kings. From the top of some arches supporting the palace of Septimius at the south-west corner I got a beautiful view in all directions. The Palatine was supplied with water by the Claudian aqueduct coming from the south, of which a few arches remain. An amusing part of the excavation is the school house on the western slope, with its walls cut and ornamented with drawings much similar to the crude pictures which our boys now perpetrate. One student of history had cut "Africanus" in the wall, much as in America one might find "Lee" or "Grant."

The Capitoline Hill is hardly less disappointing, because absolutely nothing ancient is left. At least two sites on the west side are claimed for the Tarpeian Rock and at neither point is the hill very high. An active man might possibly jump down and get only a bad shaking up. The site of the great temple was at one end and the Arx at the other, and scholars have now about agreed that the Arx was at the northern or higher end, where the present church of Ara Cœli stands. The hill is shaped somewhat like a saddle, and since Michael Angelo's time the hollow in the middle has been called Piazza del Campidoglio, flanked on three sides by handsome public buildings but open to the north, whence it is approached from the modern city by a flight of flat asphalt steps and a winding driveway. In the middle of the Campidoglio is an ancient bronze equestrian statue of Marcus Aurelius. The horse, like all ancient steeds, has his mane cropped short. The building opposite the main approach is the Palazzo del Senatore, the handsome municipal buildings erected above the ancient Tabularium. " S. P. Q. R." is still used on municipal documents, but Senatus Populusque Romanus are but a shadow now. To the left of the Piazza is the Capitoline Museum, containing amongst other things the Dying Gladiator or Gaul, a fine head of Alexander, the beautiful Capitoline Venus with abundant hair tied in a bow knot on top. The Venus was found walled up for protection. In this museum ancient skeletons lie in their original sarcophagi, and we saw also many marble fragments of an official plan of Rome, made during the reign of Septimius Severus, A.D. 193-211.

Trajan cut away a large part of the north end of the Capitoline Hill to give access from the Campus Martius to the Forum, and now on the other hand the present

Italian government is engaged in enlarging this hill where Trajan cut it away in order on its highest point to gain room to erect a marble memorial hall to Victor Emanuel, the restorer of Italian unity. So far but a few columns have been completed and they thus seem rather in keeping with the fragmentary ruins in the Forum they overlook. Strangers are not admitted and when I slipped in the soldiers on guard promptly arrested me and turned me out. It was while musing near here in the church of Ara Cœli that Gibbon conceived the design of writing his great work on the Decline and Fall of the Roman Empire.

Rome is growing much like an American city, and many of the more interesting ruins have to be sought amidst modern buildings. The vast Colosseum is overlooked in part by modern flats. This famous structure was erected by Titus where Nero had had an artificial lake in the gardens for which the burning of Rome furnished room. The site is still low. The Colosseum—named not from its own size but from the colossal statue of Nero once standing near it—was an ellipse six hundred and fifteen feet long by five hundred and ten wide, and one hundred and fifty-six feet high, in four stories without roof. The three lower stories were arcades, the ground floor being Doric, the next Ionic, the third Corinthian, and the fourth a wall with windows. The outside main wall is now standing only on the north side, and the stones of the cornice in several places look very insecure. Corbels and sockets are visible on the outside near the top for stepping the masts which supported the protecting awnings. Inside is the arena, two hundred and seventy-nine by one hundred and seventy-four feet, now excavated in part, showing chambers below in which beasts and gladiators were probably housed. From the inside the view is impressive, but it is that of a complete wreck. Four tiers of seats, for eighty-seven thousand people, were there, but now only tier upon tier of the stone or masonry on which the seats once rested. It looks like a stone building after a fire, and in some way you think you see the ribs of some vast pre-adamite monster. Part of the internal flights of steps to reach the seats remain or are restored and can be ascended to the third story, and places for others are visible all about. A number of popes have restored parts of the structure or by brick supports preserved portions in danger of falling, and these pontiffs have in each case inserted an inscription in their own honor. The size and ruin of the Colosseum may be better realized from the statement that in it grow 420 species of plants, many peculiar to it.

Between the Colosseum and the Palatine Hill is the triumphal arch of Constantine. It has a central driveway and arches at either side for foot passengers. A significant commentary on his times is that the best sculptures on it are taken bodily from an earlier and handsomer arch of Trajan, and that what was executed in Constantine's time, say 311 A.D., is far inferior. And yet we moderns, because Constantine embraced the Christian faith, generally think of his time as one of great progress and prosperity.

In the valley west of the Palatine Hill was formerly the Circus Maximus, but the neighborhood is now well built up and showed few ruins as we passed over the site in street cars. Continuing to the south and after a while turning from the walled highway into a branch road, we came to the majestic, isolated Baths of Caracalla, near the extreme southern point of ancient Rome. About this great structure was once a court, and behind a race course. The Baths are in ruins, but enough remains to indicate the arrangement. It was originally a lofty building with a portico at each end, and within in the central one of the three large chambers perpendicular to these porches were warm baths in four basins, while to the one side was the cold bath with great swimming basin, and to the other the smaller round hot bath. These were called respectively the tepidarium, frigidarium, and caldarium. Each of these was a large, vaulted apartment, the roof now gone, however, and the coarse mosaic pavement painfully uneven. The caldarium had double floors and walls for warm air and underneath I noticed what seemed to be a furnace blackened with soot. The architectural ornaments showed the decline of art into a kind of rococo, the capitals, for instance, being composite and decorated with human figures. Over the caldarium the guide pointed out the remains of an aqueduct which supplied the water. The guide was compulsory, but as he was included in the one lira admission fee we did not object much. From these Baths came the Farnese Hercules, Flora and the Hercules Torso, and there were fragments of other statuary still there, but of no especial value.

The Baths of Diocletian are at the other end of the city, and the Baths of Titus, where the Laocoön group was discovered, are in a field near the Colosseum. Leo X., who had an untiring assistant in Raphael, never passed such discoveries without well rewarding the finder.

There are other well known monuments in different parts of the city. Not to dwell on the beautiful little round Corinthian temple near the river at the foot of the

Palatine, called for Vesta, and the so-called temple of Janus Quadrifrons near by, which was more probably an exchange connected with an adjacent cattle market, (forum boarium,) one of the most interesting of the ancient structures is the Pantheon, built by Agrippa, the well known friend of Augustus, A.D. 27, in the Campus Martius. Within, time has wrought few changes, for its colored marbles, tasteful pillars, vast flat dome, which has been the model of all subsequent architects and through whose round opening the building is lighted, are well preserved. The diameter and height are each 140 feet and the simple grandeur of the vast interior is impressive. The thick walls exclude all external noise and priests and people go quietly about in worship from altar to altar. For it has been a Christian church since it was dedicated to the Martyrs in 609 on the first All-Saints' Day, when many wagon-loads of bones were brought from the Catacombs and re-interred under the high altar. In later times Raphael was buried in this church amid great popular grief at his sudden death in 1520, and in our own day Victor Emanuel also, near the high altar. At his tomb shortly after our visit occurred the hostile demonstration by French pilgrims which was resented so roughly by the Italians that the pope has thought it proper to re-consecrate the building. The Pantheon's noble Corinthian portico was approached by a flight of steps, but they are buried under modern accumulations and one actually descends now to enter.

Not far away is the rifled Mausoleum of Augustus, apparently in somebody's back yard and now used for a cheap theatre. It is round and Hadrian's would seem to have been copied from it. Within we were shown a niche in a dark passage where the ashes of Augustus and his family once reposed, but the monument has outlasted what it was built to contain, and no one knows where now is "imperial Cæsar, dead and turned to clay."

Away off from here, in the south-eastern corner of Rome, are the church and palace of St. John Lateran. The palace is said to have been presented by Constantine to Pope Sylvester and was the usual papal residence until the removal to Avignon. The tradition is that when the death of a pope is imminent the bones of Sylvester rattle in the palace. This is now a museum, whose profane department is not of much interest, but in the Christian division let into the walls are numberless inscriptions and sculptures from the catacombs. There were some rude biblical scenes, generally symbolic of the resurrection or some doctrine, such as Moses striking the rock, Daniel among the lions, and a remarkable Jonah with a whale of his own size. We saw few crosses but a good many fish, the Greek word for fish (ichthus) containing the first letters of the Greek for "Jesus Christ, son of God, Saviour." The earliest inscriptions were brief, such as In Pace, Requiescat, Pray for us, and the like, and many of the oldest in Greek, for Christianity was first preached from the Grecian East. There were few historical representations.

In the old church of St. John Lateran were held many famous councils. The present structure is in the handsome Italian style of the last century. It is rather a museum itself, for they claim that some small columns of an altar came from the great temple of Jupiter Capitolinus, in the square pilasters are the ancient pillars of Constantine's church, St. Peter's table is within the altar and that the heads of Paul and Peter are buried under it.

Not far off in another building are the sacred stairs of marble from Pilate's palace at Jerusalem, brought here by that indefatigable discoverer, the Empress Helena, mother of Constantine. On each side of them is a flight of steps, up and down which the curious go to gaze at well-dressed people as well as those in rags ascending the Scala Santa on their knees, reciting prayers as they climb. The twenty-eight steps are cased in wood to prevent their being worn out as well as the clothing of the faithful. It was while ascending these that it flashed on Luther "the just shall live by faith" and not by such acts, and so here where one would least expect it is found one of the fountain heads of the Reformation.

From the high terrace near the Lateran is a beautiful view southward over the Campagna. Many ruins are in sight and huge aqueduct arches stalk across the plain from the blue Alban mountains, while from the vicinity of the church one of the new avenues, rapidly building up, runs northward to the modern quarters of Rome again. So closely in the Eternal City tread ancient, mediæval, and modern on each other!

CHAPTER XIV.

ST. PETER'S AND THE VATICAN.

WE saw St. Peter's of course. A 'bus line runs regularly from the Piazza Venezia to the northern of the two colonnades of Bernini which all but surround the Piazza S. Pietro in front of the church. The route took us along narrow thoroughfares of the old Campus Martius, past the corner where stands the broken Greek warrior known as Pasquin, a statue on which wits paste their satires and landlords their rent notices. We then crossed the Tiber at the round castle of St. Angelo with its famous prison cells, (formerly the mausoleum of Hadrian,) and thence were taken straight to St. Peter's. The castle of St. Angelo commanded Rome from the opposite bank, and, as the great military stronghold of the popes, was once connected by a covered passage with the Vatican, the papal residence.

This trans-Tiberine quarter of Rome, the Borgo, is very unattractive and would hardly be selected on its own account as the place for the grandest ecclesiastical building of Christendom. The early emperors had gardens and a circus here outside the walls of Rome, and to light them up Nero burned Christians on crosses. Peter is said also to have been crucified near by and buried here, and, while there is very little satisfactory proof of this, not unnaturally a church was as early as the time of Constantine erected on the traditional site. Here A.D. 800 in old St. Peter's Charlemagne was crowned, and a few years later the invading Saracens took from its altar the sacred ornaments.

When in the fifteenth century Pope Julius II. conceived the plan of a grand church edifice he tore down this historic church. The present basilica is the result of the great efforts of this pontiff and Leo X., and of several centuries of work for them and their successors by such architects as Bramante, Michael Angelo and Bernini, each to some extent undoing what his predecessor had done. The necessities of the papal treasury growing out of this undertaking caused the sale of the indulgences in the time of Leo X., which aroused Luther and precipitated the Reformamation. The original and better design of Bramante was that of an equilateral Greek cross, but the church as now built is a Latin cross in shape, the main arm being 615 feet long, the transverse arm 450 feet. The nave is 150 feet high and the magnificent dome over the intersection of the nave and transept rises 435 feet. The dome is not seen to advantage in the immediate vicinity, as in front the portico unfortunately hides it, but from the Campagna outside and from many points in the city it looms up the most prominent object in Rome. Since the Eiffel tower in Paris was built 984 feet into the air, St. Peter's, the Pyramids and all other works of man formerly thought high cease to aspire to grandeur on account of height alone, but in other respects no other structure compares with this church. From the entrance doors you feel only that you are in a large and beautiful building; its proportions you appreciate at once, but the dimensions one cannot take in except by degrees. A man at a distance looks like a child, and from the doors a pair of cherubs holding a basin of holy water by a side pillar looked of normal baby size. We went up to them and found their hands larger than ours and the infants taller than even cousin Dan. By the time we had walked the length of the church we realized the distance better. At the back in the tribune is a gilt chair high above the floor, said to contain the original wooden chair of St. Peter. The bronze canopy under the dome covers the great altar,—which is not at the end of the church as is usual,—and under that is the supposed tomb of St. Peter. Before the tomb below kneels Canova's marble statute of Pius VI. as he often did in life. The canopy, or baldachino, made of metal taken from the Pantheon, rests gracefully upon its four twisted columns, but does not look its height of 96 feet. The pen in the hand of the mosaic St. Luke high above, at the base of the dome, is seven feet long, but seems only as many inches. The inscription running around the great dome, "Tu es Petrus," etc., is in mosaic letters four feet ten inches in height. But we could realize none of these dimensions except by comparing them when possible with human figures near.

In the side aisles and transepts are chapels with statuary, altar pieces, and pictures in mosaic that rival the original paintings, and in many of the chapels are tombs of popes and distinguished people. The north transept was partitioned off in 1870 and used by the council which proclaimed the Infallibility of the Pope. At a pillar in the nave near the dome is the celebrated seated bronze statue of St. Peter, with a foot projecting beyond the base, and I rubbed the toes with my handkerchief and kissed the foot like the other visitors. I suspect it is a statue of Jupiter and not Peter, but I could not afford to go to Rome and not kiss St. Peter's foot.

Of the monuments that executed by Canova for George IV. to "James III." and his sons, the exiled Stuarts, struck us very much, for it is one of George's few creditable actions. The marble group across the church, the "Pieta" of Michael Angelo, Mary with the dead Christ on her lap, is of course finely executed, but until I can share the Catholic reverence for it because of Mary I must feel averse to so ghastly a subject. It is interesting, however, to locate the resting places of distinguished men, and St. Peter's contains the graves of many famous people. Of the better known are St. Peter, Leo I., (the Great,) Gregory I., (the Great,) famous for his music, St. Gregory Nazianzen, Julius II., the fighting pope, the composer Palestrina, Gregory XIII. who reformed the calendar, and others, but many of the monuments here, as in Westminster Abbey, are in honor of illustrious dead who are buried elsewhere. The tomb of Julius II. is marked only by a flat slab instead of the magnificent monument designed by Michael Angelo and for which he carved the colossal and majestic Moses, now in S. Pietro in Vincoli, the Fettered Slaves in the Louvre, and other great works. The impatient Julius quarrelled with the sculptor about the cost and slowness of this undertaking, upon which Michael Angelo indignantly left Rome for Florence. Even after their reconciliation Julius preferred to put the artist to work in the Sistine Chapel, and the tomb was never finished.

Of all men Leo X. should have been buried in St. Peter's. He built the church, and was, next to Augustus, perhaps the greatest patron of the arts that the world has known. After his sudden and mysterious death, however, in 1521, he was interred in the Vatican and his remains were finally removed with those of his kinsman Clement VII., who reigned shortly after him, to the church of Sta. Maria Sopra Minerva on the other side of the Tiber. In the choir behind the altar there I found the tombs of these two Medici pontiffs, the monument of Leo representing him as seated, but so short is the greatest fame that a monk in the church could not point out to me Leo's grave.

Tasso is buried in an elaborate tomb at the church of S. Onofrio near St. Peter's. In its garden is his oak, now hollow, under which he so often sat and gazed on Rome. Upstairs in the convent is his room, and on the wall opposite the door is painted a speaking likeness of the poet, pausing as if surprised at the intrusion, his lightly bearded face kind and pensive. The room has its old rafters and about are a number of souvenirs.

The Vatican adjoins St. Peter's on the north. Since the Italians in 1870 deprived Pius IX. of his temporal dominions, the popes have chosen to regard and represent themselves as prisoners in this palace and have never gone outside its limits. Its rooms are counted by the thousand, although most of them are used as art galleries and not for habitation. It dates back to before the time of Charlemagne but has only gradually assumed its present shape and dimensions. Pope Nicholas V. (1447-1455) was the projector of its vast plan, and Leo X. did much to join its disconnected parts and ornament them with paintings. Externally it is not handsome and from a distance looks a great deal like an American grain elevator. The main entrance is from the Piazza of St. Peter's and after passing by the Swiss guards, (in Michael Angelo's slashed yellow, red and black uniform,) and up a long hall, we ascended a flight of steps, the Scala Regia, where at a landing a man took our parcels. On the first floor is the Sistine Chapel, on the second are the wall paintings of Raphael, and on the third is the picture gallery. When one has climbed up all the stairways,—some winding, others narrow and dark, a few magnificent,—he wishes that His Holiness would buy and put in a modern passenger elevator. Some enterprising American manufacturer could afford to present one gratis for the advertisement, and would thus earn the gratitude of travellers and popes forever.

The Sistine Chapel, whose wall paintings were by Michael Angelo in the time of Julius II., is supposed by some critics to be the finest work of pictorial art, but Rachel and I sat back in our chairs in that room and found difficulty in realizing the claim. It is a large chapel with altar at one end, and above the altar is the dim Last Judgment of Michael Angelo, finished 1541 after seven years' labor. It is made up of figures in half a dozen groups on clouds about the Saviour. The ceiling above us was covered with grand prophets, almost breathing sibyls and familiar Bible scenes, all by the same great hand. I liked best of the sibyls the Cumæan hag, possibly because I had visited her sounding caves and known her sea-girt haunts. Michael Angelo drew his figures nude and clothed them afterwards, if at all, and it has always seemed to me that he thus was led to insist too much on muscular development and on uncomfortable and awkward positions of the body both in his paintings and sculptures. Art no doubt has other aims than mere grace, but surely among them is not to displease by constantly picturing prize fighters and contortionists. In the Last Judgment, however, there is perhaps room for the grotesque. In the centre is Christ the Judge, as muscular as Hercules, by his side kneels Mary, above them appear angels with trumpets, to his right are the ascending saints, fought over by angels and demons, to his left the miserable wicked, while below are Charon, hell and devils, the last with regulation horn and tail. The figures were all nude until two of the popes had them more or less draped, putting on Mary a blue dress, hardly becoming and now much faded.

On the floor above we passed through several rooms of gigantic and impressive modern paintings to the Stanze of Raphael, a series of connected rooms, formerly constituting the papal apartments. The ceilings and walls here, too, are covered with frescoes, but the greater part of the north wall of each stanza is taken up by a large window which lights the room. Raphael was a pupil of Perugino, who originally worked here, but Raphael became so efficient that to him eventually was committed the whole. Julius II. had the honor of ordering the execution of the paintings in the first room and two paintings in the second of this suite, while the others and the loggie adjacent were painted for Leo X., of whose reign Raphael was the most distinguished ornament in the realm of art. There seems to have been a mutual repugnance between this pontiff and Michael Angelo, and that artist spent the eight years of this pontificate at Florence, not in idleness, but without producing any great work. In these frescoes Raphael by way of flattery introduces the portraits of his pontifical patrons. The most celebrated of these paintings are in the Camera della Segnature, the second room but painted first. On its walls are represented the Christian Faith, Apollo playing to the Muses, and the School of Athens. The last impressed me most. It is the familiar picture of Plato and Aristotle talking in a vaulted hall, Plato pointing upwards, and on the steps or ground are famous characters in animated discourse, and amongst them we easily recognized ugly Socrates. In the next room among other frescoes are Peter released from prison and Attila repulsed by Leo I.,—really the expulsion of the French from Italy in the time of Leo X., the goal of the political efforts of that patriotic if unscrupulous pope. A fresco to suit the present time would perhaps reverse this and be the French welcomed to Rome by Leo XIII. In the first stanza the only picture by Raphael's own hand is the Conflagration of the Borgo and its extinguishment by the sign of the cross made by Leo IV.

We had become interested in this and I was looking at a man in the picture dropping from a wall or house, when some official rushed through, shouting Italian and waving his arms excitedly. We all thought that there was another fire, and all visitors and copyists were rushed out to a gallery shut in with glass,—the Loggie of Raphael. These overlook the courtyard of S. Damaso, on the other side of which are the pope's living apartments. We have never been quite certain what was the matter, but think that His Holiness wished to pass through privately. We were shut up in this hot place for about half an hour, during which I craned my neck in the study of Raphael's excellent and familiar Bible scenes, from the Creation to the Last Supper, painted in the thirteen vaults of the gallery ceiling. In the Fall we noticed that the serpent had a woman's head. The pictures were exposed to the weather for several centuries, with the natural result of destruction of some and injury to the rest. When permitted we returned to the stanze and finished them. The fourth relates almost exclusively to Constantine, and contains the large Battle with Maxentius, the Baptism of Constantine, Constantine presenting Rome to Pope Sylvester I., and the familiar picture of the Cross in the Heavens. These were by pupils of Raphael from his designs and hardly up to his standard.

The picture gallery above is not as large as many others but contains valuable works. After the fall of Napoleon in 1815 the paintings were restored which he had taken out of Italian churches, and the pope received them and in his turn appropriated them to found a gallery, to which many others acquired by donation or otherwise have been added since. Almost all are on religious subjects. The three most celebrated are in one room,—Raphael's Transfiguration, his Madonna di Foligno with the sun for a glory behind her, and Domenichino's Communion of Jerome. In the Transfiguration the benignant Christ with Moses and Elias are in the air, on the mountain below are the three dazed disciples, thus making up the upper part of the picture, while in the lower half the disciples in the valley try in vain to heal the squint-eyed demoniac boy. This picture was at Raphael's head as his masterpiece when his body lay in state. In the Communion, St. Jerome, old, earnest, pallid and dying, is supported on his knees to take the sacrament. This was painted for the monks of Ara Cœli but these critics finally put it in a lumber room.

Guido Reni has a crucifixion of Peter in this gallery following the tradition that Peter was at his own request crucified with his head down and feet up, as he was not worthy to die in the same manner as his Lord. Poussin's striking Martyrdom of St. Erasmus is also there,—the saint meeting death by the horrible torture of having the smaller intestine drawn from the abdomen by a revolving wheel.

The Vatican sculpture galleries are probably the finest in the world and why His Holiness does not make them accessible from the main entrance of the palace we could not imagine. The only way open is to go clear around St. Peter's until you are under the windows of the Sistine Chapel and then walk half as far again up a court to the entrance steps, a distance of at least half a mile, and in our case all under the hot sun. The galleries themselves then stretch on for as much further, and sight seeing becomes almost a burden. There we saw among other sculptures the recumbent, graceful, deserted Ariadne, the shaggy bust of Zeus of Otricoli with big bump on his forehead, the beautiful bust of young Augustus, the stern, older Augustus in full armor with low reliefs, the athlete throwing the discus, the marble *biga* with two prancing yoked horses, Father Nile with children playing over him, stern, bearded Demosthenes, and his opponent, the pleasanter faced Æschines. In the arcades about the octagonal Belvidere court are the most famous pieces of the gallery, among them the Apollo and Laocoön. The thin Apollo has just shot his bow, and stands looking intently and perhaps scornfully in the direction of his aim. As it is the correct thing to undo the past and prove ourselves better informed than our fathers, it is now given out that Apollo was not shooting a bow at all, but was shaking his ægis. As his left hand was not found, of course we cannot tell what he really held in it, and it is a free-for-all contest of guessers as to this as well as so many other pieces of statuary. His hair is abundant and bound up in a knot, and his sandals, by the way, are double soled. The agonized Laocoön group is finer than any copy I have seen, although the figures are smaller than one would anticipate, and the children are rather small men than boys. The son to his left, entwined by the same serpent as the father, appeals to him for help, but the other boy is too much entangled by a second serpent even to ask for aid. In another room of the arcade is the godlike Meleager, no longer yellow like ivory, as in Addison's day, and Canova's animated Boxers in another compartment to our minds compared favorably with the works of the ancients. In the centre of a vestibule near by we found a mass of marble without much shape, but marked by all guide books as worthy of great attention. On close examination we discovered that it was the trunk of a seated human body, without head or arms, legs gone below the knees, and even what remains rather injured too. This is the Greek Torso of the first century B.C. so admired by Michael Angelo.

There is, of course, much else fine in the Vatican collections. We saw the highly polished and imposing Egyptian figures and sarcophagi, the iridescent Tuscan vases and bottles, the recumbent terra cotta figures on the Etrurian tombs, always resting on the left arm, the long brown tufa box used once as the tomb of the Scipios, surmounted by a bust, the beautiful ancient floor mosaics from the Baths and other places, the large porphyry vases and tombs, besides thousands of other pieces of sculpture. As the statuary is all on pedestals, I could not help noticing, too, the prosaic subject of *toes*. The little toe is curled up in the same supernumerary manner as now-a-days, but the one next never bends under the third, and the big and second toes are widely separated. The different effects of their sandals and our shoes are thus very noticeable, if indeed the sculptors followed actual life. There was one room of sculpture that surprised Rachel very much,—full of crabs, lobsters, monkeys, and other marble animals. There was a rude sow with little pigs, an animated camel's head, a pelican with pouch, and a little fighting cock with bristling feathers. In another room were some anatomical studies in marble,—one of the human body with flesh cut off to the ribs, another cut further until the bladder shows. We do not think generally of the Romans as caring for natural history or anatomy, and, scientific as is this age, even we do not thus perpetuate our studies.

In one room I found a very different exhibit,—the faded Tapestries of Raphael, designed for the side walls of the Sistine Chapel and illustrating scenes from the Book of Acts, such as Paul on Mars Hill, Peter and John raising the cripple, etc., the originals of the familiar types we find in many engravings. These tapestries were woven in the Netherlands, and the cartoons from which they were made found their way to England and after long neglect were placed at Hampton Court and then in the South Kensington Museum, where they are still exhibited.

It would take many visits to become even casually acquainted with all the treasures of the Vatican. Each time we saw something new, each time we learned more about what we had seen before. The long, vaulted galleries, with stucco and gilt ornamentation, the handsome marble columns, the domes, the views from porticos, are themselves interesting and beautiful, even without regard to the works of art arranged along the walls.

The many interesting churches and the mediæval palaces of the city with their paintings and monuments would themselves fill a volume, but after all we look back to the Vatican, St. Peter's and the Forum as the chief of the many glories of Rome.

CHAPTER XV.

ENVIRONS OF ROME.

ON my earlier tour a friend and I took trips in the outskirts and neighborhood of Rome and saw some things not down in the guide books. The Alban country and even the falls of Terni were visited, as well as the Via Appia and Catacombs nearer the city walls.

On one occasion after passing Monte Testaccio, a high ancient mound made of pottery, from no one knows what source, but commanding beautiful views, I visited the interesting Protestant cemetery just within the ancient walls near the south-west corner of the city. There at the foot of the ancient sepulchral pyramid of Cestius is a square grave bordered with a tiny hedge, containing the heart of the great but erratic poet, Shelley, who was drowned in a storm near Leghorn. He was in his sail boat going home and was last seen sitting in the stern reading a book. His remains were washed ashore and there in a desolate spot were cremated by his friends Byron and Trelawny as a matter of necessity, but the heart—*cor cordium*—would not burn and they rescued it and brought it here for interment. Near the entrance, surrounded by a higher box hedge, is the nameless grave of that twin genius, Keats. The inscription speaks of him as a young English poet who desired on his death bed that there be written on his tombstone, "His name was writ in water." Based on this Robert Bridges in a poem composed at Princeton College has beautifully made an angel descend in mid-ocean at the poet's death and write in the sea the name of Keats, and this the winds take up and repeat in love and sorrow the wide world over.

At another time we took a tramp southward on the Appian Way, going also to the Grotto of Egeria and to St. Paul's. We started out one morning rather late, after nine, going past the tomb of the Scipios, of which but a confused mass of brick and pillars appeared above the wall bounding the road. We then went under the plain stone arch of Drusus, which has remains of an aqueduct on top, through the mediæval looking Porta S. Paolo, and were on the Via Appia without the walls, but the Via Appia modernized by the small square stones now used for paving in Rome, and indeed further out it was macadamized. It ran below the level of the fields until we reached the neighborhood of the Catacombs, and as we were shut in between walls we saw little even of the brick tombs along the side.

At these Catacombs, originally called Cœmeteria, of S. Calixtus, the best known of the many about Rome, the Christians lived, worshipped, and were buried during the imperial persecutions before Constantine. They are lighted now in part by piercings in the roof, if I may call it such, made after they had ceased to be places of refuge and burial and had become the resorts of pilgrims from all over the Christianized world, who came to worship at the graves of the martyrs. From about the fifth century no extensions were made of the Catacombs, as the dead were now interred near the churches. It was a courageous but awful thing to live there underground amid decaying bodies for conscience' sake. The bones have now nearly all been removed, some by popes to the Pantheon and other churches, some by reverent barbarian invaders to sell in the north as sacred relics, and the interesting inscriptions have been taken to the Lateran. This aids scientific study, but it detracts from the Catacombs themselves, and leaves them rather bare to take away the martyrs to the churches and their works to the museums.

We went down holding the tallow dips handed us and followed the guide along passages hardly a yard wide and not over high, crossing at angles, generally level but sometimes at varying slopes. After four or five sharp turns I lost my reckoning entirely. I touched the dry wall, and it seemed to crumble as if the passages were cut in sand or some soft tufa rock. Along the sides were deep grooves to receive bodies, originally covered in with inscribed marble slabs. At frequent intervals were openings into vaults for families or distinguished people, popes and others, and around these also were shelves cut to receive bodies. I saw two large marble sarcophagi in a vault, one containing, even yet, a mummy and the other a skeleton, for the Christians, influenced by their belief in a resurrection, buried their dead instead of cremating like the heathen Romans about them. The ornamentation was simple and the sculpture rude. A few rooms had marble, and one, which was pointed out as the vault of a distinguished family, was striped with colors and showed a kind of barbaric refinement. Another contained the tombs of several popes, in yet another had lain St. Cecilia, and there I noticed stiff paintings of Christ with Cecilia and Urban, and in these productions of the seventh century the artist used what is even now the type for our Lord. It was a weird feeling to hurry about behind a guide and see by candlelight room after room in whose shelves and stone boxes once reposed the early Christian dead, and it was with a feeling of some relief that we re-ascended to daylight and the surface of the earth again, about five hundred yards from where we had gone down.

My friend from here returned to Rome. The Via Appia continued straight as an arrow, but undulating with hill and valley, until it reached the summit at Albano, but I branched off from it and made my way across uncultivated fields to the grotto of Egeria, enjoying beautiful views all the way. Behind me was Rome with the Lateran of many statues and the great dome of St. Peter's, in front the familiar Alban mount with its crown of trees, to its left Frascati, on its other side Albano and other villages, while away to my left stretched the high Sabine peaks, and all about me was the rolling Campagna,—an historic landscape. I passed an ancient building modernized into a church, and behind it in a vaulted ruin cows gathered from the heat. A man, of course, could also be seen sleeping there, for you can find an Italian asleep almost anywhere at noon.

The grotto where Numa nightly met the wise nymph Egeria is visible only from the Almo valley, being in the side of a hill, and this brook flows past in a brick channel above the level of the ground. The grotto is a brick vault, but a piece of its old marble facing is on the floor. In a large niche at the back is the recumbent statue of the tutelary deity, now sans head but clearly a man, and behind was an opening in the wall whence comes no water, for that gushes from a hole in the first of the three niches in the left wall and nearly floods the pavement. The right wall has three corresponding niches, all arched, and at the entrance towards the Almo the sides widen out into a transept with a niche at each end, but there is no wall at all on the side towards the brook. The front is overgrown with creeping plants and a kind of ivy hangs down partially over the entrance. It was a pretty picture indeed.

By a cross road I regained the Via Appia and a little further on left it to visit the Circus of Maxentius. This is at least a quarter of a mile long and had tiers of brick seats the whole way up. There are remains of the *spina* or division in the centre of the course, with a brick mound at each extremity where the racers turned. The Rome end of the Circus has two towers, and apparently was open, and made its shape a U. The other is hemmed in by the curve of seats, broken only by an arch for entry or exit. The remains of the walls and seats are curiously honeycombed with large earthen jars in the concrete of brick and mortar,—I suppose to economize material, as, with these internal hollows acting somewhat as arches, the structure would be strong enough. Daisies were all over the grass-grown course, which is now at one end ten feet above the ancient level, as the partly buried arch and *meta* or goal testify. This structure was not roofed in.

Near was the round tomb of Cæcilia Metella, the wife of the triumvir Crassus. The frieze is of bulls' heads and horns, much injured by time, and above are queer slit battlements of the middle ages. Inside, the huge monument is hollow and evidently was once vaulted, but I noticed no stairs in the thick walls by which to ascend.

The structure is joined now by walls to mediæval fortifications, and as it is cased in white marble is visible far and wide over the flat Campagna. During the middle ages it was used as a castle by the Roman robber nobles, as were also many of the larger monuments in the city, such as the mausoleum of Hadrian, the arch of Constantine and the Colosseum itself.

After returning on the Via Appia a short distance, I took a cross road south over to St. Paul's, called for part of the way Via Paradisa, but it was near two o'clock and the hot sunshine reminded me more of a broader way. As is common where there is not a wall, the road was bordered by a thick thorn hedge, with an upper and lower line of canes thatched in horizontally to keep it regular. In one place I saw men pitching stones at a mark, much like quoits, and while in Italy often noticed this game and that of throwing to knock one stone off another. I saw a few people hoeing and as usual many groups of curious loafers in the shade, some of course asleep. As everywhere else, there were frequent chapels or at least shrines with Mary and the Child,—the pictures judiciously protected from desecration by a wire screen, for I have seen, as near Terni, some sacred pictures cut and pencilled past recognition. In the cities there are similar shrines on the street corners, and frequently even in stores are such pictures with a candle burning before them.

The imposing summit of St. Paul's was visible long before I reached it. This basilica, restored on the site of the ancient one after the fire of 1823, is T shaped with campanile at the place where the upper arm of a cross should be. The church made a deep impression on me. The nave is of two stories, rising to the same height as the transepts, while the four other aisles, two on each side of the nave, have but one story. The upper story has windows, and between these are good paintings of scenes from the life of Paul. Beneath them all around are medallion portraits of the popes, including Leo XIII. Alexander XII. about 1700 was the last pope with a beard,—and he had not much,—while before him for a dozen all had beards and before that on upwards the large majority were bearded. The columns,—of marble or monolithic granite,—were of the Corinthian order and the flat ceiling was divided into square gilded coffers. Despite the stained glass windows, which St. Peter's has not, this church unlike St. Peter's had a light, cheerful appearance. The altar is at the crossing of the nave and transept, under the old triumphal arch on which are hideous mosaics of Christ, with Paul on his left, and to his right Peter, of the present type although made in the fifth century, and under the altar rest the remains of Paul except his head, which with Peter's is in St. John Lateran. I walked back to the city from St. Paul's pretty tired but well re-paid for my long tramp in the neighborhood of Rome.

On another occasion we spent several days near the Alban Lake, the scene of early Latin history before Rome was founded. We know now that the Latins were not fugitive Trojans as Virgil makes out and that Æneas and his son Ascanius, who is said to have founded Alba Longa, are mythical. But these poetical creations will not down at the bidding of modern critics, and they still walk the hills and sail the lakes as real as Pompey and Cicero, who did live there. Here was the seat of the Latin race when history dawns, and from here branched off the settlement on the Tiber which soon dominated the league of which it was a member and then little by little conquered the world. The country is beautiful and at every step rises some famous view or historical or literary association. Here often resided famous men of the republic, after them the emperors, and until our own times, too, the popes.

To reach Albano we went by rail south from Rome for one hour and at the modest Hotel de Russie secured rooms at the unheard of price of two francs per diem, "tutto compresso." The morning after our arrival we undertook a trip to Frascati afoot, leaving shortly before eleven A.M.,—it had rained up to that time,—and made it with many stops for views in about three and a half hours. We went past the Alban Lake and saw it, deep in the hollow of an extinct volcano, stretching two miles or so. On its west bank is a country or summer residence of the popes, Castel Gandolfo, with exterritorial rights. The views are very pleasant, embracing the water with its tiny waves and the steep, wooded shores. Leaving the lake we passed over the Aqua Ferentina, the meeting place of the ancient Latin league, to Marino, and noticed in the gorge above the stream women washing clothes in a common stone trough with slanting sides, the water fed by a spring. Frascati is a modern town of six thousand, and there we had an excellent dinner for two francs at the Trattoria Nuova. Above is the brick and plaster villa once owned by Lucien Bonaparte and the probable site of Cicero's Tusculanum. Marble cornices and statues, a soldier for one, and parts of columns found there are distributed around the grounds. The villa commands a wide view of the green Campagna, almost devoid of woodland, and Rome too was just visible—although the day was misty—and blue mountains closed the horizon. Here Cicero at Tusculanum drowned his grief over his daughter's death in philosophic composition. I stood where were written those Disputations which I had read with so much interest at Princeton.

Further up the hill was Tusculum itself, razed 1191 by the Romans on account of its Ghibelline propensities. First the ancient basalt road led past a small amphitheatre in a hollow without the walls, and in it a lazy shepherd watched his flock. Inside the Tusculum walls, mere ruins now, was a house with statues imbedded in it, and further was a small theatre with seats intact and a cistern under the stage. It was so cloudy that we did not visit the arx for the view.

We attempted to return to Albano by the east side of the lake, leaving the paved main road to Rocca di Papa at seven o'clock to go through woods. It was soon so dark that we could only tell the soaked road by the shimmer of the central part, which had been tramped into liquid mud. We had to walk at the side, treading in puddles and ditches and guarding our faces with our hands from the overhanging brush. So we went on for an hour and a half, lighting an occasional match to consult Baedeker's small map. The road divided in two often only to re-unite, and we would go different ways to test it, but at the one real separation we after all took the wrong branch, that away from the lake. It began to rain. Both of us were tired, my companion almost dropping in his tracks. The road became worse, and we finally knocked at the door of the second house, although like the first no light was visible. After a linguistic struggle which would have been amusing under other circumstances, we learned that we were six miles wrong, on the road to Velletri. They led us up a ladder into a big room with a fireplace almost as large, and in this they re-kindled the bark fire and in monosyllabic Italian we discussed our situation with the gray whiskered peasant, the children, even to the baby, gathered in the fireplace. They invited us to spend the night and we did not hesitate long about accepting and eating some dubious fried fish and bread. They showed us then to the room of the old couple and we retired,—but not to sleep. My toes caught in the holes of the sheet as I got in. Then began attacks by all beasts of the bed that creep and crawl. Scratching but aggravated the evil. My friend suffered as much but stood it more philosophically, being more experienced, while I took a savage delight in throwing what I caught over on the young man of the family in the corner. Only towards morning did I obtain a little sleep. We left as early as possible, each giving two lire. They seemed disappointed, but we thought that this more than paid for our rest. We found our way to Albano without difficulty, and the remainder of the morning we employed in sleep and in the chase with encouraging results.

In the evening we went through Ariccia and Genzano to the Nemi Lake, I having been baulked earlier the same day by rain. On the way we had from a viaduct of three superimposed arcades a fine view of the Ariccian Valley, well under cultivation,—it also the flat crater of an old volcano. At Ariccia, by the way, Horace tells us he once spent the night. The women and children of these two small towns with dark skin and black hair well sustained their reputation for beauty. Lake Nemi was small, but three hundred feet deep, its banks as high again, and worthy the ancient name " Diana's Mirror."

Perfectly unruffled, "calm as cherished hate," it reflects marvellously both shore and sky.

Monday we just missed the train from the baggage and ticket men's not being in their places, and had to spend another day at Albano. After dinner I ascended Monte Cavo, the ancient Mons Albanus, going the inland road zigzag up the mountain side. Part of the way I walked the ancient Via Triumphalis, of irregular basalt polygons and five paces wide, with a raised stone edge in which at regular intervals some stones were higher than others. The Roman generals to whom the Senate refused a triumph celebrated one here for themselves, going up this steep road to the Latin temple of Jupiter Latiaris. A plain monastery of Passionist Fathers, founded by Cardinal York, the last of the Stuarts, is now at the top, and its round garden wall contains some stones of the ancient temple foundations. The temple must have been very large. Of the many fragments of columns some are marble, some stone. I walked into the enclosure, knocked at the door, and asked the good-humored looking monk for water. He led me to a room and brought both claret and water. Upon my producing a couple of hard boiled eggs, pepper, salt and bread, he smilingly added roast chestnuts. My tramp had made me so thirsty that I came near drinking the whole flagon of wine, served in the usual round water flasks. On the walls of this room I saw several pictures of the Passionist Church at Hoboken, N. J., and the passage way was hung with scriptural and legendary pictures. As suggested by the guide-book I put in the chapel box fifty centessimi to make up for the entertainment.

The view from without was beautiful and showed the neighboring places as in a panorama, for Monte Cavo is over three thousand feet above the sea level, the tallest of the hills surrounding the inner crater of a dead volcano. This inner crater is called Campo di Annibale, the supposed site of Hannibal's camp, and is broken at the rock of Rocca di Papa, while the ridge about the outer crater is interrupted by lakes Albano and Nemi. On this outer ridge to the other side lies Tusculum, and just beyond it, and invisible, Frascati. Several ranges were seen further to the south fading off into sharp peaks beautifully blue, and to the north on a line with the longer axis of the Alban Lake lay Rome,—large, white but indistinct. The Tiber was visible at its bends, at this distance silvery in appearance, and the mountains beyond faded into haze. Rome was but a dot in the vast, uncultivated Campagna.

Naturally my descent was rapid and disregarded roads. I returned *via* Palazzuola on the Alban Lake, just under the long white hewn cliffs of unrecognizable Alba Longa, the chief of the Latin towns before Rome's supremacy. Having yet time before dark,—I had left the hotel at two, got to the convent at four, left at five, and it was now six and a half,—I went from Albano for a walk along the modernized Appian Way. I soon passed the so-called tomb of Pompey,—four superimposed and lessening stories of brick with marble beams projecting. Pompey's villa was somewhere in the present Albano. Not far from the tomb I found the exit of the *emissarius* for the high water of the lake. The stream is but a small rivulet, feeding wash troughs. This work dates back at least to the siege of Veii by the Romans, B.C. 397, when this rock tunnel—seven feet high and thirty-six hundred feet long—was hewn to prevent a disastrous overflow.

Albano is south of Rome, and four hours to the northeast of Rome is Terni, celebrated for the falls of the Velino. The channels precipitating the river over the cliff were cut by the Romans less for beauty than to prevent it from overflowing the country on the plateau, having therefore somewhat the same object as the *emissarius* of the Alban Lake. I was once in Terni overnight, and a preliminary walk revealed the most tumble-down town I ever saw. The open stairways to the second floor are often in front on the street, for there is no sidewalk, and as usual there were many children about, some quite pretty.

After passing a night at Terni, uncomfortable because of fleas, I went out by the new road along the banks of the Nera to see the falls. The road was excellent, as most are in Italy, the river rushing by its side in a very picturesque manner, shallow and all broken by rocks. The falls were beautiful but not grand enough to deserve Byron's appellation of "a hell of waters." They are precipitated from a plateau into a pleasant valley, which extends in either direction. The central fall, with its tremendous main leap of three hundred feet, is between two smaller ones, of which the one to the left, however, is insignificant. I climbed a high hill on the opposite side of the valley by clinging to the young oak growth on its steep sides, and thence discovered that the plateau where the water came from was very flat, and I determined to get the view from above also. It was hot work at noon in April, but further down the road I found a bridge and was kindly shown by a farmer the path running zigzag up. He surprised me by refusing to accept a fee,—an unprecedented occurrence. Perhaps I offered too little. After a long detour on the plateau, the road passed over Velino on a bridge built upon a lower Roman one with inscription, and at last from a house on a spur projecting in front of the cataracts I got an excellent view of them, as they fell into spray resembling heavy white smoke. A yet better view was obtained from the keeper's garden, and I then returned to Terni by the old road along the high mountain edge. Below me the streams joined and ran towards the town, on the other side was the new road, so far below that the little donkeys on it appeared no larger than ants, and on every hand were beautiful mountain and valley views that must be finer yet later in the spring when the trees are green.

In all directions from Rome are ruins of towns or roads, and months could be delightfully spent in excursions. Rome itself, however, generally absorbs the attention of travellers, and its interesting and beautiful environs are too little known. Much as I regretted it, Terni, the Alban region, and the Appian Way were all I could visit, and my time in Rome itself drew to a close all too soon.

CHAPTER XVI.

THE RIVIERA ROUTE TO PARIS.

ROME was as far south as we dared to go in hot September and so I gave up the plan of re-visiting Naples and Pompeii. Early on the morning of Monday, September 7th, we turned our faces towards the north and from then on gradually worked our way homeward, the immediate goal being Paris, to be reached by easy stages, which with stops consumed five days. Time permitted hardly more than a week's stay even at Rome, Paris and London, and somewhat less at smaller places, so that we were often *en route* and found that we could not well endure more than six or seven hours at a time of cramped confinement in the European compartment cars.

The railroad from Rome first skirts the south side of the ancient city, passing over the Appian Way by a span and giving us farewell views of the nearer mountains. In the Campagna we noticed canals for its better drainage. Anciently Rome was surrounded by a well settled country, in which were some of the thirty cities of Latium, but with the decay of small farms from the later times of the republic and the growth of great ownerships and pasturages less care was exercised, and malaria, no longer counteracted by the industry of man, has assumed full sway in this low country. Hardly one tenth of the land is now under cultivation.

In a short while the beautiful blue of the Mediterranean came in view and for four days was almost constantly on our left. Here on the Maremme shore there was often a sandy beach, and, even where there were rocks, they were not precipices as we found them further north. The views were restful and pleasant rather than striking. The one of most interest to me was distant Elba, the island given to Napoleon as a little empire after his abdication, and intended really as an honorable prison, from which, however, he escaped to fight Waterloo.

Our train avoided Leghorn and we were therefore called on to disembark at Pisa rather unexpectedly. The town is solidly built, but is not impressive and looks dead. We never would have dreamed from its present appearance that it was during the early Crusades an important seat of maritime commerce, rivalling Venice and Genoa. For many years it ably and desperately resisted the arms of Florence, to whom, however, it became finally subject in 1509.

Our hotel Nettuno on the Arno was good and reasonable, and after rest and dinner we sauntered through narrow and deserted streets, now cooler than at our arrival, to the square at the north-west corner of the town, which contains the four great monuments,—the Duomo, Campanile, Baptistery and Campo Santo.

The Cathedral looks dingy and needs scrubbing off, as we saw them doing to the cathedral at Florence, to St. Mark's and to St. Peter's, but it is handsome withal. It has nave, double side aisles, transepts, an oval dome over the intersection, and towards the Campanile is a round apse. Externally it is, like the adjacent Baptistery and Campo Santo, of white and black marble, and, while a spire or higher dome would improve the building, the façade of five tiers of semicircular arches is singular and imposing. In the front is buried its architect Busketus. Within the church the effect of the black and white marble is beautiful. The triforium, or walk around the nave at the height of the side aisles, crosses over the transepts under the dome to the choir apse. The multitude of semicircular arches gives the place a Romanesque appearance, aided too by the flat lacunar ceiling and the classic pillars, fruits of Pisan victories in Italy and in Greece. The cathedral was begun in 1063 to commemorate the great victory at Palermo over the Saracen fleet. In the nave still hangs from the ceiling by a long rod the swaying lamp that suggested to Galileo the theory of the pendulum. It is of open iron-work with cupids or cherubs on it, and hung so low that I could reach it on tiptoe.

Opposite the cathedral façade is the round and domed Baptistery, itself ornate and containing a fine font and pulpit. We heard the remarkable echo there in all its beauty. The custodian uttered four successive notes and the conical vault took them up and repeated them for some time with flute-like variations.

The Campo Santo or cemetery seen from the square is a low building approached by doors in its solid walls. Within, it is a marble colonnade surrounding an open court, dating back to the twelfth century, and the open mullioned arches facing the court are distinctly Gothic. It is a covered cemetery, the soil coming from Mount

Calvary. Quaint mediæval paintings are on the wall, and monuments and tombs, many handsome indeed, along the sides. At one end are hung the great rusty chains which were unsuccessfully used to bar up the Pisan harbor. They were captured by the enemy, long suspended before the Baptistery in Florence, and only lately have been returned by the Florentines.

Behind the cathedral is the white marble Campanile or leaning belfry one hundred and seventy-nine feet high, in eight stories of arcades. The steps ascend spirally around a central well, and in the arches of the open summit chamber are a number of bells that do their duty vigorously even yet. Rachel was too tired to ascend, but I did and dropped a piece of pottery and a piece of iron from the edge at the top and on my descent found them out twenty feet from the base. Wind may have somewhat influenced them, as the tower is said to be thirteen feet out of the perpendicular. This leaning is probably intentional, as it is not uniform. There is less of it at or near the ground. The structure is so solid that I did not experience the common feeling that it is going over. Except at the top there is no rail, and I was a little apprehensive on that account that *I* might go over, but my confidence was perfect that the mediæval building would not.

The next day we made Genoa by rail. On the beach not far west of Pisa, but invisible from the train, was where poor Shelley's body was found cast up by the sea. When we reached the coast it was only to go through tunnel after tunnel, each long and noisy, with flashing views of a wild rocky coast and angry waves dashing on it into foam. The Mediterranean here near the shore was green, not blue as further south. We had unpleasant company for a while. Three or four rough country people, with more odor than manners, sat facing us in the narrow compartment, and their big feet left no safe place on the floor for ours. My Italian was poor and even the language of scowls seemed lost on them. The trip was thus not a very pleasant one, and only relieved by our discovering in Baedeker's list for Genoa the "*Hotel Smith.*" The name was almost like home again and we selected that hostlery without hesitation.

In front of the station at Genoa is a large monument with statue and allegorical figures and on it the inscription, "His Country to Columbus." He was not born here, however, but probably at Cogoleto, a few stations further on towards Nice. The American consul told us that even this is doubtful and that very little at all can be found out about the great discoverer except that his birth was probably 1436. Columbus led a seafaring life and as he says there was no place where ships sail that he had not been. After his study convinced him that the Indies could be reached by sailing to the west, he patriotically sought first to induce the Genoese government to make the expedition, but they declined. The king of Portugal declined also, and even Ferdinand and Isabella, busy with expulsion of the Moors, refused more than once before they finally patronized the pious and persevering mariner and reaped the fruit in the great discovery of October 12, 1492.

Mr. Smith of the hotel turned out to be a pleasant Englishman who discovered that I was not one by my asking for an "elevator" instead of a "lift." But his comfortable house, entered from an alley and immediately facing the gulf, had not this convenience, which we had heretofore found rather common in Italy. Here for the first time in many days we enjoyed the luxuries of hot water for bathing, milk toast to eat, The Times and Standard of London to read, and also a high double bed. Continental beds are all single, although often they put two of them in one room.

Genoa rises beautifully in a series of terraces from the curved harbor which it half surrounds, and is the busiest city we saw in Italy. Its commerce is much greater now than that of its ancient rival, Venice. The masts on the water before us and the many lights of the shipping at night proclaimed that we had reached again a stirring commercial centre. Within the past quarter century the harbor has been improved by the government and by private munificence until now Genoa is the largest port in the kingdom.

Genoa early conquered from Pisa supremacy over the western Mediterranean. She had eastern settlements, too, and for a long time contended on equal terms with Venice herself, but from the War of Chioggia she yielded the palm, and the growth of the Turkish dominion reduced her power, too, as it did her rival's. Her government was never so firm as the Venetian, and the terrible civil contests of noble families, in which they opened the gates to foreign princes in order to wreak vengeance on each other, prevented Genoa from becoming a great Italian power, even before the famous invasion of Charles VIII. in 1494 introduced other than native arms and tendencies into Italian history. The noble palaces remain, but thus seem often monuments of family pride and unpatriotic struggles.

Much of the next day we spent on the road to Nice, crossing the French frontier between Ventimiglia and the beautiful coast resort Mentone. The whole Riviera from Genoa to Nice has somewhat the same attractive character. The railroad when not one continuous tunnel, runs in sight of the water, often on its edge. On the one side is the blue sea beating on the bare rocks or coming up peacefully to wharves of towns, and on the other are the ever shifting mountains and valleys of the Maritime Alps, their sunny slopes covered with vines, fig, orange and lemon trees and the less familiar knarled and stumpy olives, or dotted with handsome villas surrounded by palms, tropical shrubbery and flowers. This coast is much frequented for its mild winters, but in summer too it looks enchanting and is resorted to for bathing.

Near Nice, under the protectorate of France, is the little principality of Monaco, containing five and three quarter square miles, belonging to the independent Grimaldi princes. Its most famous spot is the luxurious gambling Casino at Monte Carlo, perched with towers and beautiful grounds on a hill above the railroad cut. It has half a million visitors a year, but the season extends from December to April and was over when we passed.

About ten miles further is Nice, the birthplace of Masséna and Garibaldi, once Phocæan, then Roman, Provençal, Italian, and since 1860 French. Near the station is an avenue of eucalypti, and the Avenue de la Gare, on which was our pleasant Hotel National, is a handsome boulevard, its sidewalks in front of the restaurants thronged at night in true French fashion. At the foot of this street we found (in Baedeker) the river Paillon, crossed by elaborate bridges and bordered by handsome parks, but in fact it was totally destitute of water, although in winter it is no doubt different.

Shade trees and gardens enabled us to enjoy the sea views with pleasure and our short stay here was very agreeable.

We had been travelling heretofore with two satchels. I was anxious to lessen my load and forward one of these to Paris, as we had to other places, after filling it with clothing that would not be needed on the way. But freight they told me was unsafe and express I found would cost me nearly five dollars, so I preferred to handle them myself and spend the few cents necessary for the efficient porters who throng every station. These are not supposed to charge but always expect a sou or two. In Nice at the Credit Lyonnais we drew some French money on our letter of credit. At this bank they were rather gruff at best. After they had paid us the officials seemed in much trepidation, re-examined my signature, and held a council of war over the fact that I had put a curved flourish under my name instead of a straight one which was on the letter itself. However, after critically eying my travel-stained gray suit and slouch hat and Rachel's face, they ungraciously let me keep the money. If there had been time before the train to go to another correspondent of Brown Brothers, I should myself have returned the money and calmed their fears.

The trip from Nice to Marseilles presented somewhat the same mountain scenery, although rougher and barer because further inland. The only interesting sight was Toulon, surrounded by lofty mountains crowned by forts, where in 1793 young Bonaparte earned his first laurels by gaining a height that commanded the highest English fort and thus compelling an evacuation. The place is now the principal Mediterranean naval port of France and as we passed a war fleet lay there at anchor. Near Fréjus further on the same man landed in 1815 on his escape from Elba, to play the last act of his eventful life and begin by a triumphal progress to Paris those famous hundred days which terminated so disastrously at Waterloo.

Marseilles is a great and busy city, steep like Genoa, and like Genoa also with harbor and shipping coming up into the town, but unlike it in having wide and handsome modern streets in all directions. That night by the electric light they were erecting a new building near our hotel in the fine Rue Cannebière, and a neighboring storekeeper, quite Yankee-like, took advantage of the watching crowd to exhibit by stereopticon attractive pictures and advertisements. Streets, after the Parisian style, changed their names every few blocks. In London this may have an historical origin in the gradual growth of the city until two streets, originally distinct, connect and become one, but in France they do this malice prepense, when they re-construct a place. It has the advantage of helping to identify localities. No. 1000 Broadway is very indefinite until New York establishes a uniform number of houses to a block. But if a place is known to be in Cheapside or on Rue Royale you can tell its general location even without any number.

The next morning early we took a carriage from our comfortable Hotel de Genève near the handsome Bourse and were soon on the accommodation train for Lyons. The railroad skirts the sea for a while, but follows the river Rhone from ancient Arles, of interesting history as capital once of a kingdom, and some of whose well preserved Roman ruins are visible from the train, and we had then pleasant views all the way up to Lyons. The accommodating nature of the train was illustrated in its stopping for an hour at white walled Avignon, which period we consumed in a drive about that ancient town.

At Avignon lived and died the Laura whom Petrarch loved and celebrated although she was married to another man and mother of a large family. Her grave at the church of the Cordeliers disappeared in the ravages of the French Revolution. Up to that event Avignon was papal property. After the long contest between Pope Boniface VIII. and Philip le Bel, king of France, the seat of papal government was moved in 1309 from turbulent Rome to more peaceful Avignon, where it remained for seventy years under French influence, and Clement VI. erected a great palace there. In its halls Petrarch was an honored guest at the time when in its dungeons lay imprisoned the man he had celebrated in verse, the great but erratic Rienzi, in the interval between the Tribune's first and second times of power. During the Great Schism, which was finally healed by the Council of Constance, French anti-popes resided in this palace after the legitimate pontiffs had gone back to Rome. We drove there and saw the tall white building, now a French barrack but with traces yet of its old grandeur. It is on a hill, and, in the shady street by which we approached, the scaffolding was not yet removed from a colossal monument to the Republic. An historic contrast! John Stuart Mill is buried at Avignon and the painters Vernet were natives of this place.

We had not been able to stop at Nîmes to see its Roman remains, nor did we see those of Orange except the triumphal arch visible from the train. Roman civilization was all powerful in Southern Gaul. Roman

THE PALACE OF THE POPES AT AVIGNON.

temples, statues, and arches are often found and the names of many towns show their Latin origin. The troubadour softness is still observed in the native speech, and history no less than poetry invests this country with peculiar charm. Orange is especially interesting to English speaking races as the place which gave its name to the Dutch princes of Orange, one of the greatest of whom became William III. of England. It had been an appanage of the house of Nassau for almost two centuries, but on the death of this William it was annexed to France by his great enemy, Louis XIV. Nearer Lyons is Valence, part of a principality once given to infamous Cæsar Borgia, and then came Vienne, with Roman ruins, one of which is popularly known as Pilate's tomb. This irresolute Roman procurator is said to have been finally banished to Vienne and to have died there, although Lucerne's mountains also claim the doubtful honor of being his last residence. In the time of barbarian invasion and earthquake in the fifth century the litany and its prayer, "Good Lord deliver us," is said to have originated at Vienne.

Lyons was found a bustling and handsome city, second only to Paris in size and greater than any other place in France as a manufacturing centre, particularly of silk. In the Hôtel des Négociants we discovered that we had patronized a Drummer's Hotel, where every one ate as hurriedly as at a railway restaurant in America and ladies were not at all expected. Even the chambermaids are men. The public places of Lyons are interesting. In the Place des Terreaux not far off the revolutionary guillotine held high carnival where earlier Richelieu had had his rival Cinq Mars executed, and in the enormous Place Bellecour on the way back to the Station next day we saw an imposing equestrian statue of Louis XIV.

Paris was now our goal, and the trip there from Marseilles consumed nine hours in a fast train which stopped but twice and even then but for a few minutes. There was such a scramble for seats on this limited express that but for a porter whom I had feed we would have fared badly. As it was, we lost our lunch, and, as there was no stop for dinner, I was glad enough at one halt to pay two francs for a cold half chicken. I do not believe that even the disagreeable French woman next us picked bones better than we did in our famished condition. She had tried to occupy three seats, and, when the bundles were discovered to be hers and had to give place to travellers, she piled them on the floor in every one's way. I removed them from in front of us, and she then tried to annoy us as much as elbows and general meanness would allow. When I ran to buy the chicken she put a satchel in my seat, and Rachel as promptly put it back on the floor. Her conduct disgusted even a benevolent priest who was in the compartment telling beads and taking snuff. If there is anything, however, I can succeed at with earnest effort it is being disagreeable, and I think that by the time she adjusted her hair and bonnet to get out at Paris she felt that we were at least as great nuisances as herself.

The road near the city went through the Forest of Fontainebleau, but does not pass in sight of the château, famous for associations connected with Henry IV. and Napoleon. At Paris we left the train at the Gare de Midi, and it was a long and interesting drive, especially to Rachel, before we reached the little Hôtel de la Concorde in the Rue Richepanse. We had found this hotel advertised in the Paris edition of the New York Herald bought on the train, and there, after much negotiation and showing of apartments, we were given a handsomely fitted front room on the second floor, to cost with early coffee, noon déjeuner and evening dinner fifty francs per week apiece.

CHAPTER XVII.

PARIS, ITS HISTORIC MONUMENTS AND ENVIRONS.

NO city equals Paris in appearance, and only Jerusalem and Rome surpass it in historical interest.

The north of Gaul became the country of the west branch of the German Franks, the capital under the Carolingians being Aachen. The East Franks lived about the Rhine in what was afterwards called Franconia, of which Frankfort survives. The noble defence of Paris by its Count Robert against the Normans in 885 marked out that city and that family as possessing great qualities, and his descendant Hugh Capet in 987 became king and ancestor of a race of sovereigns who reigned almost until our own day.

Paris was at first confined to the island in the Seine, which here runs from east to west with a great bend northwardly. On this island a palace was built by Hugh Capet and the church of Notre Dame erected during a later reign, but its bridges gradually made the suburbs on the mainland essential parts of the town. To the north of this island is the present heart of the city, clustered about the palace of the Louvre and its continuation to the west, the Tuileries and Champs Elysées.

To the south of the island is the Latin quarter, where the college of the Sorbonne dates from 1250 in St. Louis' time. The Louvre was begun under Francis I., who much improved the whole city, and the later Tuileries are about coeval with the massacre of St. Bartholemew in 1572. Henry IV. built a new stone bridge, Pont Neuf, from the north to the old city, Richelieu erected the present Palais Royal in the next reign, and Louis XIV. established the first boulevards, so named from the "bulwarks" whose sites they took, and erected many of the prominent structures of the city. Under Napoleon Paris was much improved by new streets, buildings, arches and in other ways, Louis Philippe also did much, while under Napoleon III. the Bois de Boulogne was opened, the city all but rebuilt, and numerous boulevards and fine buildings everywhere made Paris accessible and handsome. The German bombardment of 1871 did not greatly injure the city, but the Communists destroyed the Tuileries, threw down the Column Vendôme, burned the Hôtel de Ville, and but for the early capture by the national government would have wrecked all the great monuments. The present republic has repaired the marks of these outrages and been able even further to beautify Paris. The place has grown steadily and now covers thirty square miles and has a population of two and a half millions,—five times what it was under Louis XIV.

The first wall was erected by Philip Augustus in the twelfth century, but after Louis XIV. constructed the "Great Boulevards" on the site of the old fortifications, there was no substantial enclosure. That of Louis XVI. was only for customs purposes, Napoleon never thought of the possibility of a capture of Paris before it happened, and it was left for Napoleon III. in 1860 thoroughly to fortify it. The Germans found the place impregnable and had to bombard and starve it into submission. Balloons and carrier pigeons got out, but few got in. The Germans were impregnable in their turn and conquered all armies of relief and repelled a number of desperate sorties from Paris itself, the siege ending January 23, 1871, after having lasted four months. The Communists failed to hold the fortifications afterwards against the national troops, who stormed them and in May fought their way through the streets over formidable barricades. This second siege was almost two months in duration.

Paris is France. A successful revolution at the capital is always acquiesced in by the rest of France. The city has been but seldom in the hands of an enemy, but whenever it has this meant the submission of France. In the time of Joan of Arc the English held Paris while the maid and king still fought and successfully at Orleans, but then France was not so consolidated as during the last few centuries. We ordinarily think of Prussia as growing at the expense of other German states and criticise its methods. But the mark of Brandenburg has acted only on the example of the earlier county of Paris, which was also a "march," or frontier principality, to protect the country behind it against the Northmen. The Parisian count became a duke, in 987 a king, and his descendants have gradually acquired by intermarriage, force or fraud, Anjou, Bretagne, Normandy, Flanders, Aquitaine, Toulouse, Provence, Arles and other states which had also grown up within the limits of Gaul, many as old and some more cultured than energetic Paris. The name of France did not rightfully belong to the Parisian country. The Carolingian kingdom, whose capital was Laon, contained the true West Franks and the name France was adopted when the Parisian dukes succeeded to the royal dignity, because the Parisian dukes were Franks, although their people were not to any great extent. These aggressive kings have also acquired parts of the Empire from time to time. Essentially France has been made by Paris. It is thoroughly loyal to Paris, too, and reverences it. Indeed, too much. The new republic did well to fix its seat at Versailles and it should have de-centralized the country by giving greater autonomy to the departments, which have since the Great Revolution been made up out of the old provinces and have superseded them. But the pressure was too great and the seat of government in 1879 went back to Paris.

A little over a block south from our hotel was the Place de la Concorde, its obelisk on the site of the revolutionary guillotine. Here died Louis XVI., Marie Antoinette, Mme. Roland, Charlotte Corday, Danton, Robespierre and nearly three thousand others. There are handsome fountains off to the sides, and it was proposed to erect a great fountain in the centre, but Chateaubriand wisely said that no water could wash away the blood stains of the place. In the reign of Louis Philippe the viceroy of Egypt presented the obelisk of Luxor, erected in Thebes by Sesostris. It took years to move and re-erect the monolith, which is seventy-six feet high. On the Place the allies camped in 1814 and 1815 and here Prussian troops too in 1871, and it was later the scene of a battle with the Communists.

From here extend to the west for miles the Champs Elysées, a much frequented park, narrowing to a favorite boulevard. Not far off on the right is the secluded Palais Elysée, where resides the president of the republic, as did Louis Napoleon when president, but originally it was the residence and property of Mme. de Pompadour, mistress of Louis XV. The vista west from the obelisk seems to end at the magnificent Arc de Triomphe of Napoleon, 160 feet high and almost as long, adorned with splendid sculptures, but from that eminence the avenue descends under other names between the Bois de Boulogne and Neuilly until it crosses a bend of the Seine and becomes the route to Josephine's Malmaison. Near by at Reuil she and her daughter Queen Hortense are buried. Indeed the same highway crosses two other bends of the Seine and reaches St. Germain, famous for its beautiful park and the château where Louis XIV. was born and the exiled James II. of England lived.

Across the Seine from the president's mansion, but a long way from it, is the Esplanade in front of the Hôtel des Invalides, whose large gilded dome is visible far and near. The building was erected by Louis XIV. for disabled soldiers, but most of them now-a-days prefer to live in their own homes on pensions. In its court on the approach of the allies in 1814 were burnt many captured flags and the sword of Frederick the Great which Napoleon had removed from the tomb at Potsdam. The veterans and the museum of war costumes and arms attract less attention, however, than the magnificent tomb of Napoleon in the Invalides church. Immediately beyond the entrance hall is the great dome and in the floor beneath is an open circular crypt, surrounded by a marble balustrade. Over this gaze at all times many visitors, who instinctively talk in whispers. The crypt is twenty feet deep and thirty-six feet wide, and around its sides keep guard twelve Victories by Pradier, while reliefs between tell of Napoleon's works of peace. From a mosaic pavement containing the names of his greatest victories rises the monolith sarcophagus of red granite, in which Louis Philippe in 1840 placed the remains of Napoleon, by agreement with England brought from St. Helena in accordance with the wish in the emperor's will that they should "repose on the banks of the Seine among the French people whom he loved so well." In the chapels in the corners of the building lie his brothers Joseph and Jerome, whom he made kings of Spain and Westphalia and who lost their crowns when he did. Napoleon's ambition aimed at a modern French empire that would represent the ancient Roman one as it existed under Charlemagne, and he had the same divine right of genius to found an empire, but the dream took no account of the intermediate growth of nationalities, and its success even under a Napoleon could be but temporary.

Can any one standing by the great tomb fail to think of the humbler one not many miles away of the devoted, deserted Josephine, divorced to secure an heir? And the heir, poor boy, never reigned, while her grandson was emperor as Napoleon III. But he too died in exile and is entombed at English Chiselhurst, and alongside him there lies his promising and unfortunate son, the Prince Imperial, killed by a Zulu while fighting under the English flag to fit himself to be French emperor. And his mother, the Spanish beauty and French leader of the world of fashion and gaiety, is now a desolate and aged woman, a modern Niobe. She lately re-visited Paris. What must have been her thoughts!

Near the back of the Invalides is the Military School, fronting northwest on the Champs de Mars, the site of the Expositions. The Champs de Mars faces the Seine and there near the river is the Eiffel Tower, 984 feet high, of open ironwork. The four immense uprights of this colossus rest on deep foundations and unite under the first platform over one hundred feet from the ground to form triumphal arches. The uprights continue above this but gradually become one at the second gallery. The tower at the top is visible from all open places in Paris. The Champs de Mars was on July 14, 1790, the scene of the Fête de la Fédération, when king and people before an altar swore to the new constitution, which it was hoped would prove a panacea. Talleyrand as bishop of Autun officiated. In about eighteen months the king was beheaded at the Place de la Concorde, a short distance off across the Seine, the Reign of Terror held down the people, and Talleyrand had been disrobed and was learning as the necessary means of preserving existence that suave dissimulation which enabled him to serve in high office republic, emperor and king with equal facility.

Returning from this visit to the Invalides and Champs de Mars towards the Place de la Concorde, chosen by us as the central point of modern Paris, we passed on the way, immediately opposite the Place, the Chamber of Deputies with its imposing front. Here two days after Sedan the crowds burst in and dissolved the Assembly, whose republican members, Gambetta among them, then met elsewhere and formed a new government. From the Place de la Concorde as we turn to face the Tuileries, on the left comes in the Rue Royale, extending but a short distance until it is cut off by the Madeleine with its high basement and Corinthian columns. This was designed by Napoleon as a Temple of Glory, but has since been finished as a church.

Going eastwardly from the obelisk along the Seine we passed through the plain Jardin des Tuileries. To our left was the site of the Manège where sat the great revolutionary conventions, and northwardly up the Rue Castiglione three blocks away is the Place Vendôme with Napoleon's column, imitating Trajan's. It is 142 feet high and its bronze reliefs of the Austerlitz campaign were cast from Russian and Austrian cannon. The Communists pulled down the column, but it was soon restored. Even Napoleon's statue is there again, taking the place of the tricolor of 1880, but he does not look safe on his thin legs.

Continuing on we came to a beautiful garden, for the blackened ruins of the Tuileries, wrecked by the Communists and standing at my visit in 1880 were gone. Here died the Swiss guard when Louis XVI. and family fled in 1792 to the Assembly in the Manège; here Napoleon lived, and so too all monarchs subsequently until the Empress Eugénie left it after Sedan. The Communists devoted this historic pile among many others to destruction and their work was here complete. The long wings connecting it with the Louvre so far as injured have been restored, but nothing could be done to this old palace of Catherine de' Medici, and the ruins have been pulled down. It leaves a great blank, as the quadrangle has now no front, and some large building or monument should be erected on the site.

The court of the Tuileries extends eastwardly between the great mansarded wings for almost half a mile to the Louvre. Within the Tuileries, but dwarfed by them, stands the triumphal Arc du Carrousel, Napoleon's smaller reproduction of the arch of Severus at Rome, intended to commemorate by reliefs the campaign of

Austerlitz. On it for a number of years were St. Mark's bronze horses from Venice, returned after Napoleon's fall at the instigation of the Austrians—who had appropriated Venice itself. The court, through which runs a busy thoroughfare to the Seine bridge outside, has been enormously enlarged under Napoleon III. by destroying the many houses intervening between the arch and the Louvre. Further east, where the court is narrowed by the double wings of Napoleon III. (themselves each with smaller interior courts), is a monument and statue of Gambetta, who in the dark days of 1871 never despaired of the State. The monument is a stone pyramid, in front of which stands in bronze the Dictator, making one of his impassioned speeches, while all around are carved striking passages from his writings.

To the right as we enter the square court of the Louvre from that of the Tuileries is the site of the original Louvre château of Francis I., but it was built over by Louis XIV. to make part of a larger and grander structure. The main face of the Louvre palace is to the east and there a noble elevated colonnade faces the open street and terminates this long connected series of public places and buildings lying between the Rue de Rivoli or its continuations on the north and the quais of the Seine on the south.

But interesting buildings do not cease here. Further to the east across the street from the Louvre is the small church of St. Germain de l'Auxerrois whose bell tolled in 1572 the massacre of St. Bartholomew on a signal from King Charles IX. In that massacre, which was not confined to Paris, at least twenty-five thousand Protestants perished, and the weak, irresolute Charles himself died some months later of remorse. To the north of the Louvre across the Rue de Rivoli are the immense Magasins du Louvre, stores which I believe interested Rachel more than the palace, and continuing eastwardly up the Rue de Rivoli or along the quai of the Seine we came in a few blocks to the Hôtel de Ville, the municipal buildings, occupying a whole square, a magnificent new erection of the French renaissance style, built on the site of the old town hall. That had been the gradual growth of nearly five centuries and around it clung memories which ought to have been sacred even to Communists, for here after the fall of the Bastille Louis XVI. assumed the tricolor cockade, made by Lafayette out of the red and blue city colors and the Bourbon white. Here Robespierre shot himself. Here in 1830 Louis Philippe embraced Lafayette, and here from the old steps on the fall of that king was proclaimed the republic of 1848. Here after Sedan Gambetta organized the national defence which lasted through the siege, although he himself escaped in a balloon to become dictator at Tours. In this old Hôtel were the Communist headquarters and at this point their main resistance. When they failed they fired the building and either perished in the flames or were shot down without mercy by the government troops as they attempted to escape. Criminals had died here before. The place to the west was anciently called the Place de Grève and was the site of executions. Ravaillac, Damiens and Cartouche died there and to its lampposts the mob hung the royalist financiers, the first victims of the great Revolution.

The event of greatest interest in that struggle was the fall of the Bastille. This oblong, gloomy fortress towered further east at a place to which leads now the Rue St.

Antoine, a continuation of the Rue de Rivoli, and the spot is marked by a bronze column, erected in 1840. The fortress or Bastille St. Antoine dates back to the fourteenth century and was originally used for state prisoners, such as the unknown Iron Mask of the time of Louis XIV. Its walls were ten feet thick and very high, with eight towers, and its cannon commanded the east entrance of the city and the restless artisan faubourg St. Antoine. On July 14, 1789, it had a garrison of little more than one hundred, many of these old veterans unable to fight, and when the mob attacked resistance was useless. Commandant De Launay surrendered at last, but he and his officers were murdered on the spot.

In the Seine are two islands, the larger of which extending from opposite the Hôtel de Ville to near the Louvre, is the site of the original town, and is still called Île de la Cité. Count Robert of Paris could walk over the island which he so valiantly defended and would not recognize it. The muddy Seine protected this, the original city, but the river now is far below the new level, and presents no views and forms no part of Parisian life. It is crossed by a number of fine bridges at this island, as well as others above and below. The west end is reached from the north bank by Henry IV's Pont Neuf, which crosses also the other arm of the river to the quarters south, and where this bridge touches the island stands an equestrian statue of Henry IV., the first and greatest of the Bourbons. The republic melted down the original statue into cannon, and on the Restoration Louis XVIII. spitefully re-cast the statue of Napoleon taken from the Column Vendôme and a statue of General Dessaix to re-make the monument of Henry IV. Going eastward the length of the island we found ex-

NOTRE DAME, FROM THE SEINE.

ten'ding all but clear across it the massive Palais de Justice, the handsome seat of the numerous higher courts, and occupying the site of the royal palace. The lower part adjoining the north branch of the Seine was the Conciergerie, a prison of the Revolution, in one of whose round towers Marie Antoinette as a prisoner became gray in a night, and the room next it was afterwards Robespierre's cell. In the central court of the Palais is a small but beautiful Gothic church sixty-six feet high with famous stained glass, the Sainte Chapelle, built by St. Louis as the palace chapel, its lower story the chapel for domestics. It has all but miraculously escaped destruction more than once when the palace around it burned, the last time being when that was destroyed by the Communists.

Further east are the Hôtel Dieu, a great hospital, and the Préfecture, the head of the system of ten thousand Parisian police, and then on the south side of the island comes Notre Dame, a handsome church, cut off on the north by high buildings but presenting a fine appearance from the south. It stood on a flight of steps, but the grade has been so much raised that the cathedral is now on the general level of the surrounding streets. Its two towers are still without spires, for, although the Gothic style originated in North France, her great metropolis has never finished this church. The main approaches in front are under the towers, and in the recessed doorways are quaint carvings, and high up in one series across the façade are the kings of France. This façade, divided into three horizontal sections and these again each into three vertical ones, dates from the thirteenth century, but the main church is in parts earlier. A marked feature of French Gothic, seen often in Paris, is the beautiful large round window. There is one in the main front of Notre Dame between the towers and one or more in the façade of each transept. Inside, the massive round pillars of the nave attest the age of the structure, and the beautiful stained glass of the main church, as well as of the high transepts, sheds around a dim religious light. In these solemn precincts Maillard, the ballet girl, was enthroned during the Revolution as the Goddess of Reason, and a great orgie was held in her honor, and here later Consul Bonaparte was crowned as Emperor Napoleon.

Behind the rear flying buttresses of the cathedral is a plain building of a very different character, the Morgue, where bodies of people found in the river are exhibited for identification. They lie naked there on the inclined marble slabs behind glass, several at a time, water pouring over them. It is a ghastly sight which cannot be forgotten and had better not be seen at all by those not of strong nerves and stomachs. There are some accidental drownings, but most are suicides, the desperate end of those ruined by pleasure, overburdened with trouble, or wild with remorse. The muddy Seine sees about eight hundred of these dramas a year.

Near the Luxembourg (where the Senate sits) south of the river is where the gallant Marshal Ney was shot for treason at the Restoration because, when sent against his old master on Napoleon's return from Elba, he yielded to his feelings. In sight of his place of execution rises the dome of the Pantheon, the resting place of distinguished Frenchmen, but not now a Christian church, although once sacred to St. Genevieve, the patron saint of Paris, who was buried here. In the vaults I saw the empty marble sarcophagus of Voltaire and a wooden one of Rousseau, whose bodies were spitefully removed to some unknown spot at the Restoration. Soufflot, Marceau, Lannes, La Grange, and Victor Hugo were also buried in the Pantheon.

Other great dead are in buildings, but there are many cemeteries also. The most interesting is Père la Chaise north of the Seine and near the east end of Paris. It is kept like a garden and is a beautiful and favorite resort. So far as art can do it death is here robbed of its terrors. Trees, flowers, lawns and sculptures border winding walks and drives over hill and dale, and great names at every step bring up past ages. I still recall some of the tombs. That of Abelard and Heloise was a Gothic canopy, Casimir Perier a statue, Thiers a chapel, St. Cyr a monument and statue, McDonald a tomb, Monod a column, so Scribe, Suchet an elaborate tomb, and Ney an uninscribed, flowery grave. To Racine was a chapel, Lafontaine and Molière were together, their sarcophagus above on pillars. Gay-Lussac had a slab with flowers, Balzac a fat bust on a column, Michelet a small tomb with open book, Cousin a large tomb, Arago a fine bust, and Musset another, bearded. Rossini was once there, but has been removed to Santa Croce. If the dead could speak, surely they would prefer the blue vault of heaven here to any other roof, with nature and art so harmoniously blended around them.

North of Paris, on a bend of the Seine, is St. Denis, where were interred the ancient kings whose remains were later, by decree of the Republic, thrown into a common pit, but restored by Louis XVIII. to the crypt. He also brought there from the Madeleine the bodies of Louis XVI. and Marie Antoinette, and is buried here himself. The cathedral is an example of the earliest

Gothic, built in the twelfth century by the abbot Suger, and its oriflamme was adopted as the royal standard, used when the king went to battle. Here Joan of Arc hung up her arms, Henry IV. became Catholic, and Napoleon married Marie Louise,—for even the suburbs of Paris are full of history.

South-west is Versailles, an inland city of fifty thousand people, built by Louis XIV. as a residence because from St. Germain he could see St. Denis and it reminded him too much of royal tombs. A worse site could not be selected and the many millions spent made after all only a flat palace, fronting on stiff and artificial grounds. At the rear, which is the approach from the town, the wings make a court, while in front the long monotonous façade looks down on an avenue in which the Tapis Vert of grass extends to the large Apollo and Steeds fountain. Beyond this is a large sheet of water in the shape of a cross, whose right arm reaches to the grounds of the châteaux known as the Trianons. The gardens are extensive and are laid off in geometrical figures, with trees trained to arch overhead or to make frames for distant views, and the pavement is but the natural earth. The fountains now play only on stated occasions, but are magnificent, especially when illuminated with colored lights.

The palace was richly gilded, mirrored and frescoed, but the finery is now tarnished. In Louis XIV's bedroom is still shown his ornate square bed behind a railing. Here he dressed in public, and here he died. In the Œil de Bœuf near by, a room with an oval window, the courtiers intrigued as they waited for the king to rise in the morning, and from a balcony in front of the bedroom the chamberlain announced his death by breaking his baton and crying, "Le Roi est mort!" and as he took up a new one he exclaimed, "Vive le roi!" The apartments of Marie Antoinette were small and upholstered in yellow, and in one corner behind a sofa mirrors meet at such an angle that in looking in them she would see herself headless. I tried it and it was startlingly realistic. Near in the magnificent Galerie des Glaces by a strange turn of fortune's wheel, Wilhelm I. was proclaimed German emperor on January 18, 1871. No French sovereign has resided in the palace since Louis XVI. was taken thence in 1791 by the mob of Parisian women, never to return, and Louis Philippe utilized it for a great collection of historical paintings, portraits and busts, brought from the Louvre and elsewhere. The many battle scenes represent only French victories, and Wilhelm must have looked over them rather grimly when as conqueror he took possession. The Prussians used the building as an hospital, Marshal MacMahon from it directed the recovery of Paris from the Commune, and the Assembly sat here from then until 1879. Off somewhat to one side in the Grand Trianon resided Mme. de Maintenon, legitimately married to Louis XIV., whom she greatly influenced, and in the Petit Trianon lived Mme. du Barry, mistress of Louis XV. after the death of Mme. de Pompadour. In the Grand Trianon in 1873 also Marshal Bazaine was tried and condemned for the surrender of Metz.

I once went from Versailles to the ruins of St. Cloud, burned by a shell during the siege of Paris, whether French or Prussian is disputed. The front was towards a hill which commands a fine view of Paris, a re-entrant court faced the Seine, and back of the château is an extensive park. Here Bonaparte dispersed the Council of Five Hundred and here he resided much as emperor, as did Napoleon III. after him. The building was thoroughly gutted when I saw it and the garden a wreck. The government has of late heartlessly auctioned off these black but historic ruins as so much rubbish. Through the great park I walked over to Sèvres near by and went through its interesting porcelain manufactory and beautiful collections, and returned to Paris by boat, but the river is so far below the city level that I could see nothing except the bridges and high stone embankments.

CHAPTER XVIII.

PARIS: THE LOUVRE AND THE STREETS.

LIFE in Paris is full of interest quite apart from the history that speaks to one on every side. The art collections are hardly equalled, the stores are attractive, the streets handsome, the wider ones with trees being called boulevards. The principal avenues are paved with noiseless asphalt or with wood, but side streets, like the Rue Richepanse on which was our hotel, are still of cobble stones. Stone is not favored by the authorities because on any uprising of the lower classes it makes too good a barricade.

Our hotel was very satisfactory. In the reading room were periodicals and French and English newspapers, there was a little parlor containing a piano of fair qualities, and the meals were beyond compare. Every morning at eight or any hour we pleased we had coffee with cold bread and butter, at noon came *déjeuner*, really a hot lunch in several courses, and at six was regular *table d'hôte*, which included soup or fish, two courses of meat, vegetables, pastry, fruit and coffee. We used to think that *gâteau* stood for cake, but we found that no word except *patisserie* would bring it. We had wine at lunch and also at dinner. Every one takes wine, even children, but it is diluted with water. We took ours with sugar and water, sangaree, to the disgust of our neighbors. Water seemed to be good, reports to the contrary notwithstanding. The sewer arrangements are not good, however, for the great sewers we hear of are mainly for surface drainage into the Seine. The sewage farms below the city at Gennevilliers, however, will probably finally solve the problem of sanitary sewerage.

We got along very well with our landlady until we asked questions as to shopping. Then suddenly persons she named to us as responsible began calling on us without solicitation, and, after we found out that these were dearer than others we went to and we would not patronize them, Madame became distant and for a while hardly treated us with civility.

As it was, money melted away in Paris faster than anywhere else. Rachel had saved up her shopping so as to avoid lugging much around. Some stores tried to pass off inferior articles, but we found good places. A great institution is the Magasin, where under one roof is everything in the clothing and house furnishing line. There are a half dozen or more of these establishments. We patronized three,—the Gagne Petit on the Avenue de l'Opera where was a clever interpreter who had lived in England, the Magasins du Louvre opposite that palace and largest of all, and the Bon Marché away south of the Seine and cheapest of the three. The Magasins answer somewhat to the Stores of London. Ladies' supplies we found best in Paris, men's in London. The French seem to affect English goods somewhat as we do in America, for there was much for sale. In the Magasins dummies stand around ready dressed, a visitor selects a dress thus shown, modistes take it from the lay and fit it to the human figure on the spot, and the next day the finished gown is delivered. The beautiful satin flowers and the gloves we found particularly cheap. We went all over the Palais Royal shops of jewelry and then found such things best and cheapest at Tiffany's. It required Rachel's French and my gesticulations to get along with the shop keepers. As we wrote home, we spoke all languages indifferently.

For sight-seeing the many connected omnibus routes afforded us fine facilities, except that on Sundays it was sometimes hard to get a seat. An inside cushioned place costs thirty centimes and the hard bench on the top half as much, but the view is so much better than from within that we always went above, despite the inconvenient little winding stair at the back. The Madeleine, hardly a square from our hotel, is a starting-place for several lines and one noisily passed our very doors, so that we were favorably situated. There are few street car lines and walking is almost out of the question for long distances.

A promenade, however, from the Madeleine down the great boulevard to the Opera and from the Opera down the Avenue de l'Opera towards the Louvre is a long walk, but the monotonously handsome buildings with mansard roofs, magnificent stores, crowds of people of every condition, the fast driving of all kinds of vehicles, and other street sights make this a fair sample of Paris, and here too are Tiffany's, the New York Herald reading room and other names familiar to Americans. It is almost at the risk of one's life sometimes that he ventures to cross the boulevard, even with the aid of the refuges provided in the streets, for the police offer no assistance and attempt no control over the furious driving. The boulevards all have trees along the sidewalks, kept up at great expense. At night chairs and tables in front of cafés are crowded until a late hour with people sipping ices or drinks. This custom prevails all over the city and indeed over France and is one of the characteristic after-dark features of French life.

The Opera—or Académie Nationale de Musique, as the inscription in front has it—is a magnificent Renaissance building of many colored marbles, erected on a terrace. It was begun by Napoleon III. and completed by the Republic. The front is a rather too uniform portico of two and a half stories, and the ends being entrance pavilions crowned with statuary, of which also there are groups between the piers below. The auditorium dome takes the shape of a crown surmounted by an Apollo group, while behind, highest of all, rises the square part containing the scenic arrangements. Within the portico is the beautiful foyer across the front, between the acts full of promenaders, and next in a great hall is the magnificent marble stairway to the upper floors, ornamented with sculptures and frescoes. The auditorium seats twenty-one hundred and fifty-six, less than several other theatres, but its appearance is unequalled. In the parquette only men seem to sit, but the boxes and shallow galleries in four tiers are patronized by both gentlemen and ladies.

During our visit in September the German opera Lohengrin was rendered amid great excitement. The French are still bitterly hostile to the Germans, and the Boulangists—for it was some days yet before their exiled leader so unexpectedly committed suicide—determined on a great demonstration against having this German piece given at the Opera, which is subsidized by the French government; although Lohengrin had already been rendered several times in France, at Rouen for example with great success. We were present at the second performance in Paris, and at times wished that we had not come. It was interesting but threatened to be a tragedy. We paid fifteen francs to the speculators for three-franc seats on the top floor and shortly after our arrival saw every seat occupied in the whole house except a few boxes. On our way through the dense crowd in the Place de l'Opera in front a policeman stopped us, but let us pass on my assuring him that we had tickets, and we entered and ascended to our places. The audience received the opera not only kindly but enthusiastically, applauding and bravoing every good part. At the end of the first act every one hurried to the foyer and the balconies in front to see the crowd outside. The scene in the streets was memorable. The open place in front was occupied by a large hollow square of gens d'armes and behind was a surging mass of men. Every few minutes the police would arrest two or three of them and march them off. In the house when before the second act the stage manager announced that the heavy villain of the opera had a bad cold and that the audience must bear with him, some man downstairs proposed that we sing the Marseillaise hymn so as to help out, and immediately the whole audience rose to their feet and went wild with bravos and hisses. The man was arrested and taken out, and no Marseillaise was sung. Up by us three or four men during this disturbance were particularly vociferous, and a handsome man in a dress suit suddenly arose and called out, "*Silence, silence, s'il vous plait,*" and jerking out a tricolor ribbon wrapped it around his waist. A dozen gens d'armes at his signal quietly slipped in and took permanent stand along the walls, and then the uproar ceased. Every now and then there was some noise, but evidently coming from a very small coterie. Our protector with the tricolor was very active. He spotted three men behind us and warned them, and shortly afterwards they took occasion in the middle of an act to get up and leave, making as much noise as they could, but Mr. Tricolor went out at the same time, and I doubt not arrested them. One was a villainous looking fellow, and deserved arrest for having such a face.

A great sight of Paris in May and June is the Salon, the annual exhibition of art at the Palais de l'Industrie —in the Champs Elysées, erected for the first French Exposition, that of 1855. Here we find the new paintings, and in the Luxembourg palace works of the past few years, but the permanent art galleries of Paris are in the Louvre. There are the great collections of paintings, statues, ancient marbles and monuments, ethnographical and naval exhibits, and historical objects of all kinds.

Many of the rooms in the Louvre are handsomely decorated and make a worthy setting for the collections. The finest is the Gallery of Apollo, decorated with wall paintings and tapestry, and on tables are objects of art under glass, some protected also by railings. The enamels there are the finest existing. Prominent is a boat epergne of the time of Louis XIV., made of lapis lazuli, and in the middle of the room, guarded by a soldier, is what is left of the crown jewels since the sale in 1887. Largest of these is the Regent diamond, an inch wide and somewhat longer, cut to a point an inch below the face. Near are the crown and sword of Napoleon, and many fine stones and jewels are in the room.

On the ground floor is the statuary, entered from the court, in the north-west part the modern and in almost all the rest ancient pieces. Among the older ancient sculptures the Egyptian and Assyrian collections are particularly famous. The Egyptian are characterized by massive solidity and fine polish, some of the earlier by naturalness. These saloons are devoted to historical, civil, and funereal objects from Egypt, including a papyrus Book of the Dead. Opposite are the Assyrian antiquities, mainly consisting of huge winged bulls with human heads, lions, men with plaited hair and beard, everything of exaggerated muscular development, and near are Phœnician and other Asiatic collections, including the Moabite column of King Mesa, which added so much to our knowledge of the races just east of the Jordan in the ninth century B.C.

Among the ancient treasures, but in a different part of the palace, are also the Persian glazed picture tiles and other antiquities from Susa and Persepolis, exhumed in 1885 by M. Dieulafoy, that have shed a flood of light on the history of the Persians. They represent the royal archer body-guard known as the Ten Thousand Immortals, besides lions and fancy designs, all enameled in beautiful colors. Egypt and Assyria have become better known to us because of religious explorations, but they were peopled by races alien to us and attract us mainly by their grandeur. Persian art is later, but it is more graceful and has the attraction of being the work of our own kin. "Cyrus, the king, the Achaemenian," as he entitled himself 529 B.C. on his rifled tomb at Pasargadae, was the first great man of our Aryan race. This

Dieulafoy collection relates mainly to the palace of Darius at Susa of about 500 B.C. The carved marble columns and doorways of Darius' palace and the columns of Xerxes' hall at Persepolis had long been known, but the discovery of these tiles takes us closer to the Persian lives of the older and better time. The Persians had left their highlands, conquered all west of them, and had somewhat degenerated before they came much in contact with the Greeks. Alexander at Issus 333 B.C. encountered their empire in its decadence, but even then in each battle the Persians beat back his famed Phalanx, and it was only by his cavalry and because opposed to a Darius who was no general, if he was not indeed a coward, that Alexander conquered his way to the Persian throne. He became himself all but Persian after he married the king's daughter.

But there is no doubt that art reached its human perfection only in the little Greek states and colonies. The abundance of marble, the æsthetic sense of the people, their fondness for travel and their popular constitutions united to produce the greatest development of art in the history of the world. They began where the orientals had left off, and left off where the moderns cannot follow them. Rome was great in war, law and organization, but even Rome borrowed her art from Greece. Greek slaves copied Greek models for the statues and paintings of Roman palaces, and most of the admired sculptures which have survived to us are such copies.

Among the Greek and Roman sculptures in the Louvre one of the most famous is the recently discovered Victory of Samothrace standing on the prow of a vessel, erected by Demetrius, son of Alexander's general Seleucus, who was equally great as a soldier and as an admiral.

I have myself a beautiful didrachm with the handsome face of Demetrius on one side and an eagle and trident on the other. The Venus of Milo, found by a peasant on that island in 1820, stands in an arcade at the end of one gallery of sculpture, and, despite the loss of both arms and the pits on the face and bosom from earth corrosion, it is still a noble work. She is over life size, draped from the waist down, and probably held a shield resting against her bent left knee and on it was recording some hero's name. If so, she was as likely a Victory as a Venus, although Venus sometimes held the shield of Mars. Who was the sculptor no one knows, and it is a great tribute to ancient art that the surviving pieces we most admire do not even seem to have attracted the special attention of the Greeks or Romans. This Venus is Greek, but ancient authors do not name it. It probably dates after Phidias, whose work on the Parthenon about 450 B.C. survives in part, but before Praxiteles, the creator of the famous Cnidian Venus in the fourth century B.C. The calm repose of this Melian goddess contrasts strongly with the mundane beauty of the Venus de'Medici at Florence,—it is the heavenly Venus on the one hand and the earthly Venus on the other. The huntress Diana here in the Louvre accompanied by a fawn, seems a companion piece to the Apollo Belvidere, as she strides along, taking an arrow from her quiver and looking earnestly forward, and the Diana like the Apollo is thought to be a Roman copy of a Greek group and to date from the last century B.C.

Historically not less interesting is one of the rooms of statuary in the original Louvre building where the Ligue met and Guise hung some of its members. There, too, Henry IV. married Margaret of Valois and in this room after his assassination in 1610 his body lay in state. Almost fifty years later Molière acted here in his own plays and thus relieved somewhat the gloom of its associations.

Among the Renaissance sculptures are Michael Angelo's two Fettered Slaves, designed as a part of the never to be finished tomb of Julius II., representing chained and dying arts, and in the modern department are numerous works and busts by Houdon, Chaudet and others, amid them Canova's Cupid and Psyche like the group on Lake Como.

The Louvre galleries contain also two thousand paintings and as a general collection this is probably the most valuable in the world. It is mainly on the first floor of the south extension of Napoleon III. The Salon Carré there has many of the finest pictures of all schools. Among them are Correggio's Betrothal of St. Catharine, his Antiope approached by Jupiter disguised as a satyr, of which in another room is a painting by Titian, Murillo's Immaculate Conception, Titian's Mistress at her Toilet, with its wonderful light and shade, Leonardo's smiling portrait of Mona Lisa, once famous for its color but now almost obscure, Raphael's St. George and Dragon, his Madonna and Child with St. John, called La Belle Jardinière, Gerard Dow's dying Dropsical Woman with her daughter weeping, and Paolo Veronese's enormous Marriage at Cana, famous for its colors and portraits. The largest room is called the Grande Galerie, in which is a female portrait by Leonardo and a Holy Family also by him, Titian's fine portrait of Francis I., not from a sitting but from a medal, his Christ and two disciples eating at Emmaus, a subject also treated by Rembrandt in the same room, Guido Reni's Ecce Homo and his Magdalen, also portraits by Velasquez, and at least historically valuable an early picture by Van Eyck. There are also in this room a great many paintings by Rubens, including the large pictures celebrating the life of Marie de Médicis, widow of Henry IV. and regent during the minority of their son Louis XIII. These were painted for the Luxembourg, which she built after her first banishment. She finally was found too intriguing and was exiled for a second time and died at Cologne.

The Louvre has naturally the finest collection of French paintings to be found anywhere. Nicolas Poussin was the first great master and his most famous picture in the Louvre is a painting representing Arcadian Shepherds finding a tomb on which they spell out " Et in Arcadia ego." Claude Lorraine's landscapes are numerous and delightful, while Watteau and Boucher represent the Rococo time of the regency and Louis XV., and the later Greuze pleasantly paints the Marriage Contract, Girl and Broken Pitcher and other humble domestic scenes. The study of the antique and the aspirations of the Revolution were represented by David, whose Sabine Women and Leonidas at Thermopylæ are well known, but rather statuesque and theatrical. There were other painters of the Napoleonic era who devoted themselves to battle scenes, in which they have many modern followers too.

In 1819 what is called the era of the Romanticists began with the exhibition of Géricault's large Raft of the Medusa, a group of survivors from shipwreck, which still commands instant attention. The romantic school painted striking scenes from history and poetry, and numbered such names as Ingres, (1781–1867,) Eugene Delacroix, (1799–1863,) Ary Scheffer, (1795–1858,) Horace Vernet, (1789–1863,) and Paul Delaroche, (1797–1856.)

In the Louvre is found Ingres' Spring, considered the most beautiful example of the nude female figure in modern times. Horace Vernet was the great painter of French army life, particularly in Algiers, while Delaroche's fame as an historical painter has lasted even longer. His Death of Queen Elizabeth attracts only less attention now than it did when first exhibited in 1829.

Under the second empire Meissonier (1815-1891) was the head of the French school. He is better known in America as a battle painter, but is thought abroad even greater in smaller pictures. Troyon and Rosa Bonheur are animal painters of the first rank. Detaille and others paint military scenes and Millet peasant life,—his two peasants in prayer at the ringing of the Angelus is well known and much copied,—but the tendency of the second empire and third republic schools is too much to sensuous and nude figures. No doubt all things are pure to the pure, but Nature and History show that a nation of sensualists is in its decline. French art and French literature may throw light on Sedan and the Commune, for with Carlyle and Kingsley I believe that morality and strength go together. France needs not a political revolution, but a moral reformation.

France is implacable for the loss of Alsace and Lorraine and is but biding her time. These provinces may have been German once but the international statute of limitations should be considered as run when an acquired province has become re-nationalized and is a perfectly satisfied, integral part of the conquering country. Alsace and Lorraine in the hundred years in which they had been incorporated with France had become thoroughly French and are so still. It will not do to push matters of original ownership too far. America celebrates in the

Columbian Exposition an unparalleled appropriation of property.

Even pleasant stays must end. At last for four dollars we sent on the trunk which had awaited us in Paris direct to our homeward bound steamer at Liverpool, while we made ready for a visit to England. One morning we paid our bill to the grasping proprietress of the Hôtel de la Concorde and left its delightful meals, *vin compris*, for the train to Dieppe. On our journey the scenery was pleasant and a view of Rouen's steeples interesting, but the trip was without special incident.

At Dieppe we went aboard the Channel steamer for a wet and rough trip across to Newhaven. To save a few sous we carried our own satchels, and in consequence Rachel, who became separated from me in the crowd, slipped in the rain and fell backwards on her head. This put her in bed for the trip and for much also of our stay in England. I thus saved half a franc porterage, and paid a doctor's bill of two pounds sterling instead. The Channel trip by this route occupied six hours and it was very uncomfortable. Rachel and I sat on a bench by the cabin until the spray and rain and the lurching of the little steamer as she was knocked about drove us below. Rachel's troubles, however, had but begun. They separate the sexes on this boat, putting the women in a room surrounded with two-story berths. Rachel had an upper one and was thrown out, striking an iron post and breaking one of the numerous basins in use by the seasick folks. I fared little better, for after crossing the ocean in safety I now surrendered to the Channel, and was humbly on my knees before a basin all the time that I was not on my back in a berth, too weak to do more than hold on. We were glad to reach land but could hardly walk ashore and get into the London train. The next time I shall take the Dover-Calais route, which requires but a little over an hour, or await the construction of the Channel tunnel, which the English so strongly oppose. At present the country is safe. It can well count on seasickness' breaking up any invading force.

We landed at Newhaven, near the great watering place Brighton, and not very far from Hastings, where William in 1066 put his conquering foot on English soil. We wished to go to Battle Abbey, erected where Harold lost his life and the crown of England to the Norman, but the Channel had incapacitated us and we went on to London. We finally got out in some big station there, and, after an interminable drive in a hansom cab at night, found a pleasant and reasonable boarding house in the West End at No. 8 Duchess Street, Portland Place.

CHAPTER XIX.

LONDON.

LONDON lies on its river not unlike Paris, but the Thames flows eastwardly to the sea and not westwardly like the Seine, and with its great docks, basins and commerce is a great factor in the life of the English metropolis. The Thames, like the Seine, makes a great bend to the north, and on the north side the Tower, as the Bastille, guards the east. The heart of the city is on that bank, and to the west as at Paris are parks. As with Paris one great street at a distance from the river but parallel to it runs east and west under different names, Oxford Street in the west, then Holborn, then Cheapside, and with yet other names until it becomes a country road in the east, and in former times the likeness was completed by a thoroughfare along the Thames answering to the Seine quais, but this Strand street of London is now inland. Buildings have encroached on the river, and indeed for part of the distance there is now another highway immediately along the bank, called Victoria Embankment, on which stands Cleopatra's Needle. South of the river at Paris were few places attractive to the traveller, and in London there are hardly any at all. A striking difference between the two places, however, is that the original City of London is on the north bank of the river, and, although it has many suburbs larger than itself, is still, unlike the French island cité, the centre of metropolitan life and contains the principal business buildings. There is the same contrast, however, between the dirty solidity of London and the bright grandeur of Paris that there is between the stolid business force of the English and the industrious but fickle nature of the French.

London may be conveniently divided into four parts, three north of the Thames and one south. The true London is the old city, from Temple Bar to the Tower, with St. Paul's and the Bank of England as the foci from which radiate the main streets. East of that is the Port with its ships, piers and docks on both sides of the river, of great commercial importance but not especially interesting to travellers. West of the city is the West End, clustering about Parliament House, the Abbey and the Parks, connected with the city by the Strand and Holborn streets. South of the Thames on the Surrey side is Southwark, called the Borough. For postal and perhaps other purposes London is divided into East, West, East Center, South West, and other parts, always indicated by initials. The population is four millions. It was one million in 1800, but the change since is due as much to annexation as to increase.

Sight seeing in this vast city begins wherever one happens to be. Rachel had a friend at Westminster Hotel, and so we first drove there, going south down Portland Place, which begins on the north at Regent's Park, with its magnificent zoölogical collection, and on the way we passed through quarters whose names are household words. Soon we crossed busy Oxford Street, which under the name of Holborn leads to the city, and then went along curved Regent Street, admiring its fashionable shops. We then turned east on Piccadilly, which comes from Hyde Park, far to the west, with its pleasant walks and roads, among them the famous drive called Rotten Row. Haymarket Street then brought us to Trafalgar Square, and soon we were at our destination.

As often afterwards we used a hansom. This style of cab has two wheels and one horse, and the driver sits in a little box or perch above at the rear, handling the reins over the top of the vehicle. The newer ones have rubber tires and run easily. In bad weather we shut the two glass front doors, that close in like the arms of the Iron Virgin at Nuremburg, but happily with pleasanter results. The cabmen are not extra polite, but we had not much trouble. There are stands all over London, and prices, while higher than on the continent, are not unreasonable.

After the continental churches Westminster is disappointing. It is a Gothic building in the shape of a Latin cross, the height 103 feet and the length 513, but from without it looks small and dingy. Within, it is dark and seems narrow and cramped, and the choir enclosure extending down into the nave contracts it yet more. The monuments generally are not to be highly regarded as works of art. Putting a bust, as lately Longfellow's, in Westminster Abbey is regarded as a great honor, but it would be more so if there was a better selection and if they were kept dusted. The great interest of the Abbey we found in its history, its graves and its chapels, but not in its monuments.

Founded in the time of Edward the Confessor, this was a Benedictine monastery, the minster being dedicated to St. Peter. Henry III. and Edward I. rebuilt the church in its present form, and Henry VIII. abolished the monastery and turned over its buildings to a dean and chapter, who still hold them. In our time Dean Stanley was long in charge and is buried there. The graves are generally below the floor and in walking around we trod over the names of great men lying beneath the stone slabs. In the nave lie Sir Isaac Newton, Charles Darwin, Sir John Herschel, Sir William Temple, David Livingston, on whose grave was a wreath of flowers, Robert Stephenson the engineer, Lord Clyde and Lord Lawrence of Indian fame, G. E. Grant, the young architect who died before completion of his great creation, the Law Courts, and Ben Jonson, with the well known epitaph,—"O rare Ben Johnson." The nave has in late years been re-paved with uniform square stones, and this looks better, but unfortunately removes the old historic gravestones like Ben Jonson's. In the north transept are Lord Chatham, William Pitt and Charles J. Fox, his rival in politics, Canning, and Henry Grattan. In the south transept are the graves of Old Parr, the musician Handel, Sheridan the statesman and author, Garrick, Dr. Samuel Johnson, Charles Dickens, and the brilliant Macaulay. A part of this transept is called the Poets' Corner from the graves and many busts of poets. Chaucer's tomb is built into the wall, Spenser's is near, and next to Browning's since our visit Tennyson has been laid to rest.

The chapels, however, are perhaps the most interesting part of the abbey and take up the whole of the short arm, the east end, of its Latin cross. They consist of the central chapel of Edward the Confessor, really the continuation of the nave, and surrounding smaller ones, the most attractive of which is the later addition immediately behind the Confessor's, the beautiful chapel of Henry VII. The chapel of Edward contains the monuments of the Confessor the founder and Henry III. who rebuilt the abbey, Edward I. his son, the English Justinian, whose warlike epitaph calls him the Hammer of the Scots, Eleanor his wife, Henry V. and his wife, whose wooing in Shakspere's play is so familiar, the great conqueror Edward III., Richard II., and a number of worthies too not of royal blood. I believe most of these monuments mark the actual graves, for they had not then risen to the civilized custom of erecting cenotaphs and monuments to men who are buried miles away and thus leading the traveller to doubt even real tombs. In this chapel is the old oaken coronation chair of Edward I. containing the large stone of Scone brought by him from the west coast of Scotland. On this reposed Jacob's head in his vision, and on it too rested dying St. Columba at Iona.

In one of the main chapels to the right of the ambulatory Lord Lytton is buried, and in another on the other side Sir Rowland Hill, to whom the world was indebted for penny postage. In all are monuments of people great in their mediæval day, often with bronze or stone figures in mail lying at full length on their tombs, but now remembered only for the quaint carving and inscriptions of their last resting places. At the extreme east end I ascended some steps and entered the chapel of Henry VII., erected in the sixteenth century, itself really a church with side aisles and chapels. In the centre is the high metal tomb of Henry VII. and his queen. and in the same vault lies James I. In this nave, too, are buried Edward VI., George II. and others, and among the monuments is one marking the grave of Dean Stanley and his wife. In the left aisle is the imposing monument of Queen Elizabeth, with whom is buried her sister Queen Mary, near rest the bones of the two murdered princes, brought here from the Tower, and not far away the author of the Spectator reposes in the vault of General Monk. Opposite in the right aisle is the monument of Mary Queen of Scots, who was executed by Elizabeth and whose remains were re-interred here in 1612 by her son James, the successor of Elizabeth. These two queens, so contrasted and hostile in their lives, now repose beneath similar and adjacent monuments, a recumbent figure under a canopy, with hands folded in prayer. Here lie also Charles II., William III. of Orange, his wife Queen Mary, and her successor Anne.

Apart from the graves this chapel of Henry VII. is interesting on account of its noble ceiling of fan tracery with pendants. The airy stone fretwork is graceful and beautiful, not excelled by anything of which I know, even in England. The Gothic was worked out in more detail here than on the continent, although perhaps Great Britain does not present buildings of the same size and grandeur as Germany and France. English Gothic had three periods. The first was in the twelfth and thirteenth centuries, the time of Richard I., John and Henry III., and is called early English, or sometimes Lancet from its narrow, pointed windows. The second is the Decorated, marked by a wider window, whose arch would contain an equilateral triangle. This flourished in the fourteenth century during the reigns of the first three Edwards, and produced possibly the richest architecture of all. Its windows are mullioned and in panels, their tracery flowing and even flamboyant, the mouldings decorated with foliage, the columns clustered, and the doorways highly ornamented. The last period has a flatter arch and in general a squarer appearance, but the ornamentation is even more elaborate and the richly carved choir stalls and screens date also from this time. This is called the Perpendicular and extends from the end of the fourteenth to the sixteenth century, from the reign of Richard II. through that of Henry VII. To the Perpendicular belongs this superb chapel, whose elaborate decoration may mark a decline from first principles, but whose elegance and finish cannot be surpassed. Afterwards came the mongrel architectural combinations of the Reformation time, and then a renaissance under Jones, and more especially under Wren, which abandoned the Gothic for Italian styles.

The old cloisters of the Abbey, adjoining this abbey church of Westminster, show yet older forms of architecture, but one has to seek elsewhere for the best remains of the rude Saxon style and of the substantial round arched Norman buildings, so interesting and often so imposing.

Seldom shown, but a part of the Abbey is the Jerusalem Chamber. There died the great King Henry IV., who recognized in this the fulfilment of a prophecy that he should die "in Jerusalem." There sat that Assembly of Divines, 150 in number, from 1643 to 1648, which drew up the Westminster Confession of Faith and Catechisms, for a while the standards of England and even now of Presbyterians the world over. From the Jerusalem Chamber too in our own day is dated the Revised Version of the English Bible. Part of the work on the

King James version, published 1611, was done at Oxford and Cambridge, but part also at Westminster.

Between Westminster Abbey and the Parliament House is St. Margaret's church, where are buried Raleigh, who was executed not far away, Admiral Blake, and Caxton, whose printing press of 1476 stood near the Abbey. In St. Margaret's the Long Parliament took the Solemn League and Covenant which brought to their cause the aid of Scotland in the war against king and prelacy, and there in our day, under far different auspices, the American Phillips Brooks often occupied the pulpit of his friend Canon Farrar.

Parliament House is a vast and sumptuous structure of Perpendicular Gothic, on the west bank of the Thames, built in 1840 on the site of old Westminster Palace. The building is on low ground, and the three majestic towers at the north end, at the middle and at the southwest corner, upwards of three hundred feet high, dwarf the rest. In the south part are the royal apartments and the House of Lords, with lobby, courts and rooms, while at the north end are the Commons Hall, lobbies and the courts, including the Speaker's residence and numerous state offices. The ornamentation and finish of all is elaborate. Statues, frescoes, stained glass, tiles, coats of arms and everything else have been used to decorate the structure, and, best of all, the parliamentary life within the walls is worthy of this setting. The interior of the House of Commons is simpler than that of the House of Peers, although the lower house is really the political centre of the empire. The Speaker, whose office is non-partisan, presides from near the north end, and on the benches to his right sit the Government majority, to his left the Opposition, the leaders of each

INTERIOR OF WESTMINSTER HALL.

in front. The seats have no desks and are reserved by the members coming early and putting their hats on the places they desire. To our notion it is strange to find places for only a little over two thirds of the six hundred and seventy members, and I have seen the seats not half full then. Division on questions is taken by counting the members as they file into lobbies, and all must vote one way or the other.

To the lover of history more interesting even than this grand modern structure is "the great hall of William Rufus" adjoining, Old Westminster Hall, originally part of the Westminster Palace in which lived the kings of England from Saxon to Tudor times. This hall is 290 feet long, 68 feet broad, and 92 feet high, its fine oaken ceiling needing no columns to uphold it. Here Edward II. and Richard II. were deposed, Charles I. tried, Cromwell declared Lord Protector, Wallace, Guy Fawkes and Strafford condemned, the Seven Bishops acquitted, and so too Warren Hastings after his long trial, made brilliant by the eloquence of Burke and Sheridan, who impeached him. Here were held many parliaments and here long sat the royal courts of justice after Magna Charta declared that they should no longer follow the king about the realm but be fixed at one place for the convenience of suitors. The vicissitudes of English history hardly equal the French, but worthy of ranking with the barbarity of the Revolution was the treatment of Cromwell's remains by the royalists. His body was taken from its grave in Westminster Abbey, the head exposed for many years on a pinnacle of this Hall, and the rest thrown in a pit at Tyburn, the place of common hanging. The skull at last fell down and was sold by a sentry.

But there is much else of London to see besides Parliament Square. To the north-west of this vicinity are the parks and palaces. The nearest is Buckingham Palace, the town residence of the Queen and the scene of her drawing-rooms. Between these grounds and Green Park is Constitution Hill, where Peel was killed in 1850 by being thrown from his horse, and here several attempts have been made on the Queen's life. Beyond it at the corner of Hyde Park stands Apsley House, the residence presented to the great Wellington by the nation. From Buckingham Palace the Mall, a drive, extends to near Trafalgar Square, passing alongside St. James Park, which is behind the Downing Street government buildings. To the north and facing the drive and park is what since a fire is left of St. James Palace, the old red brick royal residence from which the English court receives its diplomatic title. Next to St. James is Marlborough House, the residence of the Prince of Wales. St. James was a royal palace from the time of Henry VIII. to George IV., and the regular residence of the sovereigns after the burning of Whitehall in 1691, and here are still held the Queen's levees.

One of the best modes of seeing London streets is at the West End to take a 'bus marked "To the Bank" and ride the whole way. We climbed on top as at Paris, but the seats face the front and not to the sides as there. An unexpected but necessary article attached to the seat is a water proof apron to pull over one in case of rain, for London weather is the worst in the world. On one dull day with the sun making but a semi-luminous halo we were told that it was a most unusually fine day. The sky is generally leaden and the streets often foggy in their best season, while in their bad weather you can hardly see the hand before your face, and the street and river traffic is practically at a standstill, perhaps for days. We missed the bad fogs but had cold wind and rain.

From the Parliament House north to where the Thames turns east this extension of the Strand is known as Whitehall. On the left we passed by Downing Street, on which and Whitehall are the stately government buildings, whence is ruled the British Empire. Near is the Horseguards, a garrison, and on the sidewalk on each side of the approach to this sits a motionless horseman in red, the wonder of passers by. I asked a policeman what it meant. He said " I don't know, but believe over a hundred years ago an officer directed them to sit there for some reason and the order has never been changed." The men are changed, though, every hour or two. Opposite is a remnant of Whitehall palace, an Italian looking building, where Charles I. was executed, going out of his old banquet window to the scaffold. He slept the night before at St. James palace and walked over to Whitehall in the morning. Then we came again to Trafalgar Square, where stands the granite Nelson pillar, one hundred and forty-five feet high, surmounted by his statue, commemorating the great naval victory in 1805, when Nelson was killed, but not until he had destroyed Napoleon's preparations for invading England from Boulogne. Between the Square and Whitehall once stood Charing Cross, a Gothic monument erected by Edward I. to mark the last halting place of his wife's coffin on its way to Westminster, and the place still preserves the name. At the Square comes in from the west Pall Mall, a handsome street of clubs, terminating at the National Gallery on a terrace.

The National Gallery has a fine selection of early Italian painters, important in the history of art, and also several noble Raphaels, but these masters are perhaps better studied on the continent. The great attraction to me was the Turner collection. This English artist is a master not perhaps of landscape but of cloudland. His buildings, sea, views, sunsets shade off into a marvellous red or yellow cloud that remind one of the simoon. Where he gets it I do not know, but it is so weirdly beautiful that it must have its original somewhere in nature. His earlier water colors are also much admired although different in style. But England has had other fine painters. The earliest was Hogarth in the first half of the last century, and in its second half came Reynolds and Gainsborough, who devoted themselves mainly to portraits, particularly of children. In our own century was the practical discovery by the English of water colors, and that they have held as their own domain, Turner and Constable being long the acknowledged leaders. Wilkie, Leslie, and Mulready painted genre pieces, but in our own generation a new school has dominated England, the Pre-Raphaelites, the advocates and practicers of accurate detail, even in backgrounds. Dante Rossetti, Holman Hunt and J. E. Millais began the movement, Ruskin eloquently preached it, and it now prevails at least in its effects. In the National Gallery all of these artists are represented as well as foreign masters, and although late in origin, the English school, particularly in landscape, may court comparison with any other, and this gallery, dating only from this century, bids fair to be one of the world's greatest collections.

The view from the portico over Trafalgar Square and its monuments is imposing, although I hardly agree with

Peel, who patriotically declared this to be the finest site in Europe. There are a number of streets from it to the river and in every other direction, including the wider Strand, which leads to the City. Near it further on to the east are Covent Garden and a number of other theatres, and Cecil, Surrey, Norfolk, and Essex streets branching off to the south show the sites of old palaces of the nobility, whose gardens faced the river. Then we came to the site of Temple Bar, a stone gate formerly leading into the City, through whose portals even the sovereign could not pass without the permit of the Lord Mayor. It was lately removed to give more room to the enormous traffic,—for here vehicles are in line for blocks together, often unable to move and seldom progressing faster than a walk. The police are autocrats in London. They rule vehicles and the streets in a very efficient manner.

Here at Temple Bar we were before the New Courts of Justice. The old English division was into Common Law courts of King's Bench, Common Pleas, and Exchequer on the one side, and Chancery on the other, all sitting in Westminster Hall, except that Chancery was for a long time at Lincoln's Inn. In 1873 the Judicature Act consolidated all into one, but made Divisions of this High Court of Justice with names similar to the old courts. This magnificent Gothic building, facing the north side of the Strand, now contains pretty much all the upper courts. Near by is Lincoln's Inn, a law school of an incorporated society of lawyers, within whose park was executed in 1683 Lord William Russell, and partly within and partly without the old City is the Temple, Inner and Middle, a similar institution, where lawyers and others live in chambers. Blackstone and Dr. Johnson resided there, Charles Lamb and Selden and Goldsmith are buried in its precincts, and further east about Fleet Street, as the continuation of the Strand within the City is called, were the haunts of the erratic Dr. Johnson. Near in Chancery Lane is the Rolls Court and in Fetter Lane is the New Record Office, containing the Domesday Book of William the Conqueror, which now-a-days we would call a Census Report, and many other valuable State papers. Within the City was Fleet Prison for debtors, removed, however, in 1844, and we have hardly got used to the name Fleet before that gives way to Ludgate Hill, a street which leads only to St. Paul's. It has been in effect continued, however, by Cannon Street, which runs from St. Paul's to the tall marble Monument near London Bridge, marking where the Great Fire of 1666 began, and may be regarded as further continued by Eastcheap and Great Tower Street to the Tower of London. Cannon is intersected midway by Victoria Street, a wide thoroughfare which the demands of traffic have compelled the authorities to cut from Blackfriars Bridge north-east to the Bank. On it is the new building of The Times, the British Thunderer, whose circulation, however, is surpassed by several American newspapers, as they in turn are by the Petit Journal of Paris, which has a million readers.

I believe St. Paul's is of white marble, but it is now blackened all over by the smoky fogs. Like all older churches it faces west. The present building was erected by Sir Christopher Wren during the thirty-five years succeeding 1675. It is in the Renaissance style, much resembling St. Peter's, although the portico is perhaps more imposing and the dome more visible, and ranks third among the world's great churches, coming next to the Milan cathedral in size. Its majestic dome,

364 feet high, can be seen to advantage only from a distance, as the yard is too small to admit of a view. Within, the church looks cold and bare compared with the rich coloring, frescoes and paintings of continental churches, but a beginning has been made in the way of mosaics in the dome.

The greatest attraction of St. Paul's is its monuments around the walls, but the resting places of the men they celebrate are in the vaults below, if in the church at all. The most recent monument I noticed was that of Chinese Gordon, a recumbent bronze statue, and probably the handsomest are those to Nelson and Wellington, who are interred in the crypt. There immediately under the dome is the great black sarcophagus of Nelson, who died in 1805 at his great victory of Trafalgar, where his last order was the well known, "England expects every man to do his duty." His coffin is made from the mainmast of the French flag ship L'Orient which blew up at his victory of Aboukir Bay and "with fragments strewed the sea." Also in the crypt is the high porphyry sarcophagus of Wellington. He died in 1852, having long outlived Napoleon, whom circumstances enabled him to conquer at Waterloo, and was alive when that emperor's will, written at St. Helena, was surrendered, and his remains permitted to be taken to France to repose in their magnificent tomb. Wellington was in peace and war the Iron Duke. He never knew fatigue or admitted failure in politics any more than in battle. The architect Christopher Wren, the painters Benjamin West, Joshua Reynolds, Thomas Lawrence, Edwin Landseer, John Opie, J. M. W. Turner and Geo. Cruikshank among artists, and Dean Milman, Bartle Frere and Sir William Jones among authors are also buried in St. Paul's. Over the north door inside the church is a tablet to the memory of Wren, with the striking conclusion, "Si monumentum requiris, circumspice."

In St. Paul's are notices not to pay the guides, who are apparently clergymen of subordinate rank. Ours after showing us all the crypt took us into a dark room and said, "That is all." We thanked him, and he, after waiting a minute, heaved a sigh as no money clinked and took us upstairs again. A more ingenious guide in the capitol at Albany, New York, once finished up the tour in the dark basement under the tower, and suggested that similar rules did not forbid my slipping half a dollar in his outside coat pocket, unknown to him. Considering my helplessness, I cheerfully complied.

Adjoining St. Paul's churchyard on the north is Paternoster Row, a short, narrow street of book stores with tempting exhibits, overlooked by a room in which in 1844 young George Williams held a prayer meeting among his fellow clerks and founded the Young Men's Christian Association which he has lived to see girdle the world with good works and noble buildings. At the west end of Paternoster Row is Stationers' Hall, in effect the British copyright office, although it belongs to a private corporation. Grub Street, famous in Dr. Johnson's time as the working place of literary hacks, is some distance north-east, beyond the street named London Wall from its site. Grub Street is now called Milton Street, from John Milton, who is buried in St. Giles church near Smithfield. This is now a meat market, but was formerly outside the walls and the place of public executions. Here died Wat Tyler, Sir William Wallace and others, and here too were burned at the stake the Protestant martyrs under Bloody Mary, the site now marked by a drinking fountain.

For the present returning to our Strand-Fleet-Cannon Street route, looking from near the Monument down the noisy street to London Bridge, I saw the greatest pack of vehicles possible, a long string in each direction, and it was with the utmost difficulty that one could cross. It is almost like waiting for the river to flow by. Fifteen thousand vehicles a day and seven times as many people on foot cross the bridge. This granite structure does not ante-date our century, but takes the place of another which went back to the twelfth century, and wooden ones before that dated back to Saxon if not to Roman times. On the gates which closed the ends of the old stone bridge, as over Temple Bar, were formerly exposed the heads of decapitated traitors, and perhaps a survival of the sentiment is still shown in making the lamp posts of captured French cannon. Until within the past hundred years London Bridge was the only one across the Thames, but there are nearly a dozen now, besides two or more tunnels.

Some of the great highways perpendicular to the river, as Victoria Street at Westminster, Gower Street and its continuations, Farringdon Road, and Bishopgate Street cross their Westminster, Waterloo, Blackfriars and London Bridges, and, continuing south on the Surrey side, gradually converge in Southwark at the Elephant and Castle Inn. Near this is the immense Tabernacle of the late Chas. H. Spurgeon, a sleepy-looking man whom I once heard there in a good, plain, earnest sermon. I remember that he accented Deutero*nomy* on the fourth syllable and prayed earnestly for rain. His convenient and well ushered church accommodates six thousand people. From London Bridge St. Paul's, Billingsgate Fish Market and other prominent buildings are in sight, and although I do not sketch I examined them with as much interest as Macaulay's New Zealand traveller will do some centuries hence. Below the Bridge are the steamships of this great port, while above it the traffic is necessarily confined to smaller steamers and light craft, and I found a trip up to Westminster Bridge on one of the penny boats full of interest. In High Street, Southwark, not far from the Bridge stood until lately Tabard Inn, whence the pilgrims in Canterbury Tales started on their journey, and not far west of the Bridge on the Bankside was once the theatre where Shakspere played, but the exact site is uncertain.

Further down the river, and just outside the old walls, stands the Tower, now an arsenal but for many centuries a prison and the scene of execution of state prisoners. Its guardians are soldiers in red with jaunty caps, who are called colloquially "beef eaters," but why is not quite certain. At the north-west corner on Tower Hill was the site of the scaffold, and opposite just within the fortress are buried many of its famous victims. There are Anne Boleyn and Catherine Howard, two of Henry VIII's queens, Lady Jane Grey and Lord Dudley her husband, Queen Elizabeth's favorite Essex, and Monmouth, the illegitimate son of James II. The two queens were executed within the Tower enclosure at a spot covered by brick. In the Tower were confined at sundry times many others of royal and noble blood, including Baliol, Bruce and Wallace of Scotland, John of France, Elizabeth while princess, Cranmer, Strafford, Laud, Jeffreys and even Marlborough. The Tower fronts the Thames on its longest side and on that and the other four sides is surrounded by castellated walls and towers, outside being a dry moat, which can be flooded. The entrance is from the south-west corner, but there is also an entrance from the river through the commonplace looking Traitor's Gate, the old route for state prisoners.

In the centre of the enclosure rises the isolated White Tower, the oldest part of all, erected by William the Conqueror on the site of a Saxon and perhaps a Roman fortress. It is very nearly a cube of one hundred feet in all dimensions. Under the stone staircase were discovered the bones of the two princes murdered by Richard III., above are the rooms occupied by Raleigh while he wrote his history in prison, higher a fine Norman chapel, and the upper floor was the scene of the abdication of the ill-fated Richard II. The White Tower now contains a collection of armor, from the leather scales or steel rings on leather of the Norman period, through the chain mail of the time of Henry III. and perfect plate armor of Henry V., down to the lighter suits of the Stuarts, after whom it was abandoned. With these are exhibited also the block, axe and executioner's mask, disused since the execution in 1747 of Lovat, a Stuart adherent. In the Tower is a collection of fire arms of all kinds, and the wall decoration is often of wreaths and ornaments of swords and bayonets. In one or other of the dozen keeps were murdered the two princes, the Duke of Clarence drowned in a butt of malmsey, and the weak-minded Henry VI. killed after the long life which saw several pseudo-kings and the struggle of his brave wife with Warwick the King-maker. The crown jewels, except the Kohinor, which is at

Windsor, are also kept in the Tower. Queen Victoria's beautiful crown of 1838 has nearly three thousand diamonds, valued at one million pounds, and its chief decorations are Maltese crosses and the great ruby once owned by the Black Prince and worn by Henry V. at Agincourt.

The other east and west route of London I named is almost as interesting. To take it from the region of docks to the west again we may say it begins at Whitechapel, so famous lately for strange murders of women. Thence by Leadenhall and Cornhill we arrive where are probably the densest crowds even in London,—the place on which fronts the Bank of England, the Royal Exchange, and the Mansion House of the Lord Mayor. Here come in King William Street from London Bridge, Lombard Street, Threadneedle, Princes Street, (to Brown, Shipley & Co.'s behind the Bank,) Poultry leading towards the West End, and several others, marking the sites of trades once carried on by the respective guilds. Here I suppose is the most valuable real estate in the world.

The Bank is a private corporation, dating back to 1691. It is the only one having the power to issue paper money, and a note when paid is immediately cancelled. The notes are small and oblong and are printed in simple devices, black on white. They are said to be difficult to counterfeit, probably on account of water marks, as the designs are neither ornate nor difficult, and as works of art do not compare with our bank notes. The Bank does its own printing and binding. Its vaults contain about twenty million pounds, and its outstanding notes aggregate somewhat more. It manages the British national debt, and is the financial centre of the world.

The plain low building takes up a whole block, and has for greater safety no external windows, being lighted from the interior courts, and is guarded by a garrison of soldiers at night. In the Exchange across the street is Lloyd's, the rooms where ship agents and underwriters do business. It is not a firm or corporation, but offices where all firms and corporations congregate.

We went westward on top of a 'bus along Poultry, which almost immediately became Cheapside, the chief trading street of old London. Off to the north up King Street is Guildhall, the seat of the municipal government, where the new Lord Mayor gives annually a great public banquet on November 9th, important because attended by the Queen's ministers, who take this occasion to outline their own policy. Beyond Cheapside is Bow Church, re-erected by Sir Christopher Wren after the Great Fire, its steeple still much admired. The true Londoner, the original Cockney, is he who is born within the sound of Bow Bells. Near are other historic spots. On Bread Street in 1608 was born John Milton, and on Cheapside between that and Friday Street was the Mermaid Tavern, where met the famous social club founded by Ben Jonson five years earlier and claiming Shakspere, Beaumont and Fletcher and others as its members. Further on we soon caught a glimpse of St. Paul's and Paternoster Row from the north, in the other direction the great building of the General Post Office, and there our street changed its name to Newgate. This it retained until we got out of the city at gloomy Newgate Prison, at the south-east corner of the street known as Old Bailey, but this is not now the principal prison of London, nor is it the scene of executions as of yore. Oates, Defoe and Penn have been confined within these walls, and in a church near by is buried John Smith, of Pocahontas fame.

Here begins the iron Holborn Viaduct, built in 1869 to connect Holborn Street with the City, from which it was separated by a ravine through which ran a stream called the Fleet, which gives its name to the parallel street nearer the river. Buildings are continuous along the sides of the Viaduct and one hardly realizes that it is a bridge. Gray's Inn Road comes in on one side of Holborn and Chancery Lane on the other, and as we went along this avenue, now become New Oxford Street, off to the right we caught glimpses through side streets of the British Museum. Further west the avenue is Oxford Street until it reaches Tyburn and Hyde Park, when as Uxbridge Road it passes the Park and Kensington Gardens and so on west out into the country towards Windsor and Oxford.

South of Kensington Gardens is the Albert Memorial, a lofty monument to the Queen's husband, who died in 1861, universally mourned. The Prince Consort is seated under a canopy, and a frieze around the monument shows the distinguished men of his time. Even a better monument is the South Kensington Museum not far away, which he founded for the education of the masses, and which has had the best results. Here are gathered together casts of almost everything of value in art, a fine picture gallery of British paintings, the original cartoons of Raphael for the Scriptural tapestries, and also valuable zoölogical and scientific collections. There is the great engine of Watts, also " Puffing Billy " the first locomotive, dating from 1813, Stephenson's " Rocket " locomotive of 1829, all clumsy enough, but meaning more than the finest Baldwin or Rogers of the present day.

The greatest collection of London, if not of the world, however, is the British Museum, and it is not yet one hundred and fifty years old. The building, which is near Oxford St., has been gradually extended and is now worthy of what it holds. In the centre is a round reading room, under a great glass dome one foot wider than St. Peter's, and to the east are the libraries of one and one half million modern books, as well as Gutenberg, Caxton and Aldine first prints, including the Mazarin Bible, the first printed. There, too, are modern autographs and famous literary originals, as well as the Codex Alexandrinus, which ranks with the Sinaiticus of St. Petersburg and the Vaticanus, they being the three oldest Biblical manuscripts. There, also, is the Syriac Genesis and Exodus of A.D. 464. In the west wings are the remains of ancient art. The Egyptian embraces the basalt Rosetta stone, discovered by the French, and whose trilingual inscription gave the key to hieroglyphics. The Assyrian collection embraces Layard's discoveries south of Nineveh and those of other explorers from the palace of Sennacherib at Nineveh itself. There are also Persian, Etruscan and other collections, the Portland vase and good Roman sculptures, including the beautiful Clytie, Boy Extracting Thorn, and the Townley Venus.

The Greek remains are priceless, among them being reliefs from the Xanthus Harpy Tomb, part of the Mausoleum at Halicarnassus, and the Elgin marbles. Lord Elgin was British ambassador at Constantinople and in the first three years of this century he brought these sculptures from the Parthenon. I am not sure about his right to them, but it would have been a good thing if some Elgin had appropriated them before the Venetians bombarded the temple in 1687 and blew up the Turkish magazine within. The marbles contain the procession of women and cavalry from the cella, the centaur metopes from the architrave, and the remains of the famous sculptures from the pediments, these last from the workshop of Phidias in the time of Pericles. The figures were suited to the spaces which they occupied,—in the centre they were standing, in the angles they were recumbent. The group in the eastern pediment represented the birth of Minerva. The centre is missing, and of the others only Theseus retains a head. The western group is still more shattered, but enough still exists of each to sustain the ancient verdict that the work was a fitting crown to this proud temple of Ictinus built on the site of the one destroyed by the Persians, and these easy and perfect figures proclaim Phidias the greatest sculptor of the world.

London is full of sites connected with authors or great men of English history. It was a Roman, then a Saxon, and then an English town, always growing, until it is now the greatest city of the world. Its streets are narrow still, except the new ones cut from time to time at enormous expense. The shops at the West End are the more fashionable, but in the City the prices are a little lower. At the co-operative Stores is everything imaginable and by borrowing the ticket of a friend we got all the articles that we wanted of the best quality and at the minimum cost.

The underground railway is a convenient method of going great distances in a few minutes and at very little expense. The cars and engines are much like those on other English roads, and the only difference in the travel is that we are in a tunnel all the time. I had two suits of clothes made at a tailor's by the Monument and went there quite often. I always took the underground if at all pressed for time, as the 'bus consumed about two hours, and the underground twenty minutes. There is a station near the Monument, and I went into a hall from the street, paid three pence at a window, and then went down the steps, where an agent punched the ticket. There are two flights of steps, as one needs the east or west bound train, which have different tracks and platforms. I never had to wait long, as the trains are frequent. When the cars came a man ran along opening the doors and all people hurriedly got to the class they wanted, the third class generally. Sometimes it was crowded and I had to stand. Then some one ran along and closed the doors, and we were off. At my destination I went up other stairs to daylight, giving up my ticket at the top. There are two routes, the Inner Circle from the Tower to Kensington, and an Outer Circle, with separate and less frequent trains, having a larger circuit, and one or the other goes near almost all points of interest, including the great terminal stations. These, by the way, have large railroad hotels connected with the stations, fitted with every comfort.

 Rachel recovered enough to ride around and also visit St. Paul's and the Abbey, but had to choose between the British Museum and Tussaud's. She naïvely chose the wax works, and that was our last sight-seeing before taking the train for Liverpool. Mme. Tussaud is dead and her own wax figure shows her as a shrivelled up little woman. Her grandson now controls the exhibition. Many of the figures are very lifelike, but many are not, especially in the hands. Some stand in groups chatting, some are seated, looking at the others, and many funny experiences are told of people asking the wax policemen questions. We were determined not to be taken in, so *we* went around suspiciously eying live ones too lest we be deceived. Little Napoleon II. in his cradle is very sweet, and a French lady asleep before her execution a perfect dream of loveliness. The figure is said even to breathe. We saw there also Napoleon's carriage, and the bed on which he died. Below is the Chamber of Horrors, with representations of prisons and executions, and there too is the original guillotine which played such havoc in the Place de la Concorde.

CHAPTER XX.

HOMEWARD BOUND.

RACHEL'S fall on the Channel steamer not only prevented her seeing much of London but made it necessary to give up our proposed flying trip to visit friends in Edinburgh. As soon as she was able to travel we made direct for Liverpool and took the Inman liner, City of Paris, for New York.

On the way from London we passed in sight of the great round tower of Windsor castle and the beautiful spires of Oxford, recalling my pleasant visits to these places in years gone by.

Windsor is about an hour's ride from London, and is the Queen's usual residence. The castle is on a hill and the terraces at one side command a wide prospect over a park and the river valley, while on the others are walls with guarded gates. Within the enclosure are two wards, in the outer of which is St. George's chapel and in the inner the royal residence. In this inner palace proper are shown the state apartments, all ornamented richly but not gaudily; they are not very large and everything there made me think this palace more homelike than any other I saw in Europe. St. George's chapel, the place of worship and interment too for the present royal family, is a beautiful church of Perpendicular Gothic, with finely carved choir stalls and fan tracery above on the ceiling. Here, where lately was buried the eldest son of the Prince of Wales, lie in plain tombs in the choir the remains of Henry VIII. and Charles I., while in the royal vaults are those of Edward IV., Henry VIII., George III., William IV. and others, and near is the elaborate mausoleum of the Prince Consort, erected by the Queen. The castle dates from Edward IV., although the Conqueror had a fortress here. It has been the royal residence only since George III. Across the river is Eton school with its handsome hall, while a short distance down towards London is the island of Runnymede, where Magna Charta was signed.

The visit to classic Oxford, too, will be long remembered. I found the university made up of some nineteen or more semi-independent colleges, situated in different parts of the town, each with its own buildings and government. As I wandered around I discovered the place to be a mine of architecture. In the town St. Mary's presents several phases of Gothic in one church, and the adjacent Gothic Martyrs' Monument marks where Cranmer and Ridley were burned as heretics in 1556. The colleges, too, are Gothic and although varying in some arrangements are all built on the same general plan. Each has one or more quadrangles, surrounded by students' quarters, chapel and lecture rooms, and either the chapel or entrance is crowned by the graceful tower so prominent from a distance. They were founded by different men from time to time, Christ Church, the largest of them all, owing much, for example, to Cardinal Wolsey. Magdalen College is one of the most interesting. In it is a fine old cloister, the tower overgrown with ivy, and in the grounds are a deer park and the leafy promenade known from one celebrated frequenter as Addison's Walk. Among other attractions of the University are the books and manuscripts of the Bodleian Library and the ivied court containing the Clarendon Press.

Cambridge is perhaps more beautiful, the college grounds there stretching down to the river on which the students love to row, but Cambridge was not on our present route. Beyond Oxford towards Liverpool is Stratford-on-Avon, the scene of the birth and death of Shakspere, whose busiest years, however, were spent in London.

The famous house of his father, now reclaimed from common uses and become a Shakspere museum, is a plain two-story building, the frame showing and filled in with brick and plaster, as is so common here in England. I entered through a door at the left-hand corner, and found myself in an entry, to the right of which were two rooms containing the Shakspere memorials that have survived, unfortunately few in number. In his chair, as is the custom with all pilgrims here, I took my seat, in the vain hope of absorbing some inspiration. In this room William assisted his father carry on a wool-combing establishment. Back of the entry was the best kitchen, and back of that two small closets, used respectively for washing and for prayer. Bacon originates the sentiment that cleanliness is next to godliness. Who knows but that the juxtaposition of washing and praying closets suggested this idea, and by way of carrying war into Africa here may be an argument that Shakspere wrote Bacon. Upstairs over the entry is the room where the world's greatest genius first saw the light. The room is clean, the fireplace large, with seats in the chimney corner, the ceiling so low that it can be reached by hand and covered by the signatures of visitors, many of them distinguished, but the custodian thought mine too humble to be permitted there. The broken plaster is held in place by metal strips and does not admit of much handling now. From the windows one sees the garden, planted with the flowers Perdita and Ophelia loved, and their sweet odors mingle with the reveries induced by this hallowed spot.

On his return to Stratford to live as a retired man of means Shakspere built himself a New Place but strangely enough only its foundations remain. Not far from where he was born stands the church under whose square tower he was buried. He lies there in the chancel, protected by the curse carved on the slab against any one that moves his bones. Above on the side wall is the well known bust or rather half figure resting on a cushion, but it is fat and coarse and staring, retaining even yet traces of the paint formerly upon it. About on noble tombs lie effigies in armor, and in front in the body of the church are the high-backed pews of the congregation. The churchyard extends down to the narrow Avon and is bounded on the town side by ivied walls.

Near Stratford are romantic Warwick and Kenilworth Castle, further beyond is dirty, modern Birmingham and the black country of the Stafford potteries, and then not far south of Liverpool came Chester. Chester was once a great port, but decayed as its river Dee gradually filled up. This gave Liverpool its opportunity. Chester is laid off regularly in squares on the lines of the Roman camp (castrum) which gave the city its name, site and shape. Its mediæval walls and characteristics still survive, the same narrow streets and Dutchy houses, the same elevated and covered sidewalks, called Rows, on which shopkeepers still show their wares.

We reached the Mersey at night and preferred the cold ferry to the tunnel route in order to see the many lights of the shipping and of Liverpool. The next day, Wednesday, September 30th, we learned that the steamer did not leave until sunset, so that we had all day to roam around the fine streets and admire the handsome buildings of Liverpool, the second city and the second port of the kingdom. Rachel bought some embroidered handkerchiefs and fancy articles as presents for friends, and I could not, despite purchases at London, resist buying a few more books.

But at last we had dinner, got our packages ready, drove down to the quay and with many others waited on the floating landing stage for the tender, investing meantime in the steamer chair which was to prove so useful. The graceful, long, black City of Paris lay there before our eyes, anchored in the river. The sidewheel tender finally came and took us off, bag and baggage, to the steamer that was to be our home on the roaring deep for almost three thousand miles of travel. It was a relief to be homeward bound, and yet it was with a sigh of regret that we left these historic shores behind us, perhaps never to be re-visited.

Plans had made us familiar with the ship's general arrangement and except that it took us some time to learn the way to our room we soon felt at home. She started off while we were at dinner in the noble dining room, a beautiful glass dome vaulting above us, and we did not at first notice that we were moving. After dark we watched the many lights ashore and on the shipping, a beautiful sight, but they finally faded away and we were out on the Irish sea.

Our big steamer we found to be in every way superior of course to the little Rotterdam. The City of Paris and its companion steamship of the same line, the City of New York, have been recently naturalized as American by special act of Congress, their names being now the Paris and the New York. Each is a three-masted, twin-screw steamer of 10,500 tons, elaborately fitted up in every respect. The three great funnels, and the engines and boiler spaces are amidships and the cabins fore and aft of these. There are four decks. The uppermost is the promenade deck, being open to walkers all along the sides, the swell $600 state rooms and the public library being in the centre. The parts of this deck adjoining the state rooms are covered with awning and here sit the readers and the invalids. Deck chairs were supplied at a rental of two shillings for the trip, but it was necessary to fee the chair steward besides, in order to receive attention. Next below is the saloon deck, and on it 120 feet from the bow is the dining saloon, its dome projecting up above the promenade deck, and near the stern are the smoking and card room, the bar and the barber shop, while on the two long passages connecting these public places are lavatories, pantries and the like. Lower is the upper deck,—showing by its name that the other two are additions to the regular structure of ships, added for convenience of the passenger traffic. On this and the last or main deck are most of the state rooms, prices varying according to floor and nearness to the side of the vessel. Ours was No. 453 on the main deck and the price was $90 for each of us.

Our cabin was thus near the water line and always needed the electric light, but through an automatic apparatus was admirably ventilated. Like most of the ship it was painted white, and with its two berths on one side and lounge opposite reminded us of our room on the Rotterdam. The satchels and steamer trunk permitted in the state rooms are labelled in red "Inman Line, Wanted." Our room was all right when we got to it, but the stairways and passages *en route* were complicated, due, I am satisfied, to the fact that originally the main and upper decks at this point had been a part of the second-class quarters, which still were above us on the saloon deck. But the second-class stairway from the promenade deck was closed for the present and to get from our steamer chairs to our berths we had to go aft and down the large stairway to the saloon deck, then descend a small flight from an entry immediately behind, next find our way back through passages on this the upper deck to an entry, where we went down one flight more on steps whose closed upper part once communicated direct with the promenade deck, and lastly go forward to our cabin on this main deck.

It took a long time for the trans-Atlantic marine to evolve such a ship as the Paris. During the first half of this century the passenger business between this country and Europe was by means of fast sailing vessels. The first two steamships arrived in New York in 1837, but they consumed so much coal on their two weeks' trip that steam did not immediately drive out the clippers. In 1840 began the Cunard steamship line, encouraged by an English subsidy, and this company had almost a monopoly, until in 1849 the American Collins line obtained similar assistance from the United States.

The Collins people added the barber shop and smoking room and made perhaps better time than the Cunarders, but lasted only six years. About that time the Inman line began and to it is due not only steerage facilities but the substitution of screw propeller for the side wheels previously in use. The White Star launched its famous Oceanic in 1870 and minimized the noise of the screw by placing the cabins amidships. Within a few years past the Inmans built the City of New York with twin screws, which do not seem materially to increase the speed but no doubt lessen the danger from accident, and also make the ship easier to handle. As each improvement is added all other lines of prominence have to follow suit. The Cunarders did not favor the twin screws, as their single screw Etruria and Umbria were all but equal to the twin screw steamers of the other lines, but even the Cunard people have built their last ship, the gigantic Campania, with two screws. Up to our return the City of Paris held the fastest undisputed westward record, five days, nineteen hours and eighteen minutes, reckoned from Roche's Point at the entrance of Queenstown harbor to Sandy Hook lightship. This time has, however, been lowered since. The Inman lines now run to Southampton.

Of late years iron and even steel have been substituted for wood and the system of water-tight compartments extending across the ship from bottom to main deck has lessened the danger from collision. The New York and Paris and perhaps others have the further improvement of dividing the engine and I think boiler spaces longitudinally, so that water might in case of accident fill one side without disabling the machinery on the other side.

I attempted to keep a journal or log on our voyage

from Liverpool to New York, but it stops abruptly. It reads as follows:—

"Wednesday, September 30.—Came on board this steamship at Liverpool by 5 P.M. tender. Could not get the hang of the stairways to our room on the fourth deck below. Dining room has glass dome. *Menu* good. Sailed about 6:30 P.M.

"Thursday, October 1.—Clear. Off Queenstown 9:30 A.M. after an easy night. We went ashore and had a half crown ride in the country on a jaunting car and returned late for lunch. Rachel seasick and had to leave the table."

I might add, parenthetically, that the Queenstown jaunt was rough, but, as the drivers were witty, the views of river and moist green country good, and our numerous company in high glee, the trip was very pleasant. On this car we sat two on a side, back to back instead of couples facing, the driver being higher in front. The cushioned seats are a little insecure despite the footboard, inasmuch as there are but two wheels. Everywhere were beggars, even the children, and poverty appeared supreme. On the dock the persistent peddlers of lace, caps and shillelahs were annoying, and one irate old woman, who seemed to control the landing, informed us after we had several times said we wanted nothing,—"Vis, ye want the grace of God." We did not think that we could obtain much of this from her, and did not worry.

"Friday, October 2.—Rainy and windy. 414 miles. Ireland out of sight by nightfall yesterday. Rachel in bed all day but easier now at night. Am reading Charlotte Brontë to her. Above 414 miles made in 23 hours against head wind. Ship pitches some but does not roll much. Many people seasick. I am not, but have not a voracious appetite.

"Saturday, October 3.—Very rough. 436 miles. With Rachel in state room most of the day, reading. Ship pitches and rolls a good deal.

"Sunday, October 4.—Stormy. 446 miles. Rachel on deck this morning until storm drove all hands inside. Since she has been seasick. Sea now somewhat more moderate but still bad. Began Kingsley's Roman and Teuton.

"Monday, October 5.—Moderate. 439 miles. Rainy and towards evening foggy. Motion of ship is not bad. Rachel on deck the whole day but not at meals. We hope to land Wednesday evening."

Here the log stops. The ship the whole way had to fight head winds and the weather was generally rainy and rough. Rachel did not go to a single meal after we left Ireland. I brought her toasted and salted crackers when she was worst off and things more substantial as she improved. The deck steward was unreliable and those who trusted to him were sometimes pretty well famished. Indeed we found the attendance in all departments poor. The call bell from our room was seldom answered, and at the table the waiters were not efficient. The bills of fare were elaborate enough, calling for everything found at a first class hotel, but what one actually got was rather indifferent in quantity and quality. The ship was over crowded, there being all told, including crew and steerage too, something like sixteen or eighteen hundred people on board, as well as we could judge.

When near home we came near trying the merits of some of the safety appliances of the Paris. By Tuesday October 6th the bad weather had developed into a severe storm and after a rough day of it we retired at night with the feeling that at all events the pulsing screw was driving us onward towards port. Something suddenly wakened us and to our alarm the beat of the propeller had ceased. We hurriedly dressed, and the ship seemed to be wearing around, gradually rocking more and more until the jerking showed we were in the trough of the sea. Articles were thrown from the berths, our two heavy satchels before I could secure them commenced charging so savagely from side to side, like the loose cannon in Victor Hugo's Ninety-three, that we could not stand on the floor. Worse yet the electric light faded out. We remembered that on a former trip this ship had in some way admitted water until the after part where we then were sank from the engine back. The dark ship was as silent as the grave except for the crash of crockery. We wanted company, and after getting ready as well as we could we slowly and painfully felt our way along the black passages and up the swaying steps until on the uppermost stairway we found several people clinging to whatever was firm and even more alarmed than ourselves. No one knew anything and as the doors to the deck were locked I could not get at the officers.

After perhaps an hour of hard work on our part keeping in one place the screw began anew and the ship righted herself, much to our relief. At first the engines worked only every few minutes, just long enough to hold the vessel up, but after a while we went on again regularly. We afterwards learned that the trouble was the automatic oiling apparatus had been deranged in some way by the lurching and allowed the engine to get overheated, but this was finally remedied. We had got behind, but we were content to give up the hope of breaking the record on condition of not breaking the engine.

I suppose there was less danger than we thought at the time. The ship could not go over. The main danger would be that if we should lie long in the trough like a log the sweeping seas might break in and swamp us. As it was a sailor and a stewardess were severely hurt during the accident, and a liberal contribution was taken up for their benefit. We learned afterwards that vessels behind us suffered worse than we did, on some there being deaths.

One gruff passenger during the excitement said the trouble was caused by our having on board some Jonahs from the Servia, which had had to put back to New York not long before on account of some accident, and he wanted these people set adrift in a life boat. I kept very quiet, as I was not certain but that I was the Jonah, since both of the ships I had patronized on my earlier voyage, the Erin and Egypt of the National line, had been lost not long afterwards.

Nothing else untoward happened except that the pounding of the sea broke into the high-priced promenade deck state rooms, and the thundering blows on the dome at meal time took away what little appetite was left. Time dragged on most miserably. Shelley and Charlotte Brontë ceased to interest us and even Kingsley's vivid account of the Barbarian invasions of the Roman empire seemed tame when read on the boisterous ocean. When we did get on deck rain drove us in again. The little newspaper which usually appears in mid ocean was this time a very lame affair and to that extent was representative.

On Thursday evening we sighted land, a silvery line at the horizon,—America once again, welcome after a summer's absence, and doubly welcome after the wretched voyage. There was a concert that night, but we were too much interested in watching the lights ashore to care much for amateur music. It was after quarantine hours, however, and we had to wait until the next morning.

It was before the cholera invasion and we were able to show a clean bill of health. As we went up the harbor, we underwent the much dreaded customs examination, but when I made my affidavit I was relieved to find that the books we had were not dutiable nor were our many unmounted photographs. In fact nothing in personal use was contraband.

We arrived at the covered pier about noon, straining our eyes in vain from the ship to see a familiar face, and after landing there we had to wait up stairs a long time for our baggage. It had arrived at Paris early and was at the bottom of the hold, and the first was thus last. All packages as unloaded were piled up in the warehouse under signs marked with letters, A, B, C, etc., the initial of the owner as shown by the red label. Ours finally came after much worry on our part and running to and from the after hatch to hurry the porters, and were placed under "H." It was at this time that we noticed our old quarters were no longer reached by the tortuous route to which we had become accustomed, but only down the steep second class stairway from the promenade deck.

While waiting we had watched the searching of other trunks, and now applied for an inspector who had seemed to be indulgent. He had passed a bundle of bloodthirsty shillelahs, and we thought that anything ought to get through the McKinley net if that did. I had asked on board if I were entitled to two overcoats, and I now found out that the lower bay inspector had marked something about it on my affidavit, as the pier examiner said, "What about the overcoat?" I said that it was mine and I needed it. So it passed, and at home in the Sunny South I have used it as it was intended,—by giving it to a friend. I told the inspectors that I did not think my intention as to donating it was any concern of Uncle Sam. They laughed and assented.

Trying to set foot on our native soil was more trouble than leaving it, but at last it was all through, and we took a carriage to our hotel to rest before the long railroad trip back home. New York seemed to have shrunk up somewhat since we had left, and the unsightly piers and common buildings near the water front struck us unpleasantly. They seemed to belong to an old tumble down place. Some parts of Broadway and the avenues, however, redeemed the city and we felt no reason there to fear comparisons.

.   .   .

Thus ended our trip abroad. Instead of six hundred dollars it had cost twelve hundred, and we had been compelled to omit part of our contemplated rambles and somewhat vary others. But withal we had adhered pretty well to the itinerary I worked out at first, and we agreeably surprised the home folks in our being able to do so. It commended itself especially to Cousin Dan, who is a railroad man.

We had seen a great deal and not unprofitably. While there is no place like America to live, across the water we can study the origin and growth of much, that, in perhaps a better developed state, is familiar to us here. The older countries have an ivied history clinging to them which our younger land cannot rival, and travel shows the current of the world's development and makes us feel that even our own great country is but a part of a greater whole.

May our Rambles in Historic Lands prove as pleasant to the reader as they were to the travellers!

INDEX.

A

Addison, 258, 281
Aix-la-Chapelle, 15
Alban Lake, 201
Alban Mount, 205
Albano, 202
Albert of Saxony, 50, 62
Alexander, 246
Alps, 83
Altdorf, 92
Apollinaris Church, 25; water, 25
Apollo Belvidere, 191
Appian Way, 196, 198, 206.
Architecture, history, 19, 152, 140
Ariadne, Dannecker's, 35
Armor, 64, 271
Art, ancient, 80, 246, 276; modern, 154, 162 (*see* Painting, Sculpture)
Assyrian remains, 245, 275
Augustus, 125, 179
Avignon, 217

B

Bach, 37, 45
Baedeker, 23
Bank of England, 272
Bastille, 231
Barbarossa, 85, 131, 138
Baroque, 63
Bavaria, 81
Bazaine, 237
Belgium, 14
Bellagio, 118
Berne, 99
Bernese Oberland, 96
Bible, 38, 275
Blücher, 26
Bohemia, 73
Bonivard, 106
Bonn, 24
Borromean Islands, 116
Borromeo, S. Carlo, 116, 123
Boulangists and Lohengrin, 253
Boulevards, 223, 241
Boulogne, 13
Breitenfeld, 53
Bridge of Sighs, 143
British Museum, 275
Brunelleschi, 153
Brünnig Pass, 95
Brussels, 14

C

Cæcilia Metella, 199
Cæsar, Julius, 171
Calvin, 102
Campagna, Roman, 206, 209
Campo Santo, Pisa, 211
Canova, 120, 145, 162
Caracalla, baths of, 177
Carlsbad, 72
Catacombs, Rome, 180, 196
Caxton, 260
Chamouny, 108
Channel, English, 251
Charlemagne, 16, 128, 183

295

Chester, 282
Chillon, 106
Cicero, 174, 202
Cimabue, 155
City of Paris, steamship, 283
Clarendon Press, 281
Claude Lorraine, 61, 157
Cloaca Maxima, 167
Cologne, 18; cathedral, 20
Colosseum, 176
Columbus, 213
Commons, House of, 260
Communion, doctrines, 103
Communists, 224, 229
Como, Lake, 118
Constance, 84; Lake, 84; Council, 85
Constantine, arch of, 177
Cook & Son, 2, 23
Corso, the, 167, 169
Cromwell, 261
Cupid and Psyche, Canova's, 120
Customs examination, 12, 15, 291
Cyrus the Achæmenian, 245

D

Dance of death, Dresden, 66
Dante, 150, 159, 164, 165
Danube, 75
David, of Michael Angelo, 162
Da Vinci, 155
Demetrius Poliorcetes, 246
Diamonds, 244, 271
Diana, Louvre, 247
Dieulafoy collection, 245
Diligences, 111
Divines, Assembly of, 259
Doge's palace, 142
Downing Street, 263
Drachenfels, 24
Dresden, 58; picture gallery, 59; Green Vault, 63; historical collection, 64; porcelain, 65; Brühl Terrace, 66
Dürer, 74, 79, 157

E

Egeria, 198
Egyptian remains, 245, 275
Ehrenbreitstein, 25
Eidgenossen, 93
Eiffel Tower, 228
Einsiedeln, 89
Eisenach, 37
Electors, 25, 33
Elgin marbles, 275
Elizabeth, Queen, 258, 270
Emperor, Roman, 126; mediæval, 16, 33, 128
Erfurt, 38
Eugenie, 227, 229

F

Ferney, 105
Fettered slaves, Michael Angelo, 248
Fire at sea, 8
Florence, 149; history, 150; cathedral, 152; baptistery, 153; Uffizi, 158; Pitti, 160; Medici chapel, 162; Loggia dei Lanzi, 163; Santa Croce, 164
Forum, Roman, 169
France and Paris, 224
Frankfort, 33
Frari, 145
Frederick II., sword of, 226

G

Galileo, 141, 165
Gambetta, 230, 231
Geneva, 101, 104; Lake, 100
Genoa, 138, 213
Genre, 65, 156
German Empire, 33
Germania, national monument, 27
Germany, military, 15, 45; Supreme Court, 45
Ghibelline and Guelf, 129, 150
Ghiberti, 154
Gibbon, 176

INDEX. 297

Giotto, 153, 165
Glacier garden, 91
Glyptothek, 80
Goethe, 34, 41, 53
Golden Bull, 34
Gothic architecture, 10 ; Italian Gothic, 122, 152 ; French, 233 ; English, 258
Grand Canal, 136, 146
Graves, famous (see Tombs)
Greek art, 246, 275
Green Vault, 63
Grindelwald, 96
Guelf and Ghibelline, 129, 150
Guillotine, 219, 225, 278
Gustavus Adolphus, 54, 64
Gutenberg, 30

H

Hansa, 19
Hansom cab, 255
Hastings, 261
Heidelberg, 30 ; castle, 30
Henry IV., 220, 232, 235, 247
Henry VII., chapel, 257
Historic relics, 64
Holy Roman Empire, 16, 33
Huguenots, 104
Huss, 40, 86

I

Ingres' Spring, 250
Interlaken, 95
Invalides, 226
Iron crown, Lombard, 120
Iron Virgin, 75
Italy, history, 128, 131
Itinerary, 3

J

Jaunting car, 287
Jerome, Communion of, 190
Jerusalem chamber, 259
Joan of Arc, 236
Josephine, Empress, 226
Julius II., 185, 188
Jungfrau, the, 96, 102, 112

K

Keats, 195
Königstein, 70

L

Lake dwellers, 89
Laocoön, 192
Last Judgment, 187
Last Supper, 121
Lateran, 180
Laura and Petrarch, 218
Lausanne, 101
Leaning Tower, Pisa, 212
Leipzig, 42 ; market, 44 ; Gewandhaus, 45 ; my room, 46 ; university, 49 ; battle of, 56
Leo X., 178, 186
League and Covenant, 260
Leonardo da Vinci, 121, 155
Lion of Lucerne, 90
Lloyd's, 273
Litany, 219
Liverpool, 283
Lohengrin at Paris, 242
London, 253 ; Westminster Abbey, 255 ; St. Margaret's, 260 ; Parliament House, 260 ; Westminster Hall, 261 ; parks and palaces, 262 ; weather, 262 ; Strand, 263 ; Trafalgar Square, 263 ; Charing Cross, 263 ; Horseguards, 263 ; National Gallery, 264 ; police, 265 ; courts and inns, 265 ; streets, 266, 268, 272 ; St. Paul's, 266 ; London Bridge, 269 ; Tower, 270 ; The Bank, 272 ; Cheapside, 273 ; South Kensington Museum, 274 ; British Museum, 275 ; Underground Railway, 276 ; Tussaud's, 277
Locomotives, old, 274
Lorelei, rock, 26
Lorenzo de' Medici, 150, 163
Louis XIV., 226, 236, 237
Louis XV., 226, 237

Louis XVI., 225, 235, 237
Louise, Queen, 23
Louvre, 230; collections, 244; gallery, 248
Lucerne, 89; Lake, 91
Lugano, Lake, 117
Luther, at Wittenberg, 39; at Worms, 30; at Wartburg, 38; at Rome, 181
Lützen, 54
Lyons, 219

M

Magasins, Paris, 240
Maggiore, Lake, 115, 119
Maintenon, Mme. de, 237
Mainz (Mayence), 29
Mamertine prison, 172
Maremme, 210
Marie Antoinette, 225, 233, 237
Marie de' Medicis, 22, 249
Marseilles, 217
Mary, Queen of Scots, 258
Maxentius, Circus, 199
Meals at Paris, 239
Medici, the, 150, 163
Melanchthon, 40
Mer de Glace, 108
Mermaid Tavern, 273
Michael Angelo, 155, 164; Florentine sculptures, 162; at Rome, 187, 188; Tomb of Julius, 185, 248
Milan, 121, 130
Mission churches, 90
Moabite Stone, 245
Molière, 235, 248
Monaco, 215
Mont Blanc, 102, 108
Monte Carlo, 215
Monte Rosa, 102
Morgue, 234
Moses, Michael Angelo, 185
Munich, 75; Pinacotheks, 77, 80; Glyptothek, 80; streets, 75
Murillo, 78, 161

N

Napoleon, 65, 112, 210, 216, 234, 236, 244, 278; at Leipzig, 56; tomb, 226; by Delaroche, 43
Napoleon III., 174, 227, 230, 238
Nelson, 263
Nemi, Lake, 204
Newgate prison, 273
Ney, Marshal, 234, 235
Nice, 215
Niobe, 159
Notre Dame, 233
Nuremberg, 74

O

Ocean travel, history, 285
Œil de Bœuf, 236
Orange, 219
Oxford, 280

P

Painting, history, 77, 154, 198; Italy, 155; Netherlands, 156; Germany, 157; France, 157, 249; England, 264
Palatinate, 31
Pantheon, 179
Paris, history, 222, 224; Place de la Concorde, 225, 228; Champs Elysées, 225; Invalides, 226; Eiffel Tower, 228; Column Vendôme, 229; Tuileries, 229; Louvre, 230, 244; Collections, 244; Hôtel de Ville, 231; Bastille, 231; Île de la Cité, 232; Sainte Chapelle, 233; Notre Dame, 233; Morgue, 234; Pantheon, 234; Père-la-Chaise, 235; paving, 239; sewers, 240; shopping, 240; magasins, 240; streets, 240, 241; opera, 242; Lohengrin, 242; Madeleine, 228, 241; Luxembourg, 234, 249

Parliament House, 260
Pasquin, 182
Passionist monastery, 205
Peel, Sir Robert, 262, 265
Père-la-Chaise, 235
Persia, history and remains, 245
Petrarch and Laura, 218
Phidias, 276
Pieta, Michael Angelo, 185
Pilate, Pontius, 95, 219
Pilatus, Mt., 95
Pinacotheks, Munich, 77, 80
Pisa, 210
Pitti Gallery, 160
Place de la Concorde, 228
Poets' Corner, 256
Police, Paris, 241; London, 265
Pompadour, Mme. de, 226
Pompey, 206
Popes, and emperors, 17, 128; beards of, 201
Porcelain, history, 65
Portier, the, 148
Printing, history, 30, 47, 260

Q

Queenstown, 287

R

Rachel, 2, 251, 277, 288
Railroad travelling, 36, 100, 209, 220, 276
Raphael, 156, 179; Florence madonnas, 160; Stanze and Loggie in Vatican, 188, 190; tapestries, 193, 274
Reformation, 181, 183
Regent diamond, 244
Rembrandt, 157
Rhine, the, 24; upper, 86; falls, 87
Rhone glacier, 98
Rialto, 136
Rietschel, 66
Rigi, 93
Ringbahn, 76
Riviera, the, 214

Robespierre, 225, 231, 233
Roland and Hildegunde, 24
Roman Empire, 16, 124
Rome, 123, 166; ancient, 167; bridges, 168; Forum, 169; Via Sacra, 170; Comitium, 171; Mamertine prison, 172; Palatine Hill, 174; Capitoline, 174; Colosseum, 176; Baths of Caracalla, 177; Pantheon, 179; Lateran, 180; Scala Santa, 181; Pasquin, 181; St. Peter's, 183; Vatican, 186; Catacombs, 196; Via Appia, 196, 198; St. Paul's, 200; Roman history, 123; lost near Rome, 203
Rosetta Stone, 275
Rothschild, 35
Rotterdam, steamship, 4
Rousseau, 102, 104, 235
Rubens, 78, 156, 161
Rütli, 92

S

St. Bartholomew, 230
St. Bernard, Pass, 109; dogs, 114
St. Cloud, 237
St. Denis, 235
St. Gall, 84
St. Gotthard Railway, 117
St. James' Palace, 262
St. Mark's, 135, 140
St. Paul's, Rome, 200; London, 266
St. Peter's, 183
Sachs, Hans, 74
Salon, 244
Salvator Rosa, 161
Santa Croce, 164
Saxon Switzerland, 70
Saxony, 67
Scala Santa, 181
Schiller, 24, 41, 53, 86
Schaffhausen, 86
School of Athens, 189
Sculptures, Munich, 80; Florence, 158, 162; Rome, 191; Paris, 245, 248; London, 275

Sea, life at, 5, 287
Sedan, 57, 228, 231
Seine, the, 232, 238
Self portraits, Florence, 160
Sèvres, 238
Shakspere, 270, 273, 281, 282
Shelley, 195, 212
Simplon Pass, 112
Sion, 109
Sistine Chapel, 187
Sistine Madonna, 59
Smith, Hotel, 213
Sprudel, 73
Spurgeon, C. H., 269
Staubbach, 96
Stratford-on-Avon, 281
Student life, German, 32, 49, 53
Switzerland, 83 ; history, 93

T

Tabard Inn, 270
Talleyrand, 228
Tasso, 186
Tell, 92
Temple Bar, 262, 269
Terni, 207
Theban Legion, 22, 107
Thorwaldsen, 43, 90, 120
Tiber, 168
Tilly, 53, 64
Times, London, 266
Titian, 145, 156, 161
Titus, arch of, 171
Toes, 193
Tombs and graves, famous, 257 :
Abelard and Héloise, 235 ;
Addison, 258 ; Anne, 258 ;
Anne Boleyn, 270 ; Alfieri,
165 ; Arago, 235 ; Augustus,
179 ; Balzac, 235 ; Beauharnais,
81 ; Blake, 260 ; Bourbons, 235,
236 ; Browning, 256 ; Busketus, 211 ; Cæcilia Metella, 199 ;
Calvin, 103 ; Canning, 256 ;
Canova, 145 ; Caxton, 260 ;
Charles I., 280 ; Charles II.,
258 ; Charlemagne, 16 ; Chaucer, 256 ; Chatham, 256 ; Clyde,
256 ; Cosmo de' Medici. 163 ;
Cousin, 235 ; Cranmer, 280 ;
Cromwell, 261 ; Cruikshank,
267 ; Darwin, 256 ; Dickens,
256 ; Duns Scotus, 18 ; Dürer,
74 ; Edward I., 257 ; Edward
III., 257 ; Elizabeth, 258 ;
Erasmus, 87 ; Essex, 270 ; Fox,
256 ; Garrick, 256 ; Grattan,
256 ; Galileo, 165 ; George III.,
280 ; Goethe, 41 ; Grey, Lady
Jane, 270 ; Handel, 256 ;
Henry VII., 257 ; Henry
VIII., 280 ; Herschel, 256 ;
Hortense, 226 ; Hugo, 235 ;
Huss, 86 ; James I., 258 ;
Samuel Johnson, 256 ; Sir Wm.
Jones, 267 ; Ben Jonson, 256 ;
Josephine, 226 ; Julius II.,
185 ; Keats, 195 ; Lafontaine,
235 ; LaGrange, 235 ; Landseer, 267 ; Leo I., 185 ; Leo X.,
186 ; Livingstone, 256 ; Louis
XVI., 235 ; Louis XVIII.,
235 ; Luther, 40 ; Lytton, 257 ;
Macaulay, 256; Marceau, 235 ;
Marie Antoinette, 235 ; Mary
Queen of Scots, 258 ; Melanchthon, 40 ; Michael Angelo,
164 ; Michelet, 235 ; Mill, 218 ;
Milman, 267 ; Molière, 235 ;
Musset, 235 ; Napoleon, 226 ;
Nelson, 267 ; Newton, 256 ;
Ney, 235 ; Niebuhr, 24 ; Parr,
256 ; Paul, 201 ; Perrier, 235 ;
Peter, 185 ; Pilate, 219 ; Pitt,
256 ; Pompey, 206 ; Racine,
235 ; Raleigh, 260 ; Raphael,
179 ; Reynolds, 267 ; Rietschel,
66 ; Rossini, 235, 165 ; Rousseau, 235 ; Sachs, 74 ; Schiller,
41 ; Schumann, 24 ; Shakspere,
282 ; Shelley, 195 ; Sheridan,
256 ; Spenser, 256 ; Stanley,
258 ; Stephenson, 256 ; Tasso,
186 ; Tennyson, 256 ; Theban
Legion, 22 ; Thiers, 235 ; Titian, 145 ; Trajan, 173 ; Turner, 267 ; Ursula, 22 ; Victor

Emanuel, 179 ; Voltaire, 234 ;
Wellington, 267 ; West, 267 ;
William of Orange, 258 ; Wren, 267
Torso, Hercules, 192
Torture, instruments, 75
Toulon, 216
Tower of London, 270
Trajan's Forum, 173
Transfiguration, 190
Tribune, Florence, 158
Tuileries, 223, 229
Turner, J. M. W., 264, 267
Tusculanum, 202
Tussaud's, 277

U

Uffizi Gallery, 158
Underground railway, London, 276

V

Vatican, 186
Vendôme Column, 229
Venice, 133, 141 ; history, 137; St. Mark's 135, 140; Rialto, 136 ; Grand Canal, 134, 146; Doge's palace, 141 ; prisons, 143 ; arsenal, 144 ; Frari, 144 ; Ghetto, 146
Venus, de' Medici, 158 ; Capitoline, 175 ; of Milo, 247 ; Canova's, 162
Versailles, 236

Via Appia, 196, 198, 206
Via Sacra, 170
Victor Emanuel Arcade, 122
Vienne, 219
Villa Carlotta, 119
Vinci, Da, 155
Voltaire, 17, 104, 105, 234

W

Wallenstein, 54, 73
Wartburg, 38
Waterloo, 15
Weimar, 40
Westminster, Abbey, 255 ; Hall, 261
Whitehall, 263
Wieland, 41
Wiesbaden, 27
Wilhelm I., 23, 237
Windscheid, 51
Windsor, 279
Wittenberg, 39
Worms, 30
Wundt, Prof., 50

Y

Y. M. C. A., origin, 368

Z

Zermatt, 110
Zürich, 87
Zwingli, 88

www.ingramcontent.com/pod-product-compliance
Lightning Source LLC
Chambersburg PA
CBHW031856220426
43663CB00006B/649